7.95

Piet,
Wonderful
Work w/ Soul,
Sal Nistico's

Jean Baptiste
Illinois Jacquet
you are the greatest I.J.

Thanks
for your
ears + eyes

Hey Piet
You capture Rhythm
you capture life N.M.R.K.
Thanks Shannon 4/10/83

To Pete
I thank you very much
From a tenor for the times
Ricky Ford

Carlos Ovens

To Pete
Best wishes always

To Pete
I thank you very much
This is But
Nothing But
Beautiful
Love
Jim 83.

To Pete
Excellent images
Keep up the good work
Please
David McKay 83.

For Pete —
Another Lefty
who can really see!
Love McCall

jam session

jam

■ Piet Klaasse

portraits of jazz and blues musicians drawn on the scene

session

jam session

jam session

DAVID & CHARLES
Newton Abbot   London

■ Mark Gardner J. Bernlef text

9/7/83

There comes a period in the development of an Artist when Love "takes over". My friend, Piet Klaasse, has reached that Level in his Art.

[signature]
9/7/83

Note to the reader

These drawings came into being because of my admiration for the indigenous music of the Black American and the often colourful and vibrantly expressive interpreters of it.

The sketches were often made under bizarre circumstances and to my surprise I noticed that I improved by leaps and bounds, making more efficient use of my materials given the short space of time I had for each drawing.

More than 800 drawings of some 350 artists were made from 1977 onward. The portraits were chosen on the grounds of the musicians being well-known or of importance to the development of jazz, as well as on the merits of the drawing itself.

Since I drew along while the musicians played — doing my bit on paper and getting into the music if only just to record the seismographic waves of rhythm — because of this I allow myself to call this book jam session.

[signature]

jam session

Jam session

The instruments

Close-up on the blues

What is jazz?

Jazz styles

The jazz life

The jazz line

Jam session

Jamming in the jungle

The jam session — that impromptu yet deliberate meeting of musical minds — is far older than America's truly original art form jazz with which jamming is so closely identified. The first jam sessions were heard in the jungles of Africa, the Red Indian Plains of the United States (before they were either united or stated by the white man), across the steaming forests of the Amazon, over the arid deserts of Australia. In all those environments homo sapiens communicated and conversed through the drum. An animal skin stretched tautly over a gourd when pounded by fingers, knuckles, sticks or bones produced a resonant sound that would carry for miles.

A new kind of language was evolved. The drum was used to sound warning, to invoke the Gods, to give courage before and during battle, to arouse sexual passion or merely to transport dancers into a hypnotic trance of rhythmic intoxication.

In primitive music the beat came first, and with it the instruments to release a rhythmic response which patterns human life in the act of reproduction, in birth itself and throughout the seven ages of man and woman.

After the rhythm came melody and harmony in the ritual chants of 1,000 tribes scattered about the globe's fragmented land surface. Even in relatively isolated Pacific islands, drums were devised for ritualistic rites, beating out messages that could be sacred or sinister, joyful or despairing.

Drums were usually employed to inspire, and one imagines that the drummers who rapped on hollows logs, carefully shaped and honed after much experimentation, must have occupied privileged positions within their disparate societies and cultures. They had the task of passing on their skills to the next generation — and those skills grew in sophistication as centuries passed. Chiefs and witchdoctors, elders and holy men needed the drummers to uplift their subjects. An oration before a suitably intense, frenzied build-up was likely to fall flat. So the drummers enjoyed a status, and of course they needed to practise their craft independently and together. And their 'rehearsals' were the first jam sessions, when new rhythmics patterns were tried and tested, accepted or rejected. Ideas were exchanged, a competitive element introduced. There was a longing to find new, more exciting rhythms of greater complexity and elaboration. In the drum jam sessions B.C. the seeds of jazz were planted.

In the tribes of West and Central Africa a particularly strong and varied array of rhythms materialized by trial and error. Fast, slow and medium tempos were used for the swaying body movements and shuffling feet of the dancers. A sudden shift of tempo could heighten the mood. As the earliest drummers jammed and then put their discoveries into actual performance, so they learned the secret and enjoyed the satisfaction of audience response and participation.

Instant creativity

In the beginning they played for themselves and each other. But an even greater spiritual fulfilment was to be achieved with positive feedback from those unable to play who could, however, sing and dance in unison. The free flow of creative thought transferred via an instrument and the talents of the musician is the axis on which jazz revolves.

The jam session is the laboratory of jazz. Within its intangible mystique styles are shaped, lessons learned, boundary lines altered, elements mixed and moulded theories expounded, explored and distilled. Intellects are concentrated on new procedures and practices. There is an absorption of the good and bad and above all the new. Musicians deal in abstracts which they are impelled to transform into realities of sound.

As we have seen the jam session is far older than jazz, but it plays a constant and continuing role in the revision and development of this most compelling form of musical expression. Jazz, it is accepted, is less than a century in age, yet down the decades it has renewed and replenished itself in a way that no other music can match. Jamming has invariably unlocked a further stylistic door when jazz seemed to be getting hidebound or moribund.

The great wealth of veins running through the body of the music is proof of its capacity to change, adapt and

7

Dizzy Gillespie. When I asked him at the end of a concert if he would write a foreword to this book he said: 'My talent lies in bringing out the best in the people I'm playing with.' Even though he is so well-known and could easily steal the show he challenges them to excel.

survive, and exude an amazing durability and flexibility. Thousands of minds have applied themselves to the task of finding a fresh perspective within the strict confines of the simple, twelve-bar blues formula, and somehow they still arrive with different answers to that same puzzle. Could any computer in existence tell us the number of possibilities within the blues form? Could a machine conceive the apparently endless diversity that encompasses the country bluesmen, their urban cousins, the Ragtimers, Boogie-Woogie players, New Orleans, Dixieland, Swing, Bebop, Jazz Funk, Rock and Free Jazz practitioners who all cooked the blues to their own recipes while abiding by the basic rules?

The past, present and future merge in the blues at a jam session. A swing drummer, a stride pianist, a fresh-faced college graduate saxophonist with his head stuffed full of John Coltraine phrases, a bebop trumpeter, an earthy blues shouter, a slick studio flautist, a white West Coaster of the soft sax school can assemble on a stage and find immediate common ground. They result may be weird, but a measure of cohesion will be there. The unusual will often spark the unpredictable. The 'star' of the proceedings can find himself blown away by an unknown. Or he may systematically demolish in musical terms those around him. Everyone involved, including those lucky enough to listen, will learn a little more about a music that leans heavily on instant creativity and the response it elicits.

James Moody/Earl Von Freeman. They were perfectly matched and the two of them replaced the sound of an entire orchestra. You can see how they both listened to both each other and themselves.

Johny Copeland. 'Jam session' example of an extremely fast, almost seismographic registration at the end of the performance.

After hours

It would be foolish in the extreme to draw positive conclusions about the state of jazz purely from recorded studio evidence or the concert and club performances of working groups and bands. These are the polished, finished offerings built upon the foundations laid in lofts and basements, rented rehearsal rooms, apartments, dingy dives and bleak bars where nobody hears. Jazz musicians are not the most disciplined of people, and generally dislike the idea of the set time rehearsal. The period for active investigation of their art is after an evening engagement when they feel played in and relaxed, ready for a challenge. As most of the world slumbers, the jazz night people break out of their familiar group roles to broaden their horizons.

The jam session is governed by unwritten laws. The unwelcome will be shunned or rapidly made to realize that they are out of their depth. A musician participating should observe the courtesies and formalities. If the majority elect a particular tune he has to go along with it. Somebody—invariably a senior participant—will not only call the tune but fix the tempo and key and solo order. If a saxophonist, trumpeter, pianist or whoever is playing interestingly he will be urged to continue his solo by cries of encouragement or helpful riffs. Should his inventive powers flag, his colleagues will peremptorily cut him short and elbow him aside. The ego-tripper who wants to hog the microphone is given short shrift.

Within the jam session will be found the virtues and faults of the single-minded individualist. A desire to learn and contribute is counter-balanced by a compulsion to be assertive and competitive. The extremities of close collaboration and cruel conquest are curiously inter-mingled. The jam session encapsulates the desire for musical fellowship and the need to gain esteem from fellow practitioners.

Many of the legendary jam sessions were good-natured

affairs at which the young tyro was tolerated amicably, although put in his place if he overstepped the mark. Suffering indignity, even humiliation, from experienced players is not easy to accept for the apprentice jazzman, but it will harden resolve and speed up the acquisition of knowledge. Lester Young, Charlie Parker and many other superlative musicians had to endure laughter and jibes early in their careers. Such treatment made them more determined to force the jokers to eat their words. On certain occasions a particular jam session has assumed epic proportions and passes into the realm of myth. When Coleman Hawkins, who almost singlehandedly gave the saxophone credibility as a jazz instrument, returned to America after a sojourn of several years in Europe, an army of eager and talented tenormen was waiting to ambush him to signal an new order and a new monarch of the instrument. Hawkins, an immensely gifted, resourceful and shrewd campaigner, knew that his reputation was on the line, and there were those willing to take him on. Like every true heavy-weight champion, the Hawk bided his time, assessed and appraised the opposition before selecting his battle ground and striking with a serpentine venom. He systematically crushed all the pretenders to his throne and set the seal on his return by recording a magnificent version of *Body And Soul* to emphasize his musical stature. His rivals were put to flight, and seldom did any aspiring tenors dare to attempt 'cutting' Hawkins after that. He was a formidable adversary to anyone seeking to score point, but with his subtle harmonic approach and melodic virtuosity he was extremely kind and helpful to younger men like Miles Davis, Hank Jones, J.J. Johnson and Fats Navarro, who were engaged in effecting the next breakthrough for the music.

Mostly, when it came to giants of Hawkins' musical stature, contemporaries were respectful, more anxious to

Monty Alexander. This is a fine example of 'togetherness'. You can see how attentive Jeff Hamilton on drums, John Clayton on bass and Monty Alexander are to each other.

'The worst thing a musician can do is not listen.' (Charles Tolliver)

show him how much they had improved rather than to flatten him in a contest of improvisation.

The centres that spawned new styles were hotbeds of jamming where musicians played around the clock, local men and strangers passing through — striving, searching, seeking to extend their vocabulary. New Orleans, Chicago, Kansas City, Detroit, Pittsburgh, Los Angeles — these were the cities where in ghettoes and red light districts jazz players opened up frontiers. When they had perfected their concept, the acid test and challenge remained New York.

Jam session as a spectacle

It is an irony that repressive laws have frequently acted as catalysts in the evolution of jazz. When the civic authorities finally cracked down on the palaces of pleasure in New Orleans, where so many fine musicians were employed, Louis Armstrong and many other pioneers moved to Chicago, and conversely with the advent of Prohibition Chicago became a wide open town with ample work for jazzmen and unlimited opportunities for jamming after hours.

Kansas City in the 1930s was another rumbustious location pouring out a stream of dynamic big bands and potent soloists. In walked the law and closed numerous clubs, thereby ensuring that the K.C. style was spread far and wide. New York's 52nd Street in the 1940s was probably the locale of the golden age of the jam session as a spectacle the public could witness. Packed into this block were a dozen clubs where for more than 20 years the finest jazz could be heard. Musicians went from one to the next to sit in. It was one continuous jam session in these spots from dusk to dawn. And it was probably there that the thought of making a commercial package of the 'All Star Session' caused a gleam in promoters' eyes.

Norman Granz was the first man to back the hunch with his famous Jazz At The Philharmonic show in Los Angeles. The notion was delightfully straightforward. Hire a bunch of star jazz names and present them jamming in a concert hall. What started as a gamble quickly became a lucrative success. For more than a decade JATP went on tours across America and around the world, taking live jazz to countries where the gifted exponents were known only from recordings. Mr Granz did an impressive public relations job for jazz, providing well-paid work for many players and gave them further exposure through his record labels, *Clef* and *Norgran*. He also insisted on integrated audiences, and in the ensembles he presented there were no colour lines; black and white played together. Yet for all that, Jazz At The Philharmonic proved to be the very antithesis of the jam session. It was a slick formula aimed at crowd-pleasing. The roster of names grew tiresomely predictable – Flip Philips, Illinois Jacquet, Oscar Peterson, Buddy Rich, Roy Eldridge, Ella Fitzgerald. Routines were set, the same ballad medleys played, the contrived tenor sax battles staged with phoney frenetics, the set-piece drum solos by Buddy Rich, Gene Krupa or Louie Bellson, the vocal interlude, and the raucous, flagwaving crescendo closer were the stock-in-trade of this travelling jazz circus. People were led to believe that this carefully prepared flying jazz package on its interminable journeyings was a real live jazz jam session. And they probably went home believing it. But they were offered a musically sterile substitute.

All gone

The belief that the spirit of the jam session can be miraculously transferred to records or tapes at studio sessions is also misguided. Rarely will the chosen mix of musicians blend under such strained circumstances. Perversely, a clash of personalities and a measure of downright ill-feeling may be the touchstone for a special record date. This was undoubtedly a factor in making the renowned Miles Davis session of Christmas Eve 1954 the remarkable affair it turned out to be. Davis found himself at odds with a man of equally strong convictions in pianist Thelonious Monk. Argument broke out, and

the trumpeter, displeased at Monk's keyboard interventions, instructed the pianist to 'stroll' (not play) behind the trumpet solos. The dispute and resultant tension added a sharp edge to the proceedings; the Davis improvisations rank with his best. But, significantly, the pair never recorded together again, although Miles frequently included Monk compositions in his repertoire.

The term

The term jam session surely refers to the numbers of musicians who would *jam* into a presumably confined space in order to play for sheer pleasure or at most minimal recompense. Flocks of perspiring tenormen, eyes closed, shirts open with neckties pulled down, pressed elbow to elbow as they unravel surprising skeins on familiar chord changes. Intense, hunched trumpeters employing lip muscle and lung power and fleet fingers in an exhausting procedure. Pianists bent over the keyboard, lost in private worlds of black and white notes, trying to find the notes between the keys. Big-handed bassists queueing up to take a turn at the big fiddle. Young athletic drummers, slim show-offs, built for endurance. A trombonist or two, nervously testing their slides and worried whether they can keep pace with all the fast-action saxes and triple-tonguing trumpets. A dim, smoke-laden, hot, airless atmosphere, shouts of acclaim from bystanders, grunts from pianist and drummer, a tightrope of tension and relaxation, a feeling of release and relief and a joy in being there when the performance concludes.

The drummer is the hub, playing the part of his predecessor of aeons past in jungle, desert and plain. He is the pulse for singers, dancers, toe-tappers, other instrumentalists. Give Art Blakey, Max Roach or Billy Higgins a hollow log, a set of skulls or ancient gourds and they could set up an infinite number of rhythmic and polyrhythmic patterns. They know far more about the techniques and science of percussion than the ancient spellbinders who pounded their stories in lost lands long ago. But Blakey, Roach and Higgins have inherited the basic beat that lends jazz its unique quality.

The drive of the drums is the engine of a jazz group, small, medium or large. That is why listeners who dislike jazz drum solos have no genuine affinity for the music. When forgotten tribes went on a bender or the warpath, those unmoved by the drums must have felt they were excluded as cultural outcasts.

The jam session is still an exclusive experience in which intellectual satisfaction is as vital as body movement response. It is the volcanic crater of creative activity in which the players perform with total honesty; no place here for the tricksters or glib phrase-stealers. In a jam session the superficial will be exposed and rejected, the craftsman improved, the genius displayed. This is where the forces of jazz are sparked and flamed. From here the influences spill out and spread to other players and into different areas of music, popular and pompous. Pop and modern straight music have shamelessly borrowed from the jazz language. Like vultures preuing on noble beasts, so much 20th century music picks at the flesh of jazz.

But why wait to encounter today's sounds in recast, distorted and emasculated forms on some unexceptional tomorrow? Listen now, and hear the untainted source in its profound richness and variety, conjured in the instant... in Jam session.

Lester Bowie. At the time I made this drawing Lester Bowie had a group called From the Roots to the Source. *It had gospel singers in it, although they are not on this drawing.*

Art Blakey

Art (Abdullah Ibn Buhaina) Blakey. Drums/Miscellaneous Percussion/ Composer. Pittsburgh, Pennsylvania, October 11 1919.

While at school, Blakey studied piano, but switched to drums out of necessity when the drummer in the local group he was working with took sick. In 1939 joined the **Fletcher Henderson** Orchestra and the following year worked with pianist **Mary Lou Williams**' group at Kelly's Stable. Had his own band for a spell at Boston's Tic-Toc Club, but was evidently back with Henderson when **Billy Eckstine** called him to be the drummer in a new orchestra formed in 1944. Blakey was with the band until it folded in 1947.

He then formed the first short-lived Jazz Messengers (small group) and fronted, albeit briefly, 17 Jazz Messengers. Blakey jobbed around New York for a couple of years, worked with **Lucky Millinder** in 1949 and was with clarinettist **Buddy DeFranco** from 1951-'53 in a quartet. Art itched to have his own group and in 1954 re-formed the Jazz Messengers, choosing three young men who were all to become leaders in their own right – **Clifford Brown**, **Lou Donaldson** and **Horace Silver** who was to stay for several years. The 1955 edition featured **Kenny Dorham** and **Hank Mobley** besides Silver and Doug Watkins. Other members of the unit in the 1950s were trumpeters Joe Gordon, Donald Byrd, Bill Hardman, **Lee Morgan**; saxophonists Jackie McLean, **Johnny Griffin**, **Benny Golson** and Wayne Shorter; pianists Sam Dockery, Walter Bishop Jr, Junior Mance, **Bobby Timmons** and Walter Davis.

Blakey was cited by Mary Lou Williams as one of the first – the other being Kenny Clarke – drummers to play bop. He received much help from Dizzy Gillespie, during their tenure in the Eckstine band, in forming his style. *One of the most aggressive, swinging and daring drummers in jazz, Blakey is a positive powerhouse, a fountain of rhythmic energy, who propels his groups with relentless energy.* Even when his Messengers have sometimes lacked originality and inspiration, Blakey's efforts have always been worth listening to. He constructs solos of logic and beauty, and his accompaniment is invariably stimulating. Blakey acts as a catalyst to those around him, and will shout words of encouragement to his sidemen, even on recording sessions. 'Blow your horn,' he will instruct a trumpeter indicating his pleasure and wish for the solo to continue. Art Blakey was closely identified with the so-called Hardbop style, a more straight ahead version of bebop, but with many of the same characteristics. Hard-bop made use of simple, riffy tunes, marches and soulful ditties that drew from blues and gospel sources. A visa for anyone auditioning for the Jazz Messengers was (and still is) the ability to swing. Despite his percussive authority, Blakey is not an overbearing leader. On some of his albums he does not even take a solo, preferring to let sidemen hold the spotlight. Art can also be a most sensitive drummer, and it is doubtful if anyone else came closer to understanding the musical aims and needs of **Thelonious Monk**.

The Monk/Blakey partnership on many recordings bears out their compatibility. Rather like Miles Davis, Blakey has an extraordinary gift for finding new talents. His magnificent sextet of the early 1960s was a prime example, containing as it did **Freddie Hubbard**, Curtis Fuller, Wayne Shorter, Cedar Walton and Reggie Workman. Hubbard, Shorter and Walton all became significant leaders within the decade.

From 1958 the Jazz Messengers embarked on regular tours of Europe, and were frequent visitors to Japan in the 1960s. When the highly successful sextet disbanded in 1965, Art put together a new unit with Chuck Mangione and **Keith Jarrett**. Others who worked with him included trumpeters Woody Shaw, **Olu Dara** and Bill Hardman; saxophonists Billy Harper, Carter Jefferson, David Schnitter, **John Gilmore** and Carlos Garnett; and pianists Cedar Walton and Joanne Brackeen (the first lady Messenger).

In the mid-1970s, the drummer got stuck in a rut, re-recording old hits like *Moanin'*, *A Night In Tunisia* and *Blues March*. He had already taken a 'Sabbatical' from leadership to tour with The Giants of Jazz (Dizzy Gillespie, Kai Winding, Sonny Stitt, Thelonious Monk, Al McKibbon) in 1971-'72, but the Jazz Messengers continued to be rather lacklustre when Blakey returned to the road. That is until 1980. In that year Art unveiled a brand-new sextet which was on a par with the group of two decades earlier. Young New Orleans trumpeter **Wynton Marsalis** proved to be the sensation of the group, but all the other members – Billy Pierce (tenor), Bobby Watson (alto), Jimmy Williams (piano) and Charles Fambrough (bass) – were fine players. Blakey was back in business! Preaching his molten message as fervently as ever. The outfit lasted less than a couple of years, but left behind an impressive collection of albums, and in 1982 Art had another terrific group with Terence Blanchard (trumpet), Donald Harrison (alto) and Jimmy O'Neal (piano).

Art Blakey once named his favourite drummers as Max Roach, Sid Catlett and Cozy Cole, but he was also influenced by Chick Webb whose dictums were swing, drive and perfect time. Blakey has never forgotten a conversation he had with Webb at the Ritz in Pittsburgh many years ago. Webb went to hear him and was not pleased by Art's showbiz antics which at that time included twirling sticks and throwing them in the air. 'Look, rhythm is on the drum – it ain't in the air!' Chick admonished him.

Blakey knows his role perfectly after more than 45 years of cooking over a hot kit. 'No jazz band is any better than its drummer. If the band is better than the drummer, then it's not a jazz band. He puts everything together there and keeps things rolling. This is what I was taught by Chick Webb and by my predecessors, and I think they're proven to be right.' Blakey is everything a drummer should be – a springboard for the entire band. And in full cry he looks like and *is* the archetypal percussionist – mouth open in a broad grin, perspiring profusely, hands and arms, feet and legs perfectly co-ordinated. Audience feet start tapping from beat one when Blakey is in charge. As Freddie Hubbard once opined: 'After you play with him (Blakey) it feels empty playing with most other drummers. He gives you so *much* support.' To the paying customers, too, Art gives his all – in every performance. His enthusiasm and capacity to groove have been untouched by the passage of time. Blakey, of the gravelly voice and sincere manner, has dedicated his life to the beat and in doing so created a special tradition of jazz drumming.

Recommended records:
The Jazz Messengers At Cafe Bohemia Vols 1 & 2
Blue Note BLP 1507/8

'I think the drum is very musical if the approach is right. The drum is the first instrument after the human voice.' (Art Blakey)

Art Blakey With The Original Jazz Messengers
Columbia 32 16 0246
Art Blakey In Paris
Epic LA 16017
Art Blakey & The Jazz Messengers/Mosaic
Blue Note BLP 4090
Art Blakey & The Jazz Messengers/Buhaina's Delight
Blue Note BLP 4104
Art Blakey's Jazz Messengers/Ugetsu
Riverside RLP 464
Art Blakey & The Jazz Messengers/Free For All
Blue Note BLP 4170
Thelonious Monk/Blue Monk
Prestige PRST 7848
Horace Silver & The Jazz Messengers
Blue Note BLP 1518
Art Blakey's Jazz Messengers With Thelonious Monk
Atlantic 1224
Jazz Messengers '70/In Japan
Japanese Victor SMJX-10086
Art Blakey & The Jazz Messengers/Live At Bubba's
Who's Who In Jazz WWLP 21019
Art Blakey in Sweden
Amigo AMLP P 839
Art Blakey & The Jazz Messengers/Album Of The Year
Timeless SJP 155
Art Blakey & The Jazz Messengers/Oh – By The Way
Timeless SJP 165

'Years ago I was talking with Thelonious and he said:"When you hit the bandstand, the bandstand is supposed to lift from the floor and the people are supposed to be lifted up too." '
(Art Blakey)

Miles Davis

Miles Dewey Jr. Trumpet/Flugel-Horn/ Composer. Alton, Illinois, May 25 1926.

His family moved to East St Louis in 1927. Miles came from a wealthy middle-class background, his father being a dentist and landowner. Davis received his first trumpet on his 13th birthday as a gift from his father. Encouraged by Clark Terry, Miles impressed Charlie Parker and Dizzy Gillespie when he sat in with the **Billy Eckstine** Orchestra in St Louis. He was later to play and record with the Eckstine band. In 1945 he studied theory at the

Juilliard School of Music in New York, but was soon getting practical jazz experience on 52nd Street in bands of **Parker** and **Coleman Hawkins**. In 1945 he appeared on the famous Parker *Ko Ko* session for *Savoy* and while touring with **Benny Carter** the following year recorded with Parker for *Dial* in Hollywood. After a stint with Eckstine he joined the Parker quintet in the spring of 1947 and stayed for 18 months, touring and recording extensively with the Bird. The first records under his own name (for *Savoy*) featured Parker on tenor sax. It was a well-organized and rehearsed date and included Miles' most assured playing up to that time.
In this early phase of his career, Davis' playing was often weak and faltering but his spare phrasing, largely in the trumpet's middle register, proved a fitting foil for Parker's fierce flights. Miles was already looking beyond the confines of the small bop combo towards a 'cool', arranged sound. In 1948 he headed a short-lived but extremely influential nine-piece band which recorded for *Capitol* the following year. Using arrangements by Gil Evans, Gerry Mulligan, John Lewis and Johnny Carisi, the band had the unusual instrumentation of trumpet, trombone, French-horn, tuba plus alto and baritone saxophones playing in front of a conventional rhythm section. Davis and saxophonists **Lee Konitz** and **Gerry Mulligan** were all to become important spokesmen for the low temperature school. Pianist **John Lewis** was to promote his own version of damped down bebop through the Modern Jazz Quartet. In 1949 Davis captivated audiences at the Paris Jazz Fair in a pick-up band with pianist **Tadd Dameron**.
The early 1950s proved to be a period of eclipse for Davis. Although he continued making outstanding recordings for *Blue Note* and *Prestige,* and still fronted his own groups, Miles had to wait for a 1955 appearance at the Newport Jazz Festival to relaunch his career. Shortly after that success he had a band with **Sonny Rollins** on tenor sax, but then he formed what proved to be another significant quintet which became the darling of fellow musicians, critics and jazz listeners. The inaugural outfit boasted **John Coltrane** (tenor), **Red Garland** (piano), **Paul Chambers** (bass) and **Philly Joe Jones** (drums). In later editions **Bill Evans** and **Wynton Kelly** took over piano duties, **Jimmy Cobb** replaced Jones, and

Cannonball Adderley (alto sax) was added. When Coltrane left, his successors were **Hank Mobley** and **George Coleman**. Meanwhile Davis resumed his striking collaboration with Gil Evans in a series of pristine orchestral recordings – *Miles Ahead, Porgy & Bess, Sketches Of Spain* – that set off his melodic trumpet and flugel-horn improvisations. Always a trend-setter, Miles' espousal of the flugel-horn immediately persuaded many of his fellow trumpeters to dabble with or switch to the larger horn. After Miles recorded *On Green Dolphin Street* or *My Funny Valentine,* dozens of musicians added the tunes to their repertoire and also made them for LP release.
In 1963 Davis disbanded and formed a new quintet with **Wayne Shorter, Herbie Hancock, Ron Carter** and **Tony Williams** – all exciting new talents who would soon graduate to leader status. Davis remained aloof, even contemptuous, of the avant garde and when told that his former sideman John Coltrane played such long solos because he didn't know how to end them, Davis remarked: 'Why doesn't he try taking the horn out of his mouth?' Given this attitude, Davis' entry into the jazz/rock arena came as a shock to his most devoted followers. One album had three pianists playing electric keyboards, and he began using an electric amplifier for his trumpet. The 'all electric' Davis tended to watch his sidemen disgorging over-long and mediocre solos. Davis sometimes and mediocre solos. Davis sometimes employed a wah-wah pedal attachment and occasionally even played keyboards himself. He despised the rock label hung on him, but was equally scathing about the 'old nostalgic junk' like *My Funny Valentine* that he formerly played. Whatever he said, Davis appeared to be moving with the commercial tide and was receiving high billing at rock festivals in the early 1970s. He broke both legs in a car accident in 1972 and this setback meant he was only sporadically active for the remainder of the decade. He was by now in the superstar bracket and could name his own price and conditions for concerts since club engagements no longer interested him.
Davis made a resounding return in 1981 with an album *We Want Miles* and a world tour. Although still surrounded by electronics his own playing had reverted to earlier modes and even some of the old favourite tunes were taken out and dusted off.

3 X
Miles Davis
Rapid '82

*This is one of the studies 'on the spot', used
for the lithography, reproduced on page 16.*

Miles Davis remains an enigma. Fond of fast cars, beautiful women and heavyweight boxing, he has never suffered fools gladly. A man of high intellect and great cultural awareness, he treats his audiences with a disregard bordering on contempt (a trick he learned from Parker), never bothering to announce a tune. These days he insists on stringent security where he plays and will not countenance the use of flash cameras in any auditorium during a concert. His use of four-letter expletives is legendary and this grating coarseness is in complete contrast to the elegant, melodic nature of so much of his playing.

Davis strikes fear into many of his contemporaries who hold him in awe, yet he can be a man of charm. In 1983 he was employing two young guitarists in his band and using an Oberheim synthesizer on stage. To keep fit he was swimming and he stopped smoking, but when he played he had to wear a truss and rubber corset to keep the abdomen muscles tight. In a rare interview with Richard Williams for the *London Times*, Davis said he was interested in writing tunes in small fragments, six-bar and ten-bar melodies that progress in a circular manner with no apparent beginning or ending. What *he* was doing in the middle sounded just as good.

Since his youth, Davis had made conscious attempts to escape from the conventions — of even modern jazz. Part of this flight was a realization that he could never play like Parker or Gillespie and really didn't want to. Yet the 1949 broadcasts from Paris with Dameron show that Davis could extemporize in the Navarro/Gillespie manner with a startling fluency, exhibiting an unsuspected virtuoso technique. His health problems in the late 1970s were not helped by his heavy use of cocaine, brandy and sleeping pills, crutches to ward off the pain of those severe leg injuries. A slight stroke jerked him away from these destructive habits and back to music. Even in his late 50s, Miles Davis is a proud rebel who will kow-tow to nobody. Once, outside Birdland, a policeman ordered him to move on. Davis refused so the cop clubbed him on the head. Blood poured down his face, but Miles steadfastly refused to budge. 'I don't move for no goddam cop. I don't move for nobody,' he told club owner Max Gordon. That single-mindedness helps to explain why Davis will only ever play what he

wants to — take it or leave it. His instruction to his musicians typifies this restless seeker after musical truth, 'Don't play what's there. Play what's not there.' Even before the death of Parker in 1955, musicians were following the Davis vision, and in contemporary jazz it is difficult to find a nook or cranny into which his influence has not percolated. Everyone will have their particular favourite Miles period, depending on when they locked in on his music, but practically all his recorded efforts from 1949 to 1964 merit the closest study. What happened after is really *the struggle of an established stylist to find alternative routes to save himself from parodying the playing of his earlier self*. Few musicians of his age concern themselves with such matters. They are content to recycle old solos and sidestep the challenge; Davis continues to confront head — on the problem of creating art. Not that he would put this abstract obsession in such fancy terms. 'Put this on the record — *all* of it!' he gruffly remarked at one tense recording session. This is precisely what Miles has done during his long career. It's *all* there on record for those prepared to listen, learn and become bewitched by the unique conception of a trumpeter who discovered the cool. Yet for all his outer hip coolness he can and does musically burn with an intense, controlled heat.

Recommended records:
Miles Davis/The Complete Birth Of The Cool
Capitol 5CO 52. 80 798
Charlie Parker/The Complete Studio Sessions
Savoy S5J 5500 — 5LP set
Miles Davis & The Modern Jazz Giants
Prestige PR 7150
The New Miles Davis Quintet
Original Jazz Classics OJC-006
Miles Davis/Miles Ahead
Columbia CL 1041
Miles Davis/Porgy & Bess
Columbia CL 1274
Miles Davis/Kind Of Blue
Columbia CL 1355
Miles Davis/Sketches Of Spain
Columbia CL 1480
Miles Davis/Someday My Prince Will Come
Columbia CL 1656
Miles Davis/E.S.P.
Columbia CL 2350

Miles Davis/Miles Smiles
Columbia CL 2601
Miles Davis/We Want Miles
CBS 88579
Miles Davis/Heard 'Round The World
CBS 88626
Miles Davis/Starpeople
CBS 25395
Miles Davis/We Want Miles
CBS C 238005

The stage is practically unlit, the hall pitch black. I'm sitting to the inside of the aisle. When it started I lay down. While lying there I was dragged away. There's a kind of paranoic guarding of the man. But with his shades on you could hardly tell it was him, and to make it even more intriguing he turned his back on the audience to boot.

The instruments

Voice and homemade instruments

The history of jazz music cannot be viewed apart from the social history of the American Negro. This also holds true for the various instruments and the periods in which they came to be used in jazz.

Prior to the abolition of slavery American Blacks were completely without rights, musically speaking too. The only means with which they could give expression to the musical heritage they had brought with them from Africa were with their voices or homemade instruments such as drums, flutes and primitively constructed guitars made from crates.

The whiteman's zeal to convert the 'primitive' blackman to Christianity brought with it the introduction of Christian hymns and the instruments on which they were played: the piano and organ.

Military brass bands

Even though the Blacks were considered primitive and seen as entertainers and makers of dance music, the whites were willing to allow them access to the arsenal of instruments which military brass bands made use of at the beginning of the twentieth century: trumpets, trombones, horns, tubas, euphonia, and saxophones. The saxophone, the last offspring in the family of wind instruments, was introduced into New Orleans from France at the end of the nineteenth century after having been rejected by the European classical world as a useless, 'suspect' instrument with a distasteful sound. It would be the American Blacks who would explore this instrument's possibilities in the course of jazz history.

It is probably no coincidence that jazz mainly uses wind instruments, for jazz has always been closely based on the human voice. To this day a jazz musician speaks of a colleague's solo as if 'he is telling a story'. It is precisely instruments like the sax, trombone and trumpet which afforded the American Black the opportunity of 'talking' on their instruments.

New instruments have easily found their way into jazz owing to the increasing element of improvisation in jazz music together with the typical jazz musicians' premise of developing as personal a sound as possible. Jazz musicians have also sought to deeply explore the expressive potential of recent developments in electronic music.

The only instruments that never really made great inroads into the jazz world were those from the violin family—these instruments being indispensable to European art music. Presumably to jazz ears this instrument did not offer a direct enough means of expression or because it was practically the symbol of white and therefore oppressive culture.

Every instrument a solo one

If in the past the rather simple distinction could be made between the typical accompaniment instruments such as the drums, piano, guitar, bass and the 'solo' instruments such as saxophone (alto, soprano, tenor, baritone), trumpet and trombone, this is no longer the case and jazz has developed along lines where every instrument can be considered a solo one.

It has been said before that the jazz musician tries to develop as personal an expression on his instrument as he can. If in Western art music the emphasis continues to lie on instrumental skill, then the jazz musician is only satisfied when he produces an immediately recognizable sound. This has led to peculiar, unconventional playing techniques often highly idiosyncratic in nature. It's exactly because the emphasis in jazz music lies on the personal and unique that it is difficult to teach it at institutions such as conservatories. Even though many European and American conservatories teach jazz, it still remains strongly linked to the experience of playing. At best, jazz can only be marginally 'learned'!

Koko Taylor. I saw her in the wings before the show. She was wearing a really shabby, faded brownish vest on top of shiny black artificial satin, shivering a little there back-stage. But once she was on stage, man what a warm powerful voice!

Koko Taylor

Forever Yours
Freddie Hubbard
"82"

22

*Freddie Hubbard. I first drew him with a coarse
graphite pencil.
In twelve strokes I got him down and thought:
don't touch it anymore.*

Koko Taylor

Cora Walton. Singer. Memphis (Shelby Co), Tennessee, September 29 1935.

She started singing in the local church choir at the age of fifteen. Like so many black people from the Southern States, she moved North to Chicago. This happened in 1953 and in the same year she married Robert Taylor. Due to a childhood preference for chocolate, she got her nickname 'Cocoa', later transformed into 'Koko'.

Her first, more or less professional, jobs in Chicago were a couple of dates with **Buddy Guy** and **Junior Wells**. The first time she entered a recording studio was in 1963, when she recorded her first '45': *Like Heaven To Me/Honky Tonky* for the *USA* label. It appeared to be the start of a long career as a recording artist. After an early sixties session for the label of her older female colleague, singer **Victoria Spivey** from New York, she was discovered by *Chess* talent scout, producer and studio musician **Willie Dixon**. Among several singles and two albums for the *Chess* label she recorded her biggest chart-topper to date, *Wang Dang Doodle,* a song that had been written for her by Willie Dixon.

Several tours across The States and in Europe followed and while Koko was happy with her success, the position of her record company did not fit with her feelings about music. Everything had been set up before she went into the studio and all she did was sing the basic tracks. However Koko continued touring, it was not until 1975 that she started recording again. This time it was Bruce Iglauer of *Alligator* records who recorded the album 'I Got What It Takes'. It appeared to be a world-wide come-back for Koko. Until now her career as both a recording artist as well as a dynamic 'live' performer seems to be an almost endless stream of success. *With her heavy sounding voice and her dedicated stage presence, she usually receives standing ovations from large audiences at such festivals as the North Sea Jazz Festival the Hague-Holland.* And there's hardly any female singer who can be compared with her. Amy O'Neal (editor Living Blues-Magazine, Chicago) wrote of Koko: 'Her voice sounds like gravel through a swamp, out-funking frogs and craw-dads. A panther' squall through black night can't scare her.'

Recommended records:
I Got What It Takes
Alligator 4706
The Earthshaker
Alligator 4711
From The Heart Of A Woman
Alligator 4724

Frank Wess must be honoured as the first musician who made the flute a fully accepted jazz instrument.

Archie Shepp

Archie Shepp. Tenor/Soprano Saxophones/Composer/Leader/Music Educator. Fort Lauderdale, Florida, May 24 1937.

Brought up in Philadelphia. As a youngster he studied piano, clarinet and alto saxophone before taking up the tenor, the instrument with which he is most closely identified. Worked in rhythm and blues field, and his first professional job was in a group including trumpeter Lee Morgan who gained fame with Art Blakey. There was little other contact with local jazz players like Henry Grimes and Bobby Timmons.

Shepp graduated from Goddard College with a degree in dramatic literature, then settled in New York with the idea of working as a playwright or actor. With no employment prospects in the theatre, Shepp returned to music. His studies of history — especially black history — and reading the works of Marx gave him a radical standpoint which he brought to jazz. It was therefore no accident that he was soon working with pianist **Cecil Taylor** whose dissonant playing was far removed from the 'norm' of jazz in 1960. He and Taylor appeared as musicians and actors in a production of *The Connection,* a controversial play about drug addiction. Shepp and trumpeter Bill Dixon co-led a quartet (no piano), and then Archie was involved with a group called the New York Contemporary Five with **Don Cherry** (cornet) and John Tchicai (alto sax). All these men were part of the 'New Wave' or 'New Thing' that permeated jazz in the early 1960s. It was a radical, rebellious movement whose spokesmen — and Shepp was one of the most articulate and perceptive — wanted to extend musical frontiers.

Shepp's early playing shocked listeners with its fierce and rough attack, but while he was a revolutionary his work was much more traditional than many of those he associated with. Shepp, whose father played banjo but not professionally, was influenced by Ben Webster, Coleman Hawkins, Charlie Parker, John Coltrane, Sonny Rollins and Ornette Coleman.

In 1964 Shepp toured Russia, Czechoslovakia and Finland with the New York Contemporary Five. He was not impressed by the Russians' chauvanistic attitude towards jazz. At the same time it was an irony that while Archie consistently pointed out that jazz was music of the black American, his own style found little favour with the black audience, his greatest champions being white intellectuals.

In 1965 Shepp worked and recorded with **John Coltrane**, who with Ornette Coleman, was the key figure in the avant garde. Also in that year his play *The Communist* was performed in New York. Controversy raged around Archie Shepp in the late 1960s. *What puzzled many listeners was the anger in Shepp's playing, but it had a sense of humour too.* The extreme nature of the New Wave inevitably evaporated as time passed and its innovations were absorbed into the jazz mainstream. The shrill shrieks of protest, in stark contrast to the soft-centred stuff of the contemporaneous 'Flower Power' pop music of the 1960s, gradually mellowed.

Archie Shepp also revised his approach, became more conservative, paid tribute in musical terms to Webster, Parker and other predecessors he admired. Shepp and composer and sometimes trumpeter Calvin Massey collaborated on a number of ventures including a musical, *Lady Day: A Musical Tragedy,* based on the life of Billie Holiday.

Shepp was to be found in Europe in 1969 working with such hardbop musicians as Philly Joe Jones and **Hank Mobley**. He continued a relentless exploration of jazz, 'ancient and modern', and the music of other cultures and countries. As a college professor, he lectured at the University of Buffalo and later the University of Massachusetts.

By the mid-1970s he was heading a quintet which included Charles 'Chuck' Greenlee, a veteran from the 1940s Dizzy Gillespie band, on trombone. On a European tour in 1976, this group recorded with Norwegian singer Karin Krog, and it proved to be a scintillating partnership on a programme that showed catholic jazz tastes, ranging from Duke Ellington to Carla Bley.

Shepp continued his reappraisal in the 1970s and many of his earlier critics (this writer among them) found his 'new' work stimulating and four-square in the jazz tradition. Shepp, it seemed, had turned full circle. Not that he had ever rejected the jazz past, but he had wanted to venture out into deeper waters; to test the temperature and to see where the current led him. According to Shepp: 'Jazz is the symbol of the triumph of the human spirit, not of its degradation. It is a lily in the swamp.' He told Valerie Wilmer in her 1970 book, *Jazz People* (London): 'The sum total of my Western formal academic training and my Southern Baptist Negro orientation was a good through-view of America. For me, personally, it's impossible to imagine playing music without seeing my entire history associated with it.'

Shepp is something of a maverick in his non-conformity and ability to surprise and disarm his detractors. 'Jazz has plenty of life to it, a very definite future,' he asserted some years ago; Shepp has been contributing to the cause. His outspoken views about the 'blackness' of jazz needed to be said at a time when the Afro-American was struggling for civil rights. Matters may have eased, but Shepp is acutely aware of the inequalities still evident in an uneasily integrated society. As a sociologist he cannot ignore these issues. In that sense the anger in Shepp's playing mirrored the plight of the people in the ghetto.

The music of Shepp and others reflected a greater political awareness than those who went before. The new guard were prepared to display their *anger* through the music. This had never really happened before. Shepp does not believe in 'art music', seeing this as a passive and bourgeois concept. Rather he regards music as a functional, living entity, a part of the community.

Recommended records:
Bill Dixon-Archie Shepp Quartet
Savey MG 12178
New York Contemporary Five, Vol 1
Polydor 623234
Archie Shepp/I Know About Life
Sackville 3026
Archie Shepp/Goin' Home
SteepleChase SCS 1079
Archie Shepp-Horace Parlan/Trouble In Mind
SteepleChase SCS 1139
Archie Shepp-Niels Henning Ørsted Pedersen/Looking At Bird
SteepleChase SCS 1149
Archie Shepp-Karin Krog/Hi-Fly
Compendium Records FIDARO 2 or Japanese Overseas Records KUX-37-V
John Coltrane/Ascension
Impulse AS-83
The World Of Cecil Taylor
Candid 59006
Cecil Taylor-Gil Evans/Into The Hot
Impulse AS-9

Archie Shepp. I made this sketch during a concert in Amsterdam's biggest jazz club, the BIM-huis in September 1983. It was so extremely packed that I could hardly move at all, but the music was so good that I was nevertheless very productive that night.

Jimmy Knepper

James M. (Jimmy) Knepper.
Trombone/BassTrombone/Baritone Horn/
Composer. Los Angeles, California,
November 22 1927.

First instrument, at age five, was the alto horn. Studied trombone from age of nine with private teacher and subsequently at Los Angeles City and State colleges. Also played baritone horn while still at school. Some of his early training was gained at military school. At 15 Knepper played his first professional engagement and went on to work with a wide variety of big bands including Charlie Barnet, Charlie Spivak, **Woody Herman**, **Claude Thornhill** and Stan Kenton. There were many dance bands that benefited from his presence, but more interestingly he gigged with **Charlie Parker**, Ray Bauduc and Art Pepper.
In 1957 Jimmy joined the **Charles Mingus** Workshop and was with the group of the volatile bassist for around four years, appearing on such important *Mingus* LPs as *Mingus Ah Um, Mingus Dynasty, Tijuana Moods, Mingus Of Yeah, The Clown* and *Blues And Roots.* The break-up from Mingus was a painful one and resulted in the loss of a tooth and damage to Knepper's embouchure. Mingus hit him in the mouth when the trombonist refused to write backgrounds for a large orchestra that was to perform and be recorded at a concert in New York's Town Hall. Knepper brought a criminal action against his former employer, and Mingus was convicted of third-degree assault.
In 1962 Knepper joined Benny Goodman for a State Department tour of Russia. After that he was in the pit band for the Broadway show *Funny Girl,* and actually with jazz work in short supply, Jimmy was employed in a number of other show orchestras, although more to his liking were the gigs and tours of Russia, Japan and Europe with the **That Jones-Mel Lewis** Orchestra.
In the 1970s Knepper was heard with Gil Evans, **Lee Konitz** and the New York Jazz Ensemble. He both played and arranged for Konitz' 1975 nonet for New York gigs. Jimmy idolized Charlie Parker and as a young man followed Bird around, recording him on a primitive wire recorder in clubs and at concerts. A number of albums by Parker have been extracted from Knepper's personal collection and released commercially.

The trombonist recalls being impressed by hearing Count Basie, Duke Ellington and Earl Hines on the radio in the late 1930s. He was still a teenager when he first visited Chicago and New York as a member of the Freddie Slack Band. Knepper, unlike so many trombonists of his age, managed to avoid sounding like J.J. Johnson. *His gruff sound and highly distinctive manner of phrasing* mark him as his own man. He has technique but is not given to employing it for its own sake. The structure of his improvisations has won him many admirers.
Critic Whitney Balliett once pronounced that Knepper was 'the first original trombonist in the modern idiom since J.J. Johnson'. Jimmy, who has observed regarding commercial bands 'the worse the music, the better they pay', puts the dedicated player's plight very succinctly: 'It's hard for a jazz musician to live a rational life, unless he has an independent income or a busy maximum of work. Even at the time I was with Mingus, we didn't work very much. Most of the jobs were either recordings or concerts, and all in all it only came to 10 or 15 weeks a year. You had to do other things besides. Working in the studios or in the theatres, whatever came your way.'
Fortunately, more interesting things came Jimmy's way in the late 1970s and early 1980s including several recording dates for the Danish *SteepleChase* and Scottish *Hep* labels. Prior to these ventures there were few records under his own leadership save for his impressive 1957 release *Idol Of The Flies* and a joint collaboration with **Pepper Adams,** aptly entitled, *Pepper And Knepper (MGM/Metrojazz).*
Jimmy has commented: *'You really have to be dedicated to the music to be able to survive.'* That's precisely what he is, dedicated, and his continued survival is an example for every aspiring jazz trombonist. He has stayed loose, receptive but unusually single-minded, although jazz for him has been no *Primrose Path* (the title of one of his compositions). Other originals authored by Jimmy Knepper are: *Ogling Ogre, Avid Admirer, Idol Of The Flies, Cunningbird, Noche Triste, Spotlight Girl, Figment Fragment, Languid, Just Tonight, Gnome On The Range, Latterday Saint* and *Adams In The Apple.*

Recommended records:
Charles Mingus/East Coasting
Bethlehem BCPS 6019
Charles Mingus/Tijuana Moods
RCA-Victor LSP 2533
Charles Mingus/Blues And Roots
Atlantic SD 1305
Charles Mingus/Mingus Dynasty
Columbia CS 8236
Pepper Adams/Jimmy Knepper/Pepper And Knepper
Japanese Metrojazz MM 2093
Jimmy Knepper/Idol Of The Flies
Bethlehem BCPS 6031
Jimmy Knepper/Cunningbird
SteepleChase SCS 1061
Jimmy Knepper/Joe Temperley/Just Friends
HEP 2003
Jimmy Knepper/Primrose Path
HEP 2012

Benny Goodman

Benjamin David Goodman.
Clarinet/Leader/Alto/Baritone
Saxophones. Chicago, Illinois,
May 30 1909.

Parents were immigrants (father from Warsaw, mother from Kovno) who married in Baltimore. Benny, the youngest son in a family of 12 children, first played clarinet in the Kehelah Jacob Synagogue rehearsal band at age 10.
Goodman received a thorough classical grounding, but also played jazz whenever he could. Benny was influenced in his early years by Ted Lewis. Worked with a number of bands around Chicago including that of Murph Podolsky, and others led by Art Kassel and Jules Herbeveaux.
At age 15 Goodman joined Ben Pollack, opening with the band at Venice, California. The trombonist/arranger with Pollack was Glenn Miller. After their stint on the West Coast, the Pollack outfit returned to Chicago. There was music galore and plenty of outlets for it. Louis Armstrong, Earl Hines, Bix Beiderbecke, King Oliver and Bessie Smith were some of the great jazz performers Goodman listened to and played alongside.
Benny's first solo on record was *He's The Last Word* with Pollack in 1926. Made a number of his own records in late 1920s and was heard on alto and baritone saxophones as well as clarinet. Left Pollack in 1929 to freelance, working in pit bands, casual dates and recording sessions. In 1933 Benny met John Hammond who persuaded him to record

Jimmy Knepper
Nov 21, 1982
Amsterdam

for *Columbia.* Hammond was to be of great help in assisting Goodman's rise to fame. Rejecting a tempting offer to join Paul Whiteman, Goodman instead decided in the spring of 1934 to start his own orchestra. Their first engagement was at Billy Rose's Music Hall, but when that job ended after three months it looked as if the band would have to break up. They were saved by landing a contract for a regular radio show on the NBC network. The radio series, *Let's Dance,* coupled with a steady flow of popular records, catapulted Goodman to fame and fortune. *Metronome* magazine voted the Goodman crew 'best swing band of 1935' – and that was the year the Swing Era was truly launched. Benny Goodman was the 'King of Swing'.

The band drew an incredible following from the teens and twenties audience, and for the first time bookers and record company executives realized the spending power of the younger generation. Armed with an expanding library of carefully selected arrangements by Fletcher and Horace Henderson, Edgar Sampson, Deane Kincaide, Benny Carter, the Goodman band was also well blessed with an impressive array of soloists in **Bunny Berigan** (trumpet), **Jess Stacy** (piano), **Gene Krupa** (drums) and of course BG himself. Singer Helen Ward also gained enormous popularity with the mass audience. The late Gene Krupa felt *Benny built a band playing musicians' music, but he didn't play over the heads of the public.*

Defining the reasons for Goodman's incredible success is difficult. The music was excellent for both listeners and dancers, but Goodman was a rather ordinary, unprepossessing fellow. Yet here he was, an idol of teenagers, a radio and record star whose concert appearances would find hundreds standing in line for tickets. His pre-eminence was to last for around nine years, until he disbanded in 1944.

Benny was not content with fronting the big band. He also had a combo to break up the programme. At first it was a trio with pianist **Teddy Wilson** and drummer Gene Krupa. Then vibraharpist **Lionel Hampton** was added to make it a quartet. In featuring Wilson and Hampton, Goodman was the first white leader to break the absurd racial divisions which then applied in jazz. Both men became highly regarded members of the Goodman package. The 'band within a

band' concept grew to sextet and septet size with the additions of black guitarist **Charlie Christian**, bassist Artie Bernstein and tenor saxophonist Georgie Auld. The combo made many recordings on its own account, and Christian's solos were influential in the development of modern jazz.

It has been argued, with justification, that there were many superior swing bands – Count Basie, Chick Webb, Jay McShann and others – led by black musicians who never won the rewards or popularity achieved by Benny, but that was hardly Goodman's fault. Benny's fame spread around the world through the band's appearances in a series of Hollywood film musicals. After the 1944 break-up, Goodman formed a new band the following year and as the 1940s wore on was obliged to give the orchestra a more modern flavour.

He had made some hard-line pronouncements about bop and its practitioners. 'They're just faking. They're just writing and playing for effect, and a lot of it doesn't swing,' he stated. But he revised his opinions and hired boppers like **Wardell Gray** (tenor), Stan Hasselgard (clarinet), Nick Travis and Doug Mettome (trumpets) and **Eddie Bert** (trombone) for his new band. Chico O'Farrill was responsible for most of the arrangements. Even Fats Navarro, most gifted of the Gillespie disciples, made one recording with Goodman. The band lasted until 1950 when Goodman decided to concentrate on concert work. He remarked that bop was on the way out and anyway, 'I never liked it.'

For the past 34 years BG has mostly led small groups, and has toured overseas on many occasions. A large orchestra was assembled with BG to record the soundtrack for *The Benny Goodman Story,* a dreadful Hollywood biopic, in 1955. Goodman also took a large ensemble to the USSR in 1962, a tremendously successful piece of cultural bridge-building, although off-stage there were many problems of a personal and political nature. Goodman also played at the Brussels International Exposition in 1958 and visited Japan in 1964. In more recent years he has elected to tour when he feels like it, usually with a sextet in which **Zoot Sims** (tenor) and Bucky Pizzarelli (guitar) have often featured. Aside from his jazz activities, Goodman has also pursued a parallel career as a classical clarinet soloist and recording

artist. Perhaps this aspect of his endeavours betrays a yearning for respectability usually denied to the jazz practitioner. Yet Goodman has been showered with honours.

Dubbed the 'King of Swing' in the 1930s, Goodman continues to play with impeccable technique and style. Leonard Feather described him as a 'peerless clarinetist', and he still receives rave reviews, despite all the changes that have swept through the music since Benny Goodman embarked on band leadership almost a half century ago.

The list of famous Goodman sidemen would fill several pages. So many went on to become leaders: Harry James, Bunny Berigan, Hampton, Krupa, Georgie Auld, Claude Thornhill, **Stan Getz**, Louie Bellson, **Red Norvo**, Cootie Williams etc. Singers with the band included Martha Tilton, Helen Ward, **Peggy Lee**, Patti Page, Dick Haymes and Buddy Greco. Goodman was the right man in the right place at the right time with the right music for that time. He became rich and famous, a pop star and symbol for an era. The music was good, sometimes great. People who put down Benny as an old square, insult and ignore not only his outstanding musicianship and achievements but also what he did to break the artificial colour line in jazz. BG has recorded prolifically in the past 58 years. This selection is intended to be representative of six decades of the Benny Goodman story.

Recommended records:
Benny Goodman/BG – 1927-1934
Brunswick BL-54010
Benny Goodman And The Giants Of Swing
Prestige PRST 7644
Benny Goodman/Arrangements By Fletcher Henderson
Columbia Special Products 524
Benny Goodman/1933
Sunbeam Records 133
Benny Goodman/On The Side, 1929-1931
Sunbeam Records 107
Jack Teagarden/King Of The Blues Trombone
Columbia Special Products 6044
Benny Goodman
French RCA 7273
1938 Carnegie Hall Jazz Concert
Columbia OSL-160
Benny Goodman/Sextet & Orchestra
Spook Jazz SJL 6602

Benny Goodman
18
Juli '82
North Sea Jazzfestival

Hamiet Bluiett

The Genius of Charlie Christian/Solo Flight
CBS M67233
Charlie Christian/With the Benny Goodman Sextet & Orchestra, Vols 1 & 2
CBS 62387/CBS 62581
Benny Goodman-Charlie Barnet/ Bebop Spoken Here
Capitol 5C05280854
Benny Goodman/Benny's Bop, Vols 1 & 2
Japanese Dan VC-5003/5023
Benny Goodman/BG In Hi-Fi
Capitol W-565
Benny Goodman/In Moscow, Vols 1 & 2
RCA Victor LOC-6008
The Benny Goodman Story/Vols 1 & 2
Decca DL 8252/3 or Coral CP 11/17
On Stage With Benny Goodman And His Sextet/Recorded Live In Copenhagen
Decca DKL 4/1 & 4/2

Hamiet Bluiett

Hamiet Bluiett. Baritone Saxophone/Alto Flute/Alto Clarinet/Composer. Lovejoy, Illinois.

At age nine began studying clarinet with George Hudson. At Southern Illinois University, Bluiett first played flute before taking up the baritone saxophone. After serving in the Navy as a musician, he played for a while with the Black Artists Group in St Louis. In 1969 Bluiett moved to New York and immediately started playing with such notable musicians as Sam Rivers, Olatunji, **Freddie Hubbard**, Elvin Jones and McCoy Tyner.
Bluiett later went on to play with **Charles Mingus** before forming his own groups. Bluiett has been recognized as an established baritone player in numerous Downbeat Jazz Critics Polls and was awarded the NYC Jazz Award 1979 for baritone saxophone.

Recommended records:
Resolution
Black Saint – BSR 0014
SOS
India Navigational – IN 1039
Steppin' With The World Saxophone Quartet
Black Saint – BSR 0027
Point Of No return
Moers Music – 01034

Sugar Blue

James Whiting. Harmonica/Singer. Harlem, New York, 1949.

New York's 'Central Park' as well as some platforms of the underground train in New York City were the first stages for harmonica player and blues singer Sugar Blue, whose musical talents came to growth when an aunt gave him a harmonica when he was eleven or twelve years old. Having a musical mother, who was a singer/dancer, he knew from his youth that music would be the most important thing in his life. After he exercised, without any remarkable results, on violin, flute and saxophone, he picked up the harmonica again to play his favourite music, the blues.
As he lived in the neighbourhood of the famous Apollo Theatre, he became familiar with blues music, went to concerts there given by such musicians as B.B. King, Muddy Waters, Albert King and Elmore James as well as several big names in soul and jazz. Outside that, there was a harmonica player around whose records he kept playing: Sonny Boy Williamson 2 (Rice Miller). Today he still mentions Sonny Boy as one of his main influences. Beside his abilities as a harmonica player, Sugar Blue is a remarkable singer as well as a composer. The lyrics of his songs usually reflect some of the sad things in today's world like discrimination, masochism and crime. During an interview for *Block* magazine he said: *'Of course I can sing songs like: Have a good time, 'n party and swing, jump up and down and... But there are enough songs like that and of course you can have a lot of fun with them in the disco. But for me the bad things that happen in the world are important as well. People get killed in the streets, are being shot or they die another awful death. Sometimes people say: "I dont want to hear this." But then I say: "Sorry but this is the reality of today's life." I hope people will keep asking, after they hear my songs, "why?." '*
After Sugar Blue recorded for the New York label *Spivey* during the late sixties and the early seventies, he gained some wider recognition when The Rolling Stones invited him to play harmonica on their album 'Some Girls' (1978). So, it's Sugar Blue's harp that can be heard on their world-wide hit, 'Miss You'. More session work for The Stones followed as

well as some performances with them. Besides more session work for artists like Johnny Shines, Roosevelt Sykes and Brownie McGhee, Sugar Blue recorded two live albums in London with Louisiana Red and he also recorded two albums under his own name. Nowadays he lives part of the year in Paris, while he spends the other time in Chicago. When he's in The States he's a member of Willie Dixon's Chicago Blues Allstars, but when he takes his 'European break' he leads his own band.

Recommended records:
Crossroads
Free Bird FLY 13
Chicago To Paris
Blue Silver BS 3012

Hamiet Bluiett. It was the first time I'd seen a baritone sax. How can you manage something like that? It's such a big instrument that it is two partners: the sax and the man.

Sugar Blue   10-7-83

Chico Freeman. He was so carried away with the drawing I'd made of him that he gave me a big hug. We left the hall arm in arm like two young friends. That accounts for the lyrical text.

Chico Freeman

Chico Freeman. Tenor/Soprano Saxophone/Flute/Alto Flute/Clarinet/Bass Clarinet/Composer. Chicago, Illinois, July 17 1949.

Father is the legendary Chicago tenor saxophonist Von Freeman who played with everybody (including Charlie Parker) in the 1940s, but did not make his first record until 1972. Chico's uncles George Freeman (guitar) and Bruz Freeman (drums) are also well-known and respected musicians. Chico studied with Muhal Richard Abrams, and in 1972 became a member of the Association for

the Advancement of Creative Musicians. Played with a number of bands, and was heard to telling effect on a number of recordings with bassist **Cecil McBee**; the two men have regularly worked together and struck up a remarkable interplay. Was generally recognized as one of the outstanding young musicians to emerge in the late 1970s.
Has a catholic taste in improvising music, having listened to Charlie Parker and Lester Young at one end of the spectrum and Albert Ayler, late John Coltrane and Pharao Sanders at the other. Played at the Camden Jazz Festival, England, in 1980. His music tends to reflect the stronger voices of the 1960s: John Coltrane and

Miles Davis. And this is understandable because he was a teenager at that time. His multi-instrumental abilities are evident on a number of his recordings, but as Brian Priestley, writing in *Jazz Journal International* (July 1981), observed: 'The apparent necessity for tenor players to double on (at least) flute and soprano these days — perhaps even more than the desire to play different kinds of material — seems to be robbing us of the immediately identifiable sounds of those who specialize on one instrument.'
Chico heard jazz first, but as a youth his first music jobs were providing backing for blues artists such as **J.B. Hutto**, Memphis Slim, Junior Wells and Lucky Carmichael

33

in Chicago. He also worked in pick-up bands behind visiting rhythm and blues acts like The Four Tops, Jackie Wilson, The Dells and The Isley Brothers. When Chico moved to New York he worked with Elvin Jones, **Don Pullen**, **Sam Rivers** and **Sun Ra** among others.

He found the year he spent with **Elvin Jones** especially helpful. 'Playing with him was great because it helped me to develop the rhythmic and percussive side of my playing,' says Freeman.

He made his recording début with the LP *Morning Prayer,* issued in Japan in 1976, and it was followed in '77 by *Chico* for *India Navigation.* In 1982 he participated in a special concert entitled 'Young Lions: Live At Carnegie Hall' which also featured Kenny Eubanks, Bobby McFerrin, **Wynton Marsalis**, Jay Hoggard, Ronnie Barruge, Hamiett Bluiett and others. *What Happened To The Dream Deferred* was Freeman's compositional contribution to this event. Also in '82, Chico had an acting and playing role in *Money*, written by LeRoi Jones and performed at La Mama in New York.

Freeman appeared with his father Von on one side of the remarkable 1982 album *Fathers And Sons* on which they showed close musical compatibility, playing 'straight' and 'free' with great fluency.

Recommended records:
Chico Freeman/Chico
India Navigation IN 1031
Chico Freeman/No Time Left
Black Saint BSR 0036
Chico Freeman/Beyond The Rain
Contemporary 7640
Chico Freeman/Kings Of Mali
India Navigation IN 1035
Chico Freeman/Spirit Sensitive
India Navigation IN 1045
Chico Freeman/Peaceful Heart, Gentle Spirit
Contemporary 14005
Chico Freeman/The Outside Within
India Navigation IN 1042
Chico Freeman/Destiny's Dance
Contemporary 14008
Fathers And Sons
Columbia FC 37972/CBS 85786
Chico Freeman/Tradition In Transition
Elektra/Musician 60163
Chico Freeman/The Search
India Navigation IN 1059
Cecil McBee Sextet/Compassion
Inner City IC 3033

Hank Jones

Henry (Hank) Jones. Piano/Composer. Pontiac, Michigan, July 31 1918.

The eldest of three musical brothers, he was a student of Carlotta Franzell. Worked with local groups in Michigan and Ohio before joining George Clarke in Buffalo. He moved to New York at the age of 26, and was greatly influenced by the younger Al Haig and to a lesser degree Bud Powell.

Jones' employers included trumpeter Hot Lips Page, **Andy Kirk** and **John Kirby**. He was **Coleman Hawkins**' pianist for two years and appeared on some of Hawk's more interesting recordings with young modernists (Max Roach, Miles Davis, J.J. Johnson, Fats Navarro etc). First toured with Jazz At The Philharmonic in 1947 and was part of that package, as **Ella Fitzgerald**'s accompanist, for five years. Subsequently played with **Benny Goodman** for several years.

From the late 1950s until 1975 he was basically a studio musician with a staff job at CBS, although he continued to be much in demand for record dates by leaders as diverse as Pepper Adams, **Chet Baker**, Lionel Hampton, **Ben Webster**, Stan Getz, **Milt Jackson**, **Bobby Hackett** and Bud Freeman. He was the first pianist with the big band co-led by his brother **Thad Jones** and **Mel Lewis**, and of the scores of albums he has contributed to, a 1952 quartet session with **Charlie Parker** shows Jones at his most responsive.

His sheer versatility has obscured his worth as a tremendous soloist when the spirit moves him. The long tenures as an accompanist for singers and the steady TV/radio network job pushed him out of the jazz limelight. Jones was part of the 1950s *Savoy* Records house rhythm section with **Wendell Marshall** (bass) and **Kenny Clarke** (drums); it was an excellent trio.

When Jones started leading groups again in the mid-1970s he used **Ron Carter** (bass) and **Tony Williams** or Ben Riley (drums). The group was fittingly billed as the Great Jazz Trio. Hank again demonstrated the depth and range of his talent by making an album of ragtime piano in most authentic fashion. But listeners were forced to acknowledge that the Jones magic was as potent as ever by the LPs he made for *Muse, Concord* and

Galaxy towards the end of the 1970s. *His deft touch, graceful phrasing and ability to turn the most unlikely material to good account* were still there for all to hear. His recasting of eight bebop classic lines, including three ballads by Thelonious Monk, served notice that Hank Jones had kept his ears open and imagination fertile during his studio hiatus. Hank is respected by the pianists of his own generation and those who came after. The late Duke Pearson, also a fine pianist, admitted to me that Hank Jones was his major influence. 'He is the most flexible pianist around and very adaptable to any given musical situation. I wish I had his touch... I only wish that someday I manage to reach the same level of his musical plateau.' Such a tribute indicates Hank's stature amongst fellow pianists who constitute a special breed of jazz player. They are the people who have to 'feed' chords to hungry hornmen and often end up struggling against the handicap of an ill-tuned instrument, minus several keys.

Certainly Jones had made his share of bland, commercial recordings because that was what the producer wanted. But it didn't harm his own style one bit, witness his productive output of the past decade. He has pumped fresh life into old novelty tunes like *Your Feet's Too Big,* along with hymns, spirituals plus Hollywood and Broadway hits.

His repertoire is amazingly large, and anything he touches musically gains an extra lustre. If there's a pretty path to take, Hank Jones will be on it, finding and investigating all the beautiful 'scenery'. He is one of only a handful of the earliest bebop pianists left, but he's also so much more — a jazz pianoman for every occasion and situation.

Recommended records:
The Quartet Of Charlie Parker
Verve MGV 8005
Hank Jones/'Bop Redux
Muse MR5 123
Jones/Brown/Smith
Concord Jazz CJ-32
Hank Jones/Just For Fun
Galaxy GXY-5105
Hank Jones/Tiptoe Tapdance
Galaxy GXY-5108
The Great Jazz Trio At The Village Vanguard
Inner City 6013

RonCarter 17 Juli 82

Ron Carter

Ronald Levin (Ron) Carter. Bass/Piccolo Bass/Electric Bass/Cello/Violin/Clarinet/ Trombone/Tuba/Composer. Ferndale, Michigan, May 4 1937.

Family were musical, and he was one of eight children who all had instrumental training. Began on cello, while still in school, at the age of 10. Early experience playing in chamber groups at concerts. Made the transition from cello to bass while at the famous Cass Tech High School in Detroit, where bassists Paul Chambers and Doug Watkins also studied.

Played bass in a local group in 1955, and led own combos in Rochester, New York, while studying for a BM at the Eastman School of Music (1956-'59). He played and recorded with the Eastman Philharmonia directed by Howard Hanson. First name jazz job was with drummer **Chico Hamilton** whom he joined in September 1959.

Carter was one of the first (Scott La Faro was another) of a new breed of bassists of great technical accomplishment who could fit into any context, no matter how advanced. Based in New York, Carter was soon in demand for recording sessions with a multitude of leaders including **Eric Dolphy, Cannonball Adderley, Jaki Byard, Randy Weston, Bobby Timmons, Mal Waldron** and **Don Ellis.** Carter was brought to the attention of many more listeners when he became a vital part of a new rhythm section for **Miles Davis** in 1963. With pianist Herbie Hancock and drummer Anthony Williams, Carter formed an almost telepathic understanding, allowing Miles and his frontline partners (George Coleman or Wayne Shorter) tremendous freedom but stirring support. They were with the trumpeter on a series of challenging and stimulating recordings including *Seven Steps To Heaven, Live In Europe, ESP, Sorcerer, Miles In The Sky* etc. Carter left Davis in 1968, and then worked with a host of different groups including the New York Bass Choir (with six other bassists), pianist/composer **Michel Legrand**, singer Lena Horne, Stanley Turrentine, Hubert Laws, **Lionel Hampton**, Joe Henderson, **George Benson** and the New York Jazz Quartet. Formed his own quartet in 1975, and played bass, cello and the unusual piccolo bass in the group. Carter, who has toured

Europe and the Far East many times, played a vital role, along with La Faro, Richard Davis, Charlie Haden and Niels-Henning Ørsted Pedersen in advancing the bass during the 1960s. He once named his favourites as Ray Brown, Percy Heath and Paul Chambers, but his work also owes a debt to Oscar Pettiford. Critic Doug Ramsey wrote of him: 'Carter is one of the contemporary giants of his instrument. He is also a fine composer, witness *Rally* and such other pieces as *Einbahnstrasse* and *Little Waltz,* which have become minor classics.' According to Nat Hentoff: 'He (Carter) is *a bassist of formidable technique who has long since learned the power of selection among his resources. And his beat is as alive as his breathing.'* Putting the musician's point of view, pianist Jaki Byard said Carter's time, tone and technique were brilliant. As a celloist, Ron also earned a favourable critical response, but it must be said that the albums under his own leadership have contained too much bass.

Carter could learn a lesson from Pettiford and Mingus who led many bands but seldom overplayed their own hands. Winner of a *Down beat* new star award on bass in 1965, Ron was on the faculty of several summer jazz clinics in the 1960s. His stock rose in the following decade and he was top bassman with *down beat* readers for three successive years (1973-'75). He wrote two books on *Building A Jazz Bass Line,* and did a good deal of television work, also touring and recording extensively.

In 1982 **Herbie Hancock** rounded up his old chums from the Davis group, Carter and Williams, adding trumpeter **Wynton Marsalis**, for a record date. Herbie, Ron and Anthony had occasionally played together as VSOP (Very Special Old Phonography!). With the additions of Wynton and his saxophonist brother Branford Marsalis VSOP II was complete. The band got back into a mid-1960s groove but in a creative way, extending that particular productive chapter of the Miles Davis tradition. On its 1983 visit to England VSOP II received a rapturous audience and critical reception. There has never been another rhythm section with the flexibility of Hancock, Carter and Williams, and to hear them working together again with such sensitive and subtle precision was a joy. This is Ron Carter's real musical family; a context in which he belongs. In the list of Ron's representative records, I have

included Miles Davis albums which do not duplicate any in the Davis biography.

Recommended records:
Eric Dolphy With Ron Carter/Where?
Prestige PRST 7843
Herbie Hancock/Empyrean Isles
Blue Note BST 84175
Herbie Hancock/Maiden Voyage
Blue Note BST 84195
Jaki Byard/Here's Jaki
Prestige PRST 8256
Jaki Byard/Hi-Fly
Prestige PRST 8273
Jaki Byard With Strings!
Prestige PRST 7573
Miles Davis/Miles In Berlin
CBS S 62976
Miles Davis/Miles In Tokyo
Japanese CBS SONX 60064R
Herbie Hancock Quartet
CBS 22219

'Until musicians really sit down and figure out why they are not making money, they will never make any and never know why they are not making it.'

'You may practise your instrument to a high point of musical proficiency, but there is no point in playing good if someone else always gets the money. That's like a farmer who spends a lifetime learning how to grow wheat, plant it, then lets the farmer next door take all the grain.'

'Freedom has its place in music and it is as valid as black power, gefilte fish, pizza or a coat and hat in the wintertime.' (Ron Carter)

Ron Carter. I had to draw him from a great distance, but it's as though you have a kind of zoom lens. Playing the music while simultaneously listening to yourself. What power in his fingers!

Milt Jackson 15 April '82 Singer Laren

Milt Jackson

Milton ('Bags') Jackson. Vibraharp/Piano/Guitar/Singer/Composer. Detroit, Michigan, January 1 1923.

Having studied music at Michigan State, Jackson, inspired by Lionel Hampton and Red Norvo, elected to make the vibraphone his main instrument. Began gigging around his hometown with saxophonist **Lucky Thompson** in 1939. The drummer and leader of that teenage band was Art Mardigan.

Trumpeter **Dizzy Gillespie**, a great talent-spotter and recruiter, heard and liked Jackson and signed him up for his first big band in 1945. At the end of that year Milt went with Dizzy to California as a member of a sextet also including **Charlie Parker**, Al Haig, Ray Brown and Stan Levey. Jackson appeared on a number of Dizzy's early recording sessions but the engineers of those days found it difficult to capture the true sound of vibes, and Milt's original style of playing.

Norvo and, to a lesser extent, Hampton had favoured a staccato approach; Jackson revelled in long, vibrating notes, often achieving almost an echo effect at the end of phrases. After the experience with Dizzy, Milt played in trumpeter **Howard McGhee**'s small group, and chalked up further experience with Tadd Dameron, Charlie Parker and Thelonious Monk.

He took over from Terry Gibbs in the **Woody Herman** Orchestra (1949-'50), but rejoined his former employer Gillespie from 1950-'52, playing both vibes and piano in Dizzy's small group. Around this time the Modern Jazz Quartet (MJQ) was at an embryonic stage. Its first records were made under Jackson's name in 1951. When it became a unit at the end of 1952, pianist **John Lewis** took over as musical director.

The group lasted with only one change in personnel (Connie Kay replaced the original drummer Kenny Clarke) for 22 years. After an eight-year break, the quartet was re-formed in 1982.

The MJQ are purveyors of subtle, subdued chamber jazz, often with European overtones. Jackson, always the instrumental star of the group, achieved a fantastic rapport with Lewis, Kay and bassist Percy Heath. Throughout its life, the MJQ has afforded Jackson a popular platform for his mercurial, inventive, blues-rooted improvising. But there are observers who feel that he has played with greater abandon in casual pick-up groups assembled for studio recordings or with units of which he was nominal leader.

In the 1950s there were interesting collaborations with **Miles Davis**, Hank Mobley and **Sonny Rollins**, but a highlight was the resumption of the old partnership with **Lucky Thompson** on a series of Savoy and Atlantic albums. 'Lucky and I grew up together back in Detroit. We know a lot about each other's style of playing. We've both always been seriously interested in music, we've gone into it conscientiously with the basic qualities and the basic foundation in mind. Lucky and I have never been interested in fads,' Milt has stated, summarizing his musical attitude.

Pianist Hank Jones, a frequent studio companion of Jackson's since their Detroit days and experience in McGhee's band, said of the vibesman: 'He has a unique way. He never seems to rush anything, yet he can play the fastest tempos with ease, and it all seems relaxed. He makes everything look and sound so easy, but he plays the most difficult things.'

That's really the measure of this exceptional musician – the ability to make the complex sound easy. *His solos flow along sweetly, lightly shaded, notes judiciously chosen so that phrases hang together and progress with an overall shape and inevitable design.*

Doug Ramsey's assessment of 'Bags' is pertinent and correct: 'Jackson is now where he has been since the 1940s, in the vanguard of dedicated creative jazz musicians who never compromise their integrity.' While he is accomplished at all tempos and in all metres, Milt appears to be at his happiest and most imaginative playing at medium pace in plain old 4/4 time on a standard such as *Out Of Nowhere*. On ballads he employs his distinctive slow vibrato. In the blues idiom he is as assured as all the great players in jazz, irrespective of era.

Bags – he earned that nickname because of the bags under his eyes – is a slim, apparently ageless man, a sharp dresser who bends over his vibraharp with total concentration. His piano playing, heard on a number of recordings, is percussive and choppy, with the right hand doing most of the work. He has occasionally played guitar, notably on an intriguing session with Ray Charles, and even broken into song.

His compositions are functional outlines sketched as springboards for improvisation. Jackson was a hit at the 1975 Montreux Jazz Festival. While with the MJQ he often co-led with **Ray Brown** a satisfying quintet featuring saxophonist **Teddy Edwards**.

In the 1970s he recorded with Dizzy Gillespie, Count Basie and Oscar Peterson among others, invariably bringing both excitement and subtlety to any project with which he was involved. Over the years he has been recorded with all manner of ensembles, large and small. The list below is a personal selection which deliberately concentrates on Milt Jackson's work outside the confines of the MJQ.

Recommended records:
Milt Jackson/The First Q
Savoy SJL 1106
Milt Jackson/Wizard Of The Vibes
Mode CMDINT 9834
Milt Jackson/Second Nature
Savoy SJL 2204
Milt Jackson Orchestra/Big Bags
Riverside RLP 429
The Complete Milt Jackson
Prestige PR 7655
Milt Jackson/At The Museum Of Modern Art
Limelight LM 82024
Milt Jackson/And The Hip String Quartet
Verve V6-8761
Milt Jackson/That's The Way It Is
Impulse AS-9189

Max Roach

Maxwell (Max) Roach. Drums/Vibraharp/Composer/Teacher. Brooklyn, New York, January 10 1925.

Began on drums while still at school. Main inspiration was Kenny Clarke who encouraged the young Max. Roach, too young then to actually get into Kelly's Stable Club to hear Kenny, was impressed by Clarke's use of the top cymbal with the left hand, superimposing rhythms. Prior to that most drummers copied Jo Jones and played sock cymbal. After leaving school in 1942 Roach went to work with **Charlie Parker** at Clarke Monroe's Uptown House, and thus found himself in on the groundfloor of a musical revolution. 'Even the way I play drums. You can say Bird was really responsible, not just because his style called for a particular kind of drumming, but because he set tempos so fast, it was impossible to play a straight, Cozy Cole, four style. So we had to work out variations,' Roach has explained.

Dizzy Gillespie also provided pointers for Max to help rather than hinder the soloist. Roach made his record debut with **Coleman Hawkins** for the *Apollo* label in February 1944, and that year was a member of the first bebop combo – the **Gilliespie/Oscar Pettiford** Quintet – on New York's 52nd Street, at the Onyx Club. Dizzy had promised a couple of years earlier that when he formed a group Roach would be the drummer.

Somewhat surprisingly, Max quit the group to join the **Benny Carter** Orchestra, but he was back in the Gillespie combo, along with Parker, for an engagement at the Three Deuces in 1945. Dizzy felt this was the apex of perfection of the new music with pianist **Bud Powell** and bassist **Curley Russell** rounding out the group. All, except Powell, were on the famous *Ko-Ko* date for *Savoy* in November 1945. But when Dizzy's sextet entrained for California the following month Stan Levey replaced Roach.

By this stage Max was regarded as the most complete modern drummer and embarked on a hectic schedule of gigging and recording activity with Hawkins, Allen Eager, Powell, **Miles Davis**, **J.J. Johnson** and many others. When Charlie Parker returned from California in the spring of 1947 he formed a new quintet with Roach on drums. Max stayed with him for more than two years, appearing on all the group's *Dial* and *Savoy* recordings.

The Parker rhythm section of either Duke Jordan or Al Haig (piano), Tommy Potter (bass) and Roach formed a magnificent team. Trumpeter Miles Davis and Max eventually left the group, and Roach provided the percussive base for the famous 'Birth of the Cool' band that Miles assembled. The drummer's stint with Parker took him to France for the Paris Jazz Festival in May 1949; three years later he was back in Europe touring with Jazz At The Philharmonic. Max continued to freelance successfully and was reunited with Parker and Gillespie for the 'Quintet of the Year' concert of 1953, also making some superlative quartet records with Parker that same year.

But Roach nurtured ambitions to have a group of his own, or at least a collaborative combo venture. In the summer of 1953, after further studies at the Manhatten School of Music, the drummer replaced Shelly Manne in bassist Howard Rumsey's Lighthouse All Stars in Los Angeles. His survey of the scene convinced him that the West Coast, after several years of a 'cool' musical diet, was ripe to receive a hard-swinging post-bop East Coast group. He called up New York, explained his ideas to the rising trumpet star **Clifford Brown**, and the pair, who had never met, determined to go West and co-lead a fresh, new group.

Carl Perkins and Teddy Edwards were the first pianist and tenor saxophonist respectively in the quintet, but were replaced by Bud Powell's younger brother Richie, on piano, and **Harold Land** (tenor) with the dependable George Morrow on bass. The group was like an extension of the Gillespie/Parker quintet, and Roach was the common denominator. Brown, a torchbearer for the modern trumpet tradition, and Powell, were members of the outfit until their tragic deaths in a car crash in June 1956. Roach had been deeply affected by the somewhat less unexpected demise of his old employer Parker the previous year; but the losses of Brown and Powell left him mortified. For several months he simply withdrew from music, and more than 20 years elapsed before he was able to listen to Clifford's records, such was the emotional hurt that he felt about fate's random removal of a brilliant musician and warm human being.

In 1958 he unearthed another superb young trumpeter in **Booker Little**, who within three years was to die of uraemia at the age of 23 – another bitter blow for Roach. Despite these setbacks, the drummer continued to provide a platform for exciting young musicians, including the brothers Stanley and Tommy Turrentine, Ray Draper (that jazz rarity – a tuba soloist), **Eric Dolphy**, **Clifford Jordan**, **Art Davis** and **Julian Priester**. Always politically aware and articulate, Max caused considerable controversy in the jazz press with his outspoken views in support of black power in the early 1960s. He and his singer/actress wife **Abbey Lincoln** (they were divorced in 1970) recorded the *Freedom Now Suite* in 1960. It contained such titles as *Freedom Day, All Africa* and *Tears For Johannesburg*. His next album reflected his political preoccupations in *Garvey's Ghost, Praise For A Martyr* and *Man From South Africa*. Also in the early 1960s Max recorded his ensemble and Miss Lincoln with a backing of a sixteen-piece choir directed by Coleridge Perkinson.

Roach has said: 'Music is the dominant force in my life. To me, the most important thing is the music. The musician and the instrument are subservient to it.' Roach was *the first drummer to play truly melodic drum solos that were tightly constructed and beautifully organized, carefully shaded with perfectly deployed dynamics.*

He believes that the innovations of Kenny Clarke, Art Blakey and himself were an extension of the possibilities opened up for drummers by Jo Jones, Sid Catlett and Chick Webb in the 1930s. Catlett was a particular idol of Roach's. 'He was a powerful man but gentle on his instrument. And he was a very generous man. He made me proud to be a drummer.'

Roach, ever the experimentalist, was the first leader to record an entire jazz album in waltz time in 1957. After leading a fine quintet with **Freddie Hubbard** (trumpet) and James Spaulding (alto sax) in the 1960s, Max's band included Cecil Bridgewater, Billy Harper and **Reggie Workman** in the 1970s.

He also created a percussion ensemble called M'Boom which featured Roach and fellow drummers Roy Brooks, Joe Chambers, Freddie Waits, Warren Smith and Omar Clay.

Roach has shown in countless solos and as a steadfast, imaginative accompanist that the drums are not to be beaten and battered, but rather brushed and blandished. He is always in absolute control of every part of the battery, and this is perhaps most easily illustrated in his three-minute solo masterpiece *For Big Sid* on his *Drums Unlimited* album.

Roach is interested in the roots of black music and culture, and has travelled widely in Africa, and has served on the selection committee of the National Board of the Nigerian Festival.

Roach has moved with the changing times without ever neglecting the basics of his craft. All of today's best drummers owe a debt to Max Roach for whether directly, or indirectly through the work of others, he has influenced them. His contribution to the evolution of jazz percussion playing techniques and procedures has been monumental. Roach's playing enhances

Max Roach. After the concert Max Roach said to me: 'I saw you, drawing on the rhythm; you are one of us!'

numerous reissue albums by Parker, Gillespie, Monk, Hawkins, J.J. Johnson, Powell etc. from the 1940s and 1950s. The choice offered here concentrates on LP's issued under his own leadership.

Recommended records:
Clifford Brown-Max Roach/Live At The Bee Hive
CBS 88453
Clifford Brown-Max Roach/Pure Genius
Elektra Musician MUS K 52388
Clifford Brown-Max Roach
EmArcy MG 36036
Clifford Brown-Max Roach/At Basin Street
EmArcy MG 36070
Max Roach/Jazz In 3/4 Time
EmArcy MG 36108
Max Roach Plus Four
EmArcy MG 36098
Max Roach/Max
Argo LP 623
Max Roach Plus Four/On The Chicago Scene
EmArcy MG 36132
Max Roach/Drums Unlimited
Atlantic 1467

Herbie Hancock

Herbert Jeffrey Hancock (Mwandishi). Piano/Composer/Electric Piano/Synthesizer. Chicago, Illinois, April 12 1940.

Family, including parents, sister and brother, involved with music. Started piano lessons at age seven. Performed at a young people's concert with Chicago Symphony, playing Mozart, at age 11. Studied classical piano through college until aged 20. First piano lessons from Mrs Whalen at Ebenezer Baptist Church, Chicago. Left college in 1960 to work in post office.
First important job with **Coleman Hawkins**, then played with Donald Byrd/Pepper Adams group, joining in December 1960 and staying until May 1963 when he left to become pianist with **Miles Davis** Quintet. First album for *Blue Note* contained hit single *Watermelon Man*. Made a series of important LPs for that label, including *Maiden Voyage, Empyrean Isles, Inventions And Dimensions, Speak Like A Child*. Also wrote score and directed soundtrack for

Carlo Ponti's new wave movie *Blow-Up* (1967). Appeared on many Miles Davis albums 1963-'68, contributing original compositions as well as excellent solos and a new concept in accompaniment in which he worked closely with **Ron Carter** (bass) and **Tony Williams** (drums). Among the best Davis records from this period are *E.S.P., Miles Smiles* and *Miles in Berlin*. Hancock's other affiliations before branching out as a leader were with Phil Woods, Oliver Nelson and **Eric Dolphy**. His compositions, such as *Dolphin Dance, Maiden Voyage, Speak Like A Child, Riot* and *Canteloupe Island*, soon gained currency in jazz circles. When he left Davis, Herbie formed a sextet and set about changing his sound by plunging into electronics, using electric guitar, electric piano and electric bass in his band plus echo-plex, synthesizer and a range of percussion. Albums like *Fat Albert Rotunda, Mwandishi, Headhunters* and *Succotash* showed an increasing preoccupation with jazz/funk and crossover sounds. Hancock is reported to have said in 1973: 'I realized that I could never be a genius in the class of Miles, Charlie Parker or Coltrane, so I might just as well forget about becoming a legend and just be satisfied to create some music to make people happy.'
In fact, Herbie operated in several areas and with the formation of the co-operative quintet VSOP for recordings and concerts he returned to the style of advanced jazz he had espoused with Miles Davis. This tradition has been continued by Hancock and his other close associates in VSOP II in the 1980s. He has also persevered with his electronic music which he has furthered by his use of the Apple computer to create synthetic sounds. His return to acoustic jazz (and piano) in 1977 showed he had lost none of his distinctive characteristics — a real pianistic touch, fine use of dynamics and long, complex, convoluted improvisational lines.
Hancock was influenced by many people. Among pianists: McCoy Tyner, Wynton Kelly, Bill Evans. Horn players: Miles Davis, John Coltrane, Eric Dolphy, Lee Morgan. And his longstanding partners-in-rhythm: Tony Williams and Ron Carter. Hancock is interested in many aspects of music and culture.
He is of the Buddhist faith and has taken the Swahili name of Mwandishi. He has recorded with pop singing star **Stevie Wonder**, had records of his own in the best-selling charts, and is widely admired

by both his contemporaries and older musicians, like Oscar Peterson. Herbie has also collaborated with **Chick Corea**, the pianist who replaced him in the Davis group of 1968.
Asked by Elliot Meadow (*Jazz Journal International,* April 1980) if there was any particular musical environment he enjoyed above all others, Hancock replied: 'The funny thing is the music I enjoy most is that which I'm working on at the given moment. I guess that makes sense otherwise I wouldn't be doing it. If you just play the notes, you haven't played the music. Feeling is the most important ingredient and that applies to every kind of musical endeavour.'
In 1983 Herbie Hancock toured Europe with VSOP II. A few months later he was back with his heavy electronic, synthesized funk. Irrespective of his efforts at the frontiers of funk, Herbie Hancock's status as a visionary jazz pianist and composer remains unobscured, except to those who have stopped listening and cannot accept his musical diversity.

Recommended records:
Herbie Hancock/Takin' Off
Blue Note BST 84109
Herbie Hancock/Empyrean Isles
Blue Note BST 84175
Herbie Hancock/Maiden Voyage
Blue Note BST 84195
Herbie Hancock/Speak Like A Child
Blue Note BST 84279
Herbie Hancock Quartet
Columbia C2 38275
Herbie Hancock/Headhunters
CBS S 65928
V.S.O.P.: The Quintet
Columbia CS-34976
An Evening With Herbie Hancock And Chick Corea
Columbia PC-32965
Donald Byrd/Free Form
Blue Note BST 84118
Donald Byrd-Pepper Adams Quintet, Vol 1/Hip-Intertainment
VGM 0002
Miles Davis/Miles In Berlin
CBS S 62 976
Miles Davis/E.S.P.
Columbia CL 2350
Miles Davis/Miles Smiles
Columbia CL 2601
Wayne Shorter/Speak No Evil
Blue Note BST 84194
Wayne Shorter/Adam's Apple
Blue Note BST 84232

Herbie Hancock with the Rockit band on the Future Shock Tour. I caught him behind his computer-programmed gadgets.

Ratcliffe
19-1-'84

Herbie
Hancock

SMOKEY smothers

Close-up on the blues

Did you ever wake up in the morning
Just about the break of day
Reach over, draw the pillow
Where your baby used to lay

Give you the blues
I'm gonna tell you that's the blues

I've got the blues so bad it hurts my tongue to talk,
I've got the blues so bad it hurts my feet to walk
Everybody knows,
I've got the blues. That's the blues!

The rich root

The blues are the rich root compost upon which the strong trunk and branches of jazz and much contemporary music have grown. They are dramatic, melodramatic, colourful, stark, powerful and highly emotional. The blues have been around for roughly a century and show no sign of decline.

Whether sophisticated or crude, the blues have an immediacy that communicates with audiences everywhere. They are living black folk music, constantly changing to express the hopes and fears, the joys and frustrations of the present. The blues tell human stories about tragedy, passion, rejection, privation, misery, pleasure, pain, heartbreak, comedy, sex, loneliness, love, work, travel, drink, drugs, lust, greed, God, the Devil, freedom, slavery, food, life and death. In short, the blues are about the body and the soul of a people.

Field hollers and early blues

The blues form, so unerringly right as a piece of musical construction, did not happen by accident. Neither was it an overnight invention. Rather it slowly evolved from the earliest slaves transported from Africa across the Atlantic to the USA, and among their descendants. The classic twelve-bar construction was probably not arrived at until the latter part of the 19th century, following the Civil War and the abolition of slavery. Research suggests that the earliest, primitive blues were eight, ten or sixteen bars in chorus length.

What came to be called the 'classic' blues stemmed directly from the work shouts and field hollers — the *work* songs — and the spirituals. Musically, the opening four bars are repeated with a slight, new melody introduced for the final four releasing and resolving bars. The shout shared with the blues the three-line structure. These songs were made up on the spot, and the reason for the repetition of the first line was to enable the lead singer to concoct a third line. And this became a convention that appears in thousands of *written* blues lyrics, being especially suited to performances at faster tempo. Sometimes just one line sufficed (either through lack of inspiration or because the composer was pleased with a good opening statement), to be repeated over and over with hypnotic effect.

A typical use of the repeat lyric line appears in Big Bill Bronzy's *Country Boy Blues* (the 1940 version he recorded with Lil Green):

I love him if he is a little old country boy,
I love him if he is a little old country boy,
Yes I love him, 'cos he fills my heart with joy.

As the blues matured as an idiom, the need to repeat a line (except for special emphasis) disappeared, and the urban, *professional* blues singers/composers would often use the second line to extend the story, as in another chorus of Rubberlegs Williams' *That's The Blues:*

Then you cry, you cry like you never cried before,
You'll even cry so loud you'll give the blues to your neighbour nextdoor,
Then you know you got the blues, Ooh-wee, you got the blues,
It'll make you feel so bad you could lay right there and die.

Nevertheless the *musical* form of the blues has generally adhered to the A (four bars) A (same four bars again) B (four bars of new melody) pattern. The earliest blues were apparently crude, raw and uncompromising. The emergence of so-called 'classic blues' was marked by a more formal, a smoother musical offering.

45

Smoky Smothers. One of the first times I worked with coloured paper. A man of the streets, nearly the definition of the blues, though his Derby hat seems like it was made to look a little older.

The blues passed into the wider spectrum of American culture, and became part of entertainment. The blues gradually assumed a meaning for *Americans,* irrespective of race. With the advent of the phonograph record, mass produced and readily available, the blues were seen to possess universal appeal.

The original bluesmen

Within the blues will be found the rhythmic beat of hammer striking rail, the clank of steam train piston and the wail of the engine's whistle, the hoot of the steam boat siren and the throb of its machinery and swooshing of its massive turning wheels. The clink of steel hitting rock was the rhythm of the chain-gang work song or blues.

Many of the early blues masters, including *Huddie Ledbetter* (Leadbelly), spent long stretches of their lives as prison inmates. Ledbetter, like so many of the black singers, led a wandering minstrel sort of life, playing his guitar anywhere that people would listen. His stock in trade were ballads, cowboy songs, hollers and shouts, and the blues he learned from *Blind Lemon Jefferson.*

In the early years of this century, the blues were only part of the travelling musician's repertoire. He would use whatever material caught his fancy, and not unnaturally was ever ready to perform his own compositions. Hearing them played by others and knowing they would be spread far and wide gave the composer much satisfaction and was a source for genuine pride.

Like a large mound of pastry flattened under a rolling pin, the blues spread across the map of America. Invaluable assistance to this dissemination of a minority music was the black vaudeville theatre along with the minstrel troupes, circus and medicine shows.

The instruments used by these pioneers to accompany their singing were inevitably the hand string-instruments of guitar and banjo. They were conveniently portable and could be strummed or plucked (picked) as songs were sung. The singers developed an instrumental facility that allowed them to rest their voices and *improvise* one or several choruses. Already we begin to perceive the crucial influence of the blues on jazz in the realms of spontaneous expression.

Among these original bluesmen there was a certain degree of rivalry (and occasionally rank hostility), but also there existed a close feeling of brotherhood. Partnerships were forged, and these increased the musical possibilities, permitted men to learn from each other and provide a more interesting and entertaining 'show'.

Blues as social history

Because neither the words nor the music of the very first primitive blues were written down, and preceded the invention of the phonograph, no unarguable evidence exists about the origins. In 19th century America few white people were interested in the music of the Negro or any other aspect of an ethnic sub-culture which had been evolving for more than two and a half centuries. To African tribal culture had been added aspects of the white man's belief and experience. Yet all this occurred almost unnoticed to whites. What could mere slaves teach *Them* about anything? So the blues were quietly stewing, garnering new ingredients and flavours. The songs that blacks hollered in cotton plantations or as they hauled heavy loads along the docks of Southern ports were based on tribal chants from Africa. When those workers returned to their cramped living-quarters after dark the melodies they sang were also their own. Father and mother passed on the words and tunes to sons and daughters. New words were added and the old forgotten, melodies changed and improved.

After the abolition of slavery thousands drifted North believing that in the Yankee States they would encounter no prejudice. The reality, of course, proved to be no Shangri-La. Actual slavery was replaced by the equally odious economic slavery imposed by the segregated confines of the ghetto. Within 40 years of the end of the Civil War all the major cities of the Mid-West and the Northern States on the East Coast were segregated. The blacks discovered they had exchanged rural poverty for urban squalor. Their plight was told in the blues of street musicians.

Meanwhile in the South, attempts to build a new order in the wake of abolition rapidly sputtered out in the face of vested interest and a white society that regarded the Negro as a chattel, an animal to be worked and abused. Blacks were soon disfranchised by State laws, and the voting rights which had been hard won in the carnage of bitter conflict were thus stripped away.

Ironically, the railroads which took free and hopeful blacks North had been built by the blistering toil of slave labour. While handling the heavy sleepers and hammering into place the hot rails under the burning sun, a new repertoire of work songs and blues was created. The railroads and their mystique also served as inspiration for a crop of black ballads, notably *John Henry* and *Railroad Bill.*

Indeed, any occupation, predicament or circumstance in which the Negro found himself was material for an

46

Pee Wee
Crayton

Willie Dixon

Willie James Dixon. Upright Bass/Guitar/Singer. Vicksburg, Mississippi, July 1 1915.

Willie Dixon is undoubtedly one of the most legendary names in the history of the Chicago Blues. Until today he's been active for more than 50 years as a songwriter/composer of countless blues songs, producer, arranger, A&R man, talent scout and musician, and his path crossed that of many of Chicago's most famous musicians in the history of the blues like Howlin' Wolf, Muddy Waters, Sonny Boy Williamson 2 (Rice Miller), Little Walter, Koko Taylor and others.

He learned to play bass in 1937 and in 1945 he recorded for *Mercury Records*. During the same year he formed the legendary Big Three Trio with Leonard Caston and **Bernardo Dennis**. Many recordings for such labels as *Columbia* and *Cobra* followed, but Willie's real big time came when he started to work for *Chess/Checker Records* in the early fifties, to this day the most influential and legendary record company in the history of the (Chicago) Blues. Giants like Howlin' Wolf, **Muddy Waters** and **Sonny Boy Williamson** usually recorded their own compositions for the *Checker/Chess* label which often featured Willie Dixon on bass, while he also was the producer and arranger in many cases. *But for the compositions of Willie Dixon they all made exceptions to this statement. And so, some of Willie's compositions, became blues classics. The legendary Muddy Waters had a chart topper with 'Hoochie Coochie Man', Howlin' Wolf scored with 'Spoonfull' and with 'Little Red Rooster', while Sonny Boy Williamson had a great success with 'Bring It On Home'. Also Koko Taylor's greatest success to date, 'Wang Dang Doodle' carried the name of Willie Dixon as the songwriter and composer.* Also artists like Chuck Berry, Bo Diddley, Jimmy Rogers and Magic Sam recorded songs written by Willie. During the '50s/'60s/'70s countless records carried his name on the label as the arranger/songwriter/producer, and in the last mentioned decade he recorded an album under his own name for *Columbia Records:* 'I Am The Blues'. It resulted in a Golden Record.

Willie Dixon visited Europe for the first time in 1962 with the American Folk Blues Festival, a visit he repeated in 1963, 1964 and 1970.

After a foot amputation in '77 Willie came to Europe as the host of The New Generation of Chicago Blues and in 1983 he visited Europe again with the present line-up of his own band which he formed in 1968: The Chicago Blues All Stars. Besides his activities as a performer, Willie continues composing new blues songs, owns a studio and a work shop for younger musicians in Chicago's South Side and, in 1984, is attempting to set up a Coast To Coast blues radio programme in The United States.

Recommended records:
The All Star Blues Word Of Maestro Willie Dixon
Spivey LD 1016
Songs Of Memphis Slim & Willie Dixon
Folkways FA 2385
Memphis Slim & Willie Dixon At The Village Gate
Folkways FA 2386
I Am The Blues
Columbia CS 9987
Willie Dixon/Chicago Blues
Spivey SPI 1003
Willie Dixon/Maestro & Chicago Blues
Spivey SPI 1016
Willie Dixon/Willie's Blues
Original OBC 501
Willie Dixon/Blues Roots Vol 12
Chess CHE 624802
Willie Dixon/Peace?
Yambo 777-15

Pee Wee Crayton

Connie Curtis Crayton. Guitar/Singer. Rockdale, Texas, December 18 1914.

From his childhood he was raised in Austin, Texas. At an early age he was interested in music and first learned to play ukelele on a self-made cigarbox instrument. A little later he played trumpet in a school band. He worked in a job outside music until the mid-1930s. From that time on he worked with various musicians at a club in Oakland, California. At the age of 33, he taught himself to play guitar. As he told Marcel M. Vos (interview *Block* 44, Oct.-Dec. '82) he performed as a guitar player one year after he bought his first guitar. 'I don't like to say it, 'cause people might explain it the wrong way, but it's not me who's playing. It's God who plays my guitar indirectly. It's a gift from God. When I play I feel that I'm another person than when I don't play.'

During his career Crayton has been influenced by such guitar-greats as Charlie Christian and T-Bone Walker. He made his first recordings for the *Four Star* label, a local from Los Angeles, California, and from then on he continued recording pretty continuously until the early 1960s. Then there was a gap in his recording career until 1968. During the fifties and the sixties he toured with many well-known musicians, mostly from the American West Coast, like Roy Milton, Dinah Washington, **Ray Charles**, Big Maybelle and The Johnny Otis Show. In '70 he played at the Monterey Jazz Festival. Although his reputation on the West Coast is comparable with that of the late T-Bone Walker in Texas, it took until 1979 before he flew over to Europe. *Today Crayton keeps up his reputation in and around Los Angeles, California, where he lives, but beside that his reputation in other parts of The States as well as in Europe seems to be growing faster than ever.*

Recommended records:
The Genius Of The Blues
Ace Records CH 23
The Things That I Used To Do
Vanguard VSD 6566

Willy Dixon. It was towards the end of the show. Luther Allison jumped up on stage and together they paid hommage to Muddy Waters. And afterwards Luther sang in praise of Willy Dixon. What an event!

Willie Dixon

North Sea
10-7-83

Luther Allison
Willie Dixon

ever expanding blues 'book'. As the eminent blues historian Paul Oliver has written (*The Story Of The Blues,* 1969): 'Seen from any point of view, the blues is both a state of mind and a music which gives voice to it. Blues is the wail of the forsaken, the cry of independence, the passion of the lusty, the anger of the frustrated and the laughter of the fatalist. It's the agony of indecision, the despair of the jobless, the anguish of the bereaved and the dry wit of the cynics. As such the blues is the personal emotion of the individual finding through music a vehicle for self-expression. But it is also a social music; the blues can be entertainment, it can be the music for dancing and drinking by, the music of a class within a segregated group.'

Blues instruments

The informal nature of the blues scene at the turn of the century was about to be overtaken by history in the shape of social and commercial change, triggered by rapid industrialization. The exodus to the North by Southern blacks quickened with the need for a massive labour force to man factories where the mass production of goods was now a reality. The automobile had arrived, and it would not be a luxury for long. With the advent of the phonograph and the realization by big business that fortunes were there to be made from the sales of sheet music and records, commerce invitingly beckoned the blues.

The tools of the trade for the working bluesman were more readily available, too. Guitars could be obtained from mail-order companies. The handyman could purchase a do-it-yourself kit and assemble his own instrument, while those lacking a carpenter's skills might easily come by a Spanish guitar imported to the South from across the nearby Mexican border. An old bottleneck cost nothing. Drawn across the strings it produced a wailing, vocal effect.

The inexpensive mouth-organ, the Jew's-harp and the tin whistle were added to the bluesman's kit. Just as the subjects that blues musicians covered would change, so their instruments would alter to accommodate new tastes. From the 1920s onwards, blues singers performed with jazz rhythm sections and ensembles. In the 1930s it was virtually de rigeur for a Kansas City swing band to have one or two featured blues singers. Those bands, with singers like *Jimmy Rushing* and *Walter Brown,* reminded the jazz community that an infusion of the blues was refreshing to a music becoming increasingly preoccupied with elaborately written scores.

War and prohibition

The blues popularity explosion had been primed several years before the USA entered the first global conflict. *W.C. (William Christopher) Handy* had already published and copyrighted a number of his most famous compositions, including *Memphis Blues, Yellow Dog Blues* and *Joe Turner Blues.* A slumbering giant was ready to awaken. World War I, just as the Civil War had done half a century earlier, acted as a catalyst on the music. The war threw together black musicians and singers from States in the North and South for service training at home and ultimately battle in the terrifying European theatre. The black regiments fought the white man's war with surprising resolve and patriotism. There was little in it for them, and even less when they returned home to unemployment. But for the blues artists conscripted the war enabled them to meet and exchange ideas. This was an important factor in the forthcoming blues boom. The music had been given a final polish and would never again exist purely as a local folk mode of expression. It would be known nationally and then internationally.

One individual who, above any other, effected the breakthrough into popularity was *Bessie Smith,* one of seven children who were orphaned when Bessie was only eight years old. She appears to have been a complete 'natural', possessing a magnificent voice which required no training other than that gained from the experience of regular work and listening to her contemporaries. Bessie's immediate predecessor in the blues firmament was *Gertrude 'Ma' Rainey,* known as the 'Mother of the Blues', who was Smith's senior by eight years. Bessie toured in tent shows with Rainey for quite a few years, and almost certainly learned a few wrinkles about dramatic presentation from Ma in the tent shows and theatres where they appeared.

Two significant events in 1920 spurred on the blues arrival at centre stage in American culture. On January 17 the manufacture, sale and consumption of alcoholic drinks was outlawed in the USA, and on August 10, Mamie Smith recorded *Crazy Blues* for *Okeh.* It was the first vocal blues record. Prohibition, far from lessening demand for alcohol, actually boosted sales of illicit liquor, presenting to organized crime its most profitable 'industry'. Outlets for the sale of booze led to the establishment of hundreds of speakeasy clubs in the cities and towns of America, and these were new places of employment for blues singers from the South. The encouraging sales of the Mamie Smith record

Jim Brewer. An example of one of those singers just off the streets. With light left in one of his eyes only. After the show in the dressing-room I asked him to sign it. I was actually a little embarrassed, but he wasn't. He held my work almost against the one eye drawing those letters.

JIMBREWER

JOHNLHOOKER

North Sea 10-7-81

John Lee Hooker. The brash colours of his
clothes tell us something about his music: it's
music from the streets, without a necktie, and
the drawing underscores this. He was sitting on
stage during the North Sea Jazz Festival,
backed by a complete band and thousands of
people all around him, and still he had
something lost and lonely about him.

Big Six, The Delta Big Four and **The Fairfield Four**.

Hooker then uprooted again and settled in Detroit where he appeared at a host of clubs and started recording. Hooker became the number one blues man in Detroit which was a jumping city with plenty of money around as the automobile industry boomed in the late 1940s. Hooker took the place by storm and built on his popularity there as a springboard to national and then international fame. Paul Oliver, in *The Story Of The Blues* (1969), assessed Hooker thus: 'He had a guitar technique which made extensive use of "hammering on" the strings and his heavy-accented foot-beat as he played was integral to his performance. A slight speech impediment in his deep and rich voice gave it an oddly expressive urgency.' The late Professor Marshall Stearns reckoned that Hooker was *'one of the few truly authentic exponents of archaic guitar style, a style which may well trace back to Civil War days.'* And writer Pete Welding thought him: 'One of the most gripping and powerful singers the blues has yet produced and a guitarist whose playing all but overwhelms one with its ferocity and rhythmic tension.' Hooker has recorded extensively during the past 35 years, and over the last three decades has toured widely, making the first of many European tours in 1962. He became a great favourite in England and appeared in that country with John Lee's Ground Hogs and **John Mayall**'s Bluesbreakers. Also heard on a number of tours with the American Folk Blues Festival package in the 1960s.

Hooker's style has changed — he has made rhythm and blues and rock and roll sessions — since his earliest records but as an illustration of the incredible stylistic span in jazz and blues it is worth mentioning that Hooker is only two months older than Dizzy Gillespie, for so long the torchbearer of musical modernity!

Hooker has been a prolific composer of original blues and some of the titles to his credit are *Hard Headed Woman, Guitar Lovin' Man, Church Bell Tone, I'm Prison Bound, Sugar Mama, I'm Bad Like Jesse James, I Need Some Money, One Way Ticket, No Shoes, Whiskey And Wimmen, If You Got A Dollar* and *Dusty Road*. His influence has been widespread and those who owe a debt to Hooker's music include Junior Parker, John Mayall, Buddy Guy and Canned Heat.

Recommended records:
John Lee Hooker/Urban Blues
BluesWay BL-6012
John Lee Hooker/Simply The Truth
BluesWay BL-6023
John Lee Hooker/The Blues
Crown CLP 5157
The Original American Folk Blues Festival
Polydor 46397
John Lee Hooker/You're Leavin' Me Baby
Riverside 673.005
John Lee Hooker/House Of The Blues
Chess LP 1438
John Lee Hooker/Detroit Special
Atlantic SD 7228
John Lee Hooker/Boogie Chillin
Fantasy F 24706
John Lee Hooker/Black Snake
Fantasy F 24722
John Lee Hooker/Everybody Rockin'
Charly CRB 1014

John Lee Hooker

John Lee Hooker. Singer/Guitar.
Clarksdale, Missouri, August 22 1917.

One of 11 children whose parents were sharecroppers. Raised on stepfather William Moore's farm. Sang spirituals in local church. Moore taught him the rudiments of guitar and they played together at dances.

At age 14, Hooker ran away from home to Memphis and worked with local groups before moving to Cincinnati in 1933, playing with such gospel groups as The

convinced the record companies that there was a large market for what came to be called 'race records'. The major firms quickly launched subsidiary labels to cater exclusively for the tastes of black buyers. New companies were formed to specialize in recording black music. One of these, *Black Swan,* a venture involving composer W.C. Handy and Harry Pace, was the first recording company owned and operated by blacks. Ironically, *Black Swan* passed up the opportunity to record Bessie Smith!

Bessie Smith

Although Mamie Smith, the pioneer of blues recording, was billed as the 'Queen of the Blues' she wasn't really a blues singer, being more at home with popular songs of the day. The top blues people of the 1920s set great store by the right billing. Bessie Smith could not be either the mother or the queen of the blues since those titles were taken, so she went one better and was imperiously styled 'Empress of the Blues'. Indeed, she was a majestic, statuesque figure whose very dark complexion contrasted with the white gowns she invariably wore.

Bessie Smith made her first records for *Columbia* in 1923 and was immediately a star. In her first year as a recording artist she sold a phenomenal two million records. By the mid-1920s she was the highest paid and most successful black performer in history up to that time. Her descent from these dizzy heights was as rapid as her climb. Her addiction to alcohol, coupled with bad management by her business advisers and changing public taste, made her an almost forgotten name by the early 1930s. Between 1931 and her death six years later she made only one recording session. The line dividing blues from jazz was narrow during Bessie Smith's heyday. She frequently recorded with jazz musicians, and on three of her record dates trumpeter *Louis Armstrong* was present. Their 1925 version of Handy's *St Louis Blues,* perhaps the most famous non-blues of all, is still regarded as definitive to this day. Armstrong, apart from being the first jazz genius, was a magnificent blues singer, but such was his trumpet talent that his vocal ability was almost an incidental. Among the notable female contemporaries of Bessie were here namesakes Clara and Trixie Smith, who were both big-voiced blues singers and recording artists in their own right. Other blueswomen of importance were *Bertha 'Chippie' Hill, Lizzie Miles, Sippie Wallace* and *Victoria Spivey.*

Country and urban blues

The blues began to fragment into different styles in the 1930s. The original country blues continued on in the Southern States, but each of the large industrial cities produced its own distillation of the blues essence. The main centres were Chicago, St Louis, Detroit, Memphis and Kansas City. In those cities were to be found the colourful names of blues history — *Big Bill Broonzy,* Tampa Red, Peetie Wheatstraw, *Roosevelt Sykes, Cow Cow Davenport,* Bumble Bee Slim, Scrapper Blackwell, *Leroy Carr,* Peg Leg Howell, Kokomo Arnold, Sonny Boy Williamson, St Louis Jimmy, Washboard Sam, Stump Johnson, *Big Joe Williams* and Jazz Gillum. Many of these men were emigrees from the South. Down-at-heel bars and cheap cafés were the outlets for Chicago's urban blues. The city that spawned organized crime and the Syndicate at least provided a nightly forum for the pianists, guitarists, harmonica players and singers to 'strut their stuff'. The blues tradition is still going strong in the Chicago of today. Equally vital in the inter-related story of the blues and jazz was Kansas City, that conveniently central railway junction of middle-America, a wide-open, jumping and lawless town in the late 1930s. Here were to be heard Joe Turner, *Jimmy Rushing,* Walter Brown, *Helen Humes* and others. The best jazz instrumentalists and black swing bands were also there in abundance — Count Basie, Andy Kirk, Harlan Leonard and Jay McShann. All these bands played blues and featured blues singers.

Blues after 1945

The blues went into an eclipse during World War II, but new names were starting to emerge — *Jimmy Witherspoon,* Joe Williams, Percy Mayfield, *Aaron 'T-Bone' Walker,* Wynonie 'Mr Blues' Harris, Dinah Washington, Elmore James, *Muddy Waters* and *John Lee Hooker.* The urban bluesmen had no hesitation about adopting the electric guitar, and T-Bone Walker, Elmore James, Buddy Guy and others put it to excellent use in blues bands. T-Bone Walker is generally acknowledged to have been the first blues guitarist to employ amplification. Many have followed his path — Muddy Waters, Otis 'Smokey' Smothers, *B.B. King, Chuck Berry,* Juke Boy Bonner, Jimmy Reed and Buddy Guy among others.

Jazz, and more particularly swing, was the popular music or the World War II years. A blues revival occurred just after the war when Huddie Ledbetter and

Lovie Lee. His posture is the epitome of the elementary power of blues accompaniment. He was Muddy Waters' piano player years ago.

Lovie Lee.
6/19/50
WINCHESTER
60636

in memoriam Muddy Waters

18 XII 83

Memphis Slim

Peter Chatman. Piano/Organ/Singer.
Memphis, Tennessee, September 3 1915.

Peter Chatmon, a.k.a. Memphis Slim, grew up in a street in Memphis with a local blues & boogie club next door. As anyone can guess, Peter was interested in music at an early age. When he was seven years old, he taught himself to play piano. A little later he played string-bass in a school band.
From 1931 on he hoboed through the Deep South to make some money in juke joints, dance halls and camps. The same year he went North to settle in Chicago. Soon after his arrival he met guitar player/singer **Big Bill Broonzy** and they worked together for about seven years. In the early 1940s he recorded with his own washboard-band for *Okeh* Records in Chicago. A long row of recordings for an almost countless amount of labels, most of them based in Chicago, followed. Soon after a date in New York's famous Carnegie Hall, he went to Europe to work concert dates with **Willie Dixon.** Many tours through several European countries followed and since the late '60s Paris, France, is Memphis Slim's permanent residence, although he keeps visiting his birthplace Memphis at least once a year to celebrate his birthday with his relatives and his friends.
Beside the fact that Memphis Slim is an outstanding performer, mastering a piano style that can hardly be compared nowadays with anyone else's, he made a career as a songwriter/composer. His composition *Everyday I Have The Blues* is one of the long-time standards in the field of blues and hardly anybody will be able to guess how many musicians covered the song.
Since Memphis Slim chose Paris as his permanent residence, he recorded for many European labels and he made extensive solo tours, while in the meantime, he entertained many people in some nightclubs in Paris, France.
Looking back on his long career the recordings he made in the sixties for *Folkways* can be considered as an artistic highlight in his career.
Of great importance are also the recordings he did with the late **Sonny Boy Williamson** (Rice Miller), during the latter's several concert dates and recording sessions in Europe in the early sixties.

Without doubt, Memphis Slim is one of the blues' biggest names... He simply is a legend in his own time.

Recommended records:
Songs By...
Folkways FA 2358
At The Village Gate
Folkways FA 2386
With Carey Bell and Lowell Fulson
Jewel LPS 5004
Southside Reunion
Blue Star 80 601

Johnny Copeland

Johnny Clyde Copeland. Guitar/Singer.
Haynesville, Louisiana, March 27 1937.

Blanton Copeland, Johnny's father was a farmer/musician. When Johnny was about a year old his parents separated and he went with his mother and his older brother to Magnolia in Arkansas. When Johnny was eight years old his father came back, but died one year later. He got his father's guitar which was, as he said in an interview, like a toy for him. When he was twelve, the Copeland family moved to Houston, Texas, where he met musicians like Joe Hughes. One day Johnny went to a music shop to buy himself a new guitar. Another customer asked him to come to his club that night. Johnny and his friends did so and the club owner bought them some amplifiers.
When Houston guitar giant Albert Collins wasn't able to work for a period of four months in 1954, Johnny took over his band for that period, which was a guarantee for him to work two nights a week for 4 dollars a night.
After occasional session work for the Houston based Duke/Peacock label, Copeland made several 45's under his own name for such labels as *Wand, Brown Sugar, Jet Stream, Atlantic, Resco* and *Golden Eagle.* He also saw the release of a more country & western orientated album, on Huey P. Meaux', Louisiana based label *Crazy Cajun.*
In 1975 Johnny made his move from Texas to New York City, where he met Dan Doyle. Doyle produced a few tapes with Copeland and went with them to *Rounder Records.* The result was Copeland's album 'Copeland Special', which received a wide acclaim from reviewers and record buyers. This

ensured an almost worldwide distribution of the album and Johnny went with his band on several tours through The States and since then, he almost annually visits Europe, where he's present at the major festivals in the field of blues and jazz music.
A second album for 2Rounder followed, 'Make My Home Where I Hang My Hat', the title song being a re-edition of an old Copeland success. Copeland uses a band that includes a horn section and apart from himself — being a singer with a strong voice and mastering an almost unique Texas flavoured guitar technique — his manager/producer Dan Doyle and his piano player/arranger Ken Vangel play an important role in Copeland's successful career.
The future seems to be all right for Johnny Copeland. His contract with *Rounder Records* guarantees some more albums and he continues to come over to Europe at least once a year. *Reviewer Marcel M. Vos of Block Magazine called him: 'The Texas Blues Tornado', and that's, considering the way Johnny takes the European and American fans by storm, the right description.* Together with musicians like Luther Allison, Jimmy Johnson and Albert Collins, Copeland belongs to the blues' most promising names nowadays.

Recommended records:
Copeland Special
Rounder 2025
Make My Home Where I Hang My Hat
Rounder 2030

57

Memphis Slim. There's a dollar sign in his autograph, but then he gave us our money's worth.

Best to Pete
May 5 - 1983
Johnny Copeland

Big Bill Broonzy were again well to the fore. They reminded listeners of the fine music which had fallen into neglect during the hysteria of the Swing Era. Wartime blues gave a new slant on the old story of two-timing women, and that was certainly the theme of Rubberlegs Williams' *4-F Blues*.

Girls, what you gonna do when Uncle Sam takes your 4-F man to war,
What you gonna do when Uncle Sam takes your 4-F man to war,
Some of you gonna drink muddy water,
sleep in a hollow log.

Took your good soldier's money and gave it to your 4-F man.
Took that good soldier's money, give it up to your 4-F man.
Now Mr Roosevelt has passed a Bill, and
brought out a brand new plan.

This recording was made in January 1945. And to show how the blues carries over from one *jazz* style to another, Dizzy Gillespie, who backed Rubberlegs Wil-liams on the above performance, recorded a traditional twelve-bar with his bebop sextet and singer Alice Roberts, 16 months later. The lyrics were those of a wronged woman, that recurring figure in blues lore, and *A Handfulla Gimme* could have been written at any time in the preceding 30 years:

I've been so lonely, ever since I put you down,
I've been so lonely, ever since I put you down,
But you've got a habit,
even worse than running around.

Every time I give you, you come running back for more,
Every time I give you, you come running back for more,
But now when you come back, daddy,
I won't even answer the door.

I bought you a suit last Monday, then you asked me for a tie,
Now you're begging for your birthday, you want a ring in July,
But you can forget it, you don't even have to give me a size,
You got a handfulla gimme,
and a mouthful of much obliged.

I play The Blues
I play it well
My name is Queen
Sylvia, and I sing like
Hell!!

Paradiso 18-10-8?

Rhythm and blues

After World War II, the blues was revived in its purest form when Huddie Ledbetter and Big Bill Broonzy emerged from obscurity. But the blues also appeared in a more forceful manner co-linked with rhythm. The resultant music, aptly termed rhythm and blues, was rather like a staging post between the blues and jazz. A fertile middle ground where young, aspiring jazz musicians could absorb the influence of bluesmen, and carry forward the benefits of that invaluable tutorship. R&B, to use the convenient appellation, covered a wide spectrum of performers and styles, and had more than its share of colourful characters such as *Screamin' Jay Hawkins,* Joe 'The Honeydripper' Liggins, Bull Moose Jackson, *Eddie 'Cleanhead' Vinson, Earl Bostic, Fats Domino,* King Kolax and Joe Morris. These men could 'put on a show' with music only part of the act. But what their singing and bands may have lacked in finesse, they more than made up for in sheer red-blooded power.

Rock and roll

From R&B to rock and roll in the 1950s. The transition was predictable and logical. R&B at its most emphatic and obvious (still employing the blues) was a commercially saleable product to a mass audience. Chuck Berry and B.B. King, among others, had hit potential. They were also listened to by the Rolling Stones and the Beatles across the Atlantic in Britain. These groups, with a superficial blues veneer inherited at third hand, led the British rock movement through the 1960s and into the 1970s. Eric Clapton was another important British rocker who liked the playing of the leading contemporary bluesmen.

The blind singer and multi-instrumentalist *Ray Charles* featured a smooth, modern blues style that enjoyed great success with black and white enthusiasts. The savage guitar style of *Jimi Hendrix* had a high blues content, and he achieved cult status, especially after his premature death at the age of 27 in 1970. Before his death from cancer in 1958, Big Bill Broonzy lived to see the blues and their advocates travel the world. He visited Europe many times from 1951, and for one memorable tour was paired with Brother John Sellers on a nation-wide concert trip around England (1956-'57). They were the heralds of a blues rush to Europe. One of those to follow was *Memphis Slim* (Peter Chatman), a fine blues singer and excellent jazz/blues pianist. Slim first went to Europe in 1959, and after finding there was more work available for him in England and on the Continent, decided to move to Paris. He has been an enormously successful figure on the European scene for more than two decades, making countless records and turning out a steady flow of original compositions. Memphis Slim is a very rich man, thanks to hits like *Every Day I Have The Blues, Rainin' In My Heart* and *The Comeback.* An authentic boogie-woogie stylist, Memphis Slim was on the first American Folk Blues festival package which toured Europe in 1962. Others in that historic assembly were. *T. Bone Walker,* the blues duo of Sonny Terry and Brownie McGhee and the vocalist/bassist *Willie Dixon.*

Dixon, an astute businessman, organizer and prolific composer has, like Memphis Slim, shown that blues artists can reap their rewards and avoid exploitation. Rated as the top blues bassist, Dixon established his own record company and saw to it that his many songs were copyrighted. He has been described as the single most influential artist in the modern blues, and that is no exaggeration.

And what of contemporary blues in the 1980s? The flamboyant *Buddy Guy* remains a powerful presence on the European scene – a showman who never sells a song short. Then there is the 'wild man' of the blues, James Brown, the swinging B.B. King, the ever dependable *Pee Wee Crayton,* whose instrumental talents run from guitar and ukelele to trumpet, *Katie Webster* (piano/organ/vocal) whose career has revived, the exciting guitarist and harmonic player *Luther Allison,* who has pointed a new course for the electronic blues players, and not to forget Albert Collins.

Musicians such as Allison have effected a far more impressive and lasting union between the blues and rock music than the many attempts by others at a jazz/rock fusion. Indeed, modern blues and contemporary rock are so close as to be almost indistinguishable, the better musicians being able to interchange the style and emphasis to accomodate either idiom, or achieve a very satisfactory synthesis.

A new young generation, open-minded and receptive, is now listening to the blues. It is less obsessed with dogma and purism than its counterpart of 40 years ago. It selects what it likes without following the pronouncements of anyone. But while this selection may be random now, it could well lead to a lifelong fascination with the blues and an exploration of jazz in the future. Any point of contact with the blues at any stage will lead the curious back through the music's history and forward to its continuing evolution.

Nick Vollebregt 'Jazzcafé Laren

What is jazz?

'If someone from Mars came here and asked where the music came from, they would have to say it was music developed and created by people of African descent who live in America. So for a title I would call it African-American music.' (Max Roach)

A way of playing, a way of feeling

What is jazz? Three little words and one enormous question are contained in that short sentence. It is a query which is continually posed, but rarely answered. No two definitions are the same because no two musicians, let alone critics and lay listeners, can agree. As Leonard Feather, the doyen of jazz writers, has stated: 'Many have tried to explain jazz in words; all have failed.' It is not the intention of the present writer to set forth yet another description of what is, after all, an entirely abstract creation about which it is impossible to be objective. Rather more constructive may be to repeat some of the better attempts at analysis, along with some amusing or absurd postulations.

No other music has been quite so bedevilled by so much controversial argument as jazz. Many of its practitioners reject the four letter word itself. For example, the late Sidney Bechet, a vital soprano saxophonist closely identified with the New Orleans style: 'Let me tell you one thing: Jazz that's the name the white people have given to the music.' Or listen to Max Roach: 'The reason I've objected to the term "jazz" was that I didn't think it gave enough respect to the individuals and I mean the geniuses, the innovators who were instrumental in bringing us up to the point where we are now in the development of the music. And "jazz" is kind of like one of those catch-all phrases, but they should really say the music of Fats Waller, the music of Duke Ellington, the music of Charlie Parker, the music of Thelonious Monk. I think that this is more appropriate.'

With dispute over the four-letter word itself, is it really surprising that a music which has a multitude of styles should continue to defy analysis. Critic George Simon opined: 'Jazz is not really a music. It's a way of playing.' And pianist Bill Evans suggested: 'Jazz is a mental attitude rather than a style. It uses a certain process of the mind expressed spontaneously through some musical instrument. I'm concerned with retaining that process.'

Sidney Bechet put his finger on one of the truths about jazz when he wrote in his autobiography, *Treat It Gentle:* 'It's a way of feeling. It's a way of listening too, and that complicates it because there's so much difference that can be listened to. A man, he's got all kinds of things in him and the music wants to talk to all of him. The music is everything that it wants to say to a man. Some of it comes from jokes and some of it comes from sorrow, but all of it has a man's feelings in it.'

Composing the moment

Emotional content is what every jazz musician is concerned about when he or she plays either straight melody (the tune) or improvises around the melody or on top of the harmony. The tonal and rhythmic inflections of the jazz performer make his music virtually impossible to put on paper. The notes themselves can be written down, but the tone, the way a note is 'bent' challenge the normal rules of notation. The only way to understand is to listen.

'In one degree or another all forms of jazz allow the musicians involved to express their own personality within the music. It is this that makes the music attractive to the performer and, I believe, ultimately to the listener,' suggested bassist/composer Graham Collier in his book, *Jazz Inside* (London, 1973). Jazz certainly affords the player more scope for freedom of personal expression than any other music, past or contemporary. Jazz exists in the moment. When a jazz performer improvises he is *composing* as well as playing. This is the essential difference between jazz and 'straight' music. Improvising is not peculiar to jazz — it has a place in the blues and gospel music and, to a limited extent, in some contemporary popular music like rock and reggae. But in jazz, improvisation is an essential ingredient. Without it the form would have lost meaning decades ago. As jazz critic Martin Williams wrote in *The Jazz Tradition* 1970: 'Jazz shares such contributions as its "blues scale" and its unique musical form, the

63

Dizzy Gillespie

John Birks Gillespie. Trumpet/Conga Drum/Tambourine & Miscellaneous Percussion/Piano/Composer/Arranger/ Leader/Singer. Cheraw, South Carolina, October 21 1917.

The last of nine children, Gillespie was born into a poor family. Father was a bricklayer who played piano with his own band at weekends. He kept the band instruments at home, and Dizzy tinkered with them. Father died when Dizzy was only ten. Started by picking out a song called *Coon Shine Lady* on the family piano at age of four. First instrument at school was slide trombone. Within a year he became equally proficient on trumpet which a friend allowed him to play. Dizzy showed so much promise that he was able to study harmony and theory at Laurinburg Institute, North Carolina. The young man learned much about rhythm by listening to the music in a local Sanctified Church. At the age of 18 Dizzy moved to Philadelphia where he had relatives, and played his first important job with a band led by **Frank Fairfax**; Charlie Shavers was another member of the trumpet section. Though having listened to earlier trumpeters like Louis Armstrong, Gillespie was naturally drawn to the work of the young stylistic pacesetter of the day, **Roy Eldridge**. Dizzy replaced Roy in the **Teddy Hill** orchestra, and the youngster. impressed his new employer. With the Hill outfit, Dizzy visited France and England in the summer of 1937. A measure of Hill's admiration for his discovery was the fact that he featured Gillespie on three numbers, *King Porter Stomp, Yours And Mine, Blue Rhythm Fantasy,* at a record date for Victor. There were factions in the band who were jealous of the young 'upstart' and gave him a tough time. On returning from Europe Dizzy jobbed around for awhile before rejoining Hill. The band began to swing in a different. more modern manner when **Kenny Clarke** took over percussion duties. The orchestra played at the World's Fair in 1939, and in the same year Dizzy impressed with a brace of super solos on a **Lionel Hampton** recording date. He worked briefly with Mercer Ellington before joining **Cab Calloway** in the autumn of 1939. Dizzy was chalking up invaluable playing experience, sitting in with the **Savoy Sultans**, a marvellous jump band,

and the orchestra of Chick Webb. It was in the Webb band that he met Cuban trumpeter **Mario Bauza** who opened Dizzy's ears to the possibilities of Latin rhythms and thus planted the seeds of Afro-Cuban jazz, a vital and lasting sector of Dizzy's music-making. It was through Bauza that Diz got the job with Calloway, and now the two men were able to play together nightly. According to Dizzy, when he first went with Calloway, his style was somewhere between Roy Eldridge and his own conception. Bauza encouraged him, in a fatherly way, and Dizzy probed new musical areas, somewhat to Calloway's annoyance as he cautioned Gillespie to 'stop playing that Chinese music'. The rift between leader and star sideman eventually resulted in an angry confrontation and then a scuffle; Calloway fired him. Dizzy joined the band fronted by singer **Ella Fitzgerald** who took over when her employer Chick Webb died. The job was short-lived and Dizzy returned to New York. While in the Calloway organization he had met **Charlie Parker** in Kansas City and found a kindred spirit. He also knew Thelonious Monk, the uncompromising pianist. In the early 1940s these men and others played together at after-hours jam sessions in Minton's. By 1942 their ideas were starting to crystallize and the bebop revolution, in which Gillespie played such a major part, was under way. Dizzy worked with **Benny Carter, Charlie Barnet, Les Hite** and **Calvin Jackson**, but he and Parker began to get exposure (though not on record) when they were recruited for a new orchestra launched by the cigar smoking pianist Earl Hines in 1942. The band had a fresh outlook with Diz, Bird, a modern drummer in Shadow Wilson and two fine singers, Billy Eckstine and Sarah Vaughan. Dizzy says: 'Charlie Parker and I had a meeting of the minds, because both of us inspired each other.' Dizzy feels that he was slightly more advanced harmonically while Parker had the rhythmic edge. Where influences began and ended is impossible to say; what mattered was that Gillespie and Parker gave the new jazz its direction and kept it on course for more than a decade. The pair also worked together in the Billy Eckstine Orchestra, the first big band to feature bop extensively, largely due to the leader's enthusiasm for the work of his contemporaries. In 1944 Gillespie quit to co-lead with **Oscar Pettiford** the first bop combo on 52nd Street. Bebop was a fact.

Nobody could ignore by 1945 – a year that was packed with activity for Dizzy Gillespie. He and Parker recorded together on all sorts of sessions, with singers and swing players, and finally together with men of their own choosing. Their interpretations of *All The Things You Are, Salt Peanuts, Groovin' High, Dizzy Atmosphere, Hot House, Shaw 'Nuff* were the anthems of the new order. They played an engagement at the Three Deuces which Dizzy recalls as the 'height of perfection' of their music. Meanwhile Dizzy launched his first big band that toured as part of a package show called Hepsations '45. At the end of the tour the orchestra was disbanded, and Dizzy re-formed the small group with Parker. Before they left for California they recorded for Savoy (Dizzy's début as a pianist). In '45, too, Dizzy popped up at a Lionel Hampton concert to contribute an astounding solo on the Parker composition *Red Cross*. In Hollywood the Gillespie Sextet (often augmented to seven pieces by tenorman Lucky Thompson) received a mixed reception. Dizzy and Bird played for Norman Granz at a few concerts, but the musicians, with the exception of Parker who stayed behind, were all glad to get back to New York. **Sonny Stitt** replaced Parker, but the sextet did'nt last long. Dizzy formed a new big band which was to bloom for 3½ years. Here at last was the setting that Gillespie had yearned for – a wholly modern orchestra, packed with talented soloists and using the work of the finest modern arrangers – Tadd Dameron, John Lewis, George Russell, Budd Johnson, Gil Fuller. Their first efforts on record were for a small independent label, but by 1947 they had signed with Victor and there followed a steady stream of classics such as *Ow, Oop-Pop-A-Da, Two Bass Hit, Stay On It, Woody 'n' You, Cool Breeze, Cubana Be, Cubana Bop, Manteca, Good Bait, Swedish Suite* etc. The band toured Scandinavia and France in 1948, toured widely at home and played a number of Carnegie Hall concerts. A majority of critics believe the band was the perfect context for Dizzy's leadership qualities and his amazingly gifted trumpet-playing. It was a driving outlet for his mercurial dynamism and terrific personality. The musicians who passed through its ranks read like a 'Who's Who' of modern jazz – saxophonists James Moody, Cecil Payne, John Coltrane, Ernie Henry, Yusef Lateef,

Dizzy Gillespie. I said to him: 'I'd really love to draw your portrait without those bulging cheeks.' He thought that was extremely kind. That broke the ice.

Dizzy Gillespie

Jimmy Heath, Paul Gonsalves; trumpeters Dave Burns, Benny Harris, Kenny Dorham, Benny Bailey and Elmon Wright; trombonists Matt Gee, Chuck Greenlea, Ted Kelly, J.J. Johnson; pianists Thelonious Monk and John Lewis; bassists Ray Brown, Al McKibbon, Nelson Boyd; drummers Kenny Clarke, Joe Harris, Teddy Stewart, Specs Wright. The vocalists included Kenny 'Pancho' Hagood, Joe 'Bebop' Carroll and the splendid baritone balladeer Johnny Hartman. In Chano Pozo, Gillespie found the most accomplished conga drummer whose complex rhythms were a great asset to the band until his untimely death. Chano was co-composer of *Monteca* (something greasy), and his drumming proved a huge influence in the Afro-Cuban jazz fusion, but Dizzy was again the catalyst in this movement. The band broke up in 1950, mainly for economic reasons.

Dizzy reverted to small groups and, in partnership with Dave Usher, founded the Dee Gee label with Gillespie as its main recording star.

Above the raw accompaniment of his 1940s big band Dizzy soared effervescently; the one musician always in charge. In the mid-1960s Dizzy introduced electric bass into his group. In the 1970s he played the international festival circuit, travelling in 1971-'72 as a member of The Giants of Jazz, four of whom — Sonny Stitt, Thelonious Monk, Al McKibbon and Art Blakey — were former Gillespie employees! Dizzy, despite his name, has always been concerned with matters religious, political and racial. He has been a staunch opponent of segregation in any form, offered himself as an independent candidate for the American presidency in 1963, and is a staunch follower of the Bahai faith which envisages a time when all mankind will be united in peace. He wrote in his autobiography. 'The highest role is the role in the service of humanity, and if I can make that, then I'll be happy. When I breathe the last time, it'll be a happy breath.' Dizzy is cherished by so many people for his numerous qualities. Thousands who have never met him are enthralled by his music. He has sent messages through his trumpet to multitudes, and made them all feel happier and better inside. On that level alone he has performed a lasting service to humanity. All we have to do is listen — and Dizzy is with us.

Recommended records:
The Men From Minton's
Smithsonian Collection R004-P13456
Coleman Hawkins & His Orchestra
Smithsonian Collection R004-P13456
Sarah Vaughan & Her All-Stars
Smithsonian Collection R004-P13456 & P13457
Dizzy Gillespie: The Small Groups (1945-1946)
Phoenix LP-2
Dizzy Gillespie/Dizzy's Delight (The Big Bands)
Phoenix LP-4
Dizzy Gillespie/1946-1949 Vols 1 & 2
French RCA PM 42408
Dizzy Gillespie/Ella Fitzgerald/Charlie Parker/It Happened One Night
Natural Organic 7000
Dizzy Gillespie/Dee Gee Days
Savoy SJL 2209
Jazz At Massey Hall
English Saga ERO 8031
Dizzy Gillespie-Stan Getz/Diz & Getz
Verve VE2-2521
Dizzy Gillespie Orchestra/At Salle Pleyel, Paris
Prestige PRST 7818
Dizzy Gillespie/Dizzy In Greece
Verve MGV 8222
Dizzy Gillespie/With Sonny Rollins & Sonny Stitt
VSP Verve 15/16
The Ebullient Mr Gillespie
Metro Records 2682 007
Dizzy Gillespie/Something Old, Something New
Philips PHM 200-091
The Dizzy Gillespie Reunion Big Band
Saba MPS 15-207 or MPS 21 29682-2
Dizzy Gillespie-Bobby Hackett-Mary Lou Williams/Giants
Perception PLP-19
Dizzy Gillespie/The Giant
Prestige 24047
Dizzy Gillespie's Big 4
Pablo 2310-719
Dizzy Gillespie y Machito/Afro-Cuban Jazz Moods
Pablo 2310-771
Dizzy Gillespie Jam – Montreux '77
Pablo 2308-211
The Giants Of Jazz
Atlantic SD 2-905
Dizzy Gillespie/Birks Works
Duke Records D-1019
Dizzy Gillespie/At The Downbeat Club, Summer 1947
Phontastic NOST 7629

Arnett Cobb

Arnett Cleophus Cobb. Tenor Saxophone/Singer. Houston, Texas, August 10 1914.

He studied piano with his grandmother, and also toyed with violin, C-melody sax and trumpet before settling for the tenor saxophone. His first professional job was with **Frank Davis** in 1933, and this was followed by stints in the bands of **Chester Boone** and **Milton Larkins**. Cobb made a big name for himself during a lengthy tenure (1942-'47) in **Lionel Hampton**'s Orchestra. He replaced Illinois Jacquet in the barn-storming Hampton outfit, exercising his lungs on such tear-ups as *Flying Home, Hamp's Boogie Woogie, Chop Chop* and *Air Mail Special*. He led a swinging sextet for a time after quitting the Hampton organization but was laid low by illness.

He suffered serious injuries in an accident in the 1950s, and more recently sustained a stroke which left him partially paralysed and restricted to a chair on stage. But the man's determination is such that, like the proverbial rubber ball, he keeps bouncing back. After the stroke, Cobb had to re-learn saxophone fingering which had been second nature to him. The English saxophonist/writer Dave Gelly has opined that all the musical college education and study will not give a young musician the swing generated by Cobb's simple yet markedly individual phrasing. *Arnett, bald, battered but spiritually unbent, has a typically meaty, expressive 'Texas tone' and while his style teeters on the brink of rhythm and blues at times it is immensely enjoyable. His raw-throated vocals are heard more often now because of his physical disability, but they are a treat in themselves.*

Cobb has visited Europe several times in recent years. Arnett is an inspiration, and the fact that he can still get up there and play with such fire and dedication makes him a hero. Those who enjoyed the groovy playing of the late Gene Ammons will find themselves in tune with the cogent Mr Cobb.

Recommended records:
Arnett Cobb/The Fabulous Apollo Sessions
Vogue CLDAP 768
Arnett Cobb/More Party Time
Prestige PRLP 7175

Arnett Cobb. No matter what the circumstances, he always draws attention with his tasteful, forceful tone.

twelve-bar blues, with other popular idioms. But jazz is the most respected Afro-American idiom, the most highly developed one, and the idiom to which improvisation is crucially important.'

Mr Williams had further observations about jazz which are basic truths and may help listeners to more fully understand and appreciate the music: 'Jazz is the music of a people who have been told by their circumstances that they are unworthy. And in jazz, these people discover their own worthiness. They discover it in terms that mankind has not experienced before.'
And again:
'Jazz is a music evolved by black men and in general best played by black men, which white men can play and sometimes play excellently. But at the same time it is a music which obviously has deep meaning for extraordinary numbers of men of all races the world over.'

Phrasing is style

Melody, harmony, rhythm make up the three foundation stones upon which jazz is laid. The one constant has been rhythm. In its more recent forms, jazz has sometimes cast off melody, shunned harmony, but it has never abandoned rhythm. Indeed when Albert Ayler, Ornette Coleman and John Coltrane were attempting to find new ways to improvise, the rhythmic element assumed a greater importance. Coleman and Eric Dolphy explored a new area of melodic extemporization while Coltrane plumbed unknown areas of harmony, but to counterbalance their particular obsessions they required the support of percussionists who would provide greater rhythmic emphasis, a stronger, more complex beat to carry their structures forward. It should be noted though, that Coleman and Ayler could work quite happily as *solo* soloists.

The way in which a musician phrases is another aspect of jazz that distinguishes it from other music, and also serves to identify one player from another. Trumpeter Dizzy Gillespie believes that phrasing *is* style, and it certainly accounts for much of individual style, together with tone or, in the case of the keyboard player, touch. How Gillespie gets from one note to the next, his placement of the notes, use of spaces (intervals), vocal effects, 'blue' notes and the tempo itself are unique. They cannot be copied, any more than his tone can be exactly reproduced. Dizzy, Miles Davis and Wynton Marsalis all play the same instrument but all sound quite different.

A music of the emotions

In trying to find a personal style, a musician has to overcome a natural fear of the unknown. How do you find that style, once you have all the technical equipment you need? A lot of it has to do with relaxation, a state extremely hard to achieve in a working atmosphere invariably filled with tension. It's a problem all the finest improvisors have recognized and attempted to clarify to their mentors with a few well chosen words. Charlie Parker used to tell Miles Davis: 'Don't be afraid. Go ahead and play.' Similarly, when Art Tatum stood behind pianist Red Carland one night he spotted that the younger man was tense. 'You're forcing. Don't play the piano. Let the piano play itself,' he advised Garland. 'What they call jazz is just the music of people's emotions. It comes from wherever there have been coloured people gathered together during the last hundred years,' wrote one of the 'professors' of jazz piano, Willie the Lion Smith, in his autobiography, *Music On My Mind* (London, 1964). His analysis, though simple, is as true as any of the others we shall encounter. Jazz is essentially a music of the emotions, and the idiom has a capacity for transmitting a wealth of feelings about love and hatred, joy and sadness, tenderness and cruelty, passion and rejection, gratitude and hurt, spiritual peace and conflict. It tells you what the player is feeling and experiencing, albeit only in artistic terms, at that moment.
Black people are no more, no less, emotional than any other group, but they are more honest about expressing and showing emotion. While they have been suppressed for centuries in white America they have not been repressed. Making and listening to music has been an emotional release in which the response is totally honest. That is why the listener reared on a diet of arid classical music finds jazz too potent to swallow. That would apply to many whites but not all. And it would be the case with a great number of white musicians. As saxophonist Ornette Coleman has said: 'I think black people in America have a superior sense when it comes to expressing their own convictions through music. Most whites tend to think that it's below their dignity to just show suffering and just show any other meaning that has to do with feeling and not with technique or analysis or whatever you call it. And this to me is why the black man has developed in the field of music that which the white man calls jazz. And basically I think that word, the sense of that word, is used to describe music that the white man feels is really inferior.' (In *Four Lives In The Bebop Business* by A.B. Spellman.)

Don't explain

Musicologists, neophytes and lifelong students of jazz have continued to wrestle with the problem of trying to analyse this evolving music. They were doing it when pianist Fats Waller was improvising solos and hit tunes at the drop of a cheque. It was Fats, comedian, jazz pianist supreme and songwriter, who when asked by an old lady: 'What is jazz, Mr Waller?' shot back the legendary retort: 'Madam, if you don't know by now, don't mess with it!' Waller, like most working musicians of his time, was too busy earning a living to brood on that particular question. He didn't need to ask it. He *knew* what jazz was and didn't have to put it into words. The fact that white people attempt to explain jazz irks contemporary black musicians. Pianist Cecil Taylor stated that neither John Cage, an American composer, nor Stravinsky had any right to make evaluations about jazz, because they did not know the tradition jazz had come out of. 'I've spent years in school learning about European music and its traditions, but these cats don't know a thing about Harlem except that it's there. Right away, when they talk about music they talk in terms of what music is to them,' Taylor told A.B. Spellman.

There is powerful logic in Cecil Taylor's point of view, but he ignores that enjoyment or appreciation of a completely abstract form is not dependent on a person having experienced the ethnic background of the artist. The Japanese are among the most knowledgeable and receptive of jazz listeners, but the majority are not familiar with life in Harlem. Each listener gives his or her *own* meaning to a jazz performance; there is no single way of interpreting it. Even the emotional response will differ from one individual to another. We are in the realms of totally subjective opinion. Is it possible to be objective about jazz? Objectivity tends to by-pass emotion, yet jazz is all about projecting emotions and responding to them.

A collective art

Practically any statement regarding jazz can be contradicted and a counter argument produced. For instance the brilliant musicologist Andre Hodeir pronounced in his book, *Toward Jazz* (New York, 1962): 'Jazz is a collective art; it is therefore normal that the artist should be affected by his environment, especially if he is given to improvising.' But jazz is not necessarily a collective art, especially if we are considering *Art* Tatum. Most of his finest playing was created as a solo pianist without accompaniment of any kind. Tatum was seemingly unworried by environment and, being blind, it mattered less to him anyway.

Yet Hodeir is correct, jazz *is* normally a collective art and the *soloist* does depend on his colleagues. If they are out-of-step, unsympathetic or incompetent the soloist will be affected. Charlie Parker could carry a bad rhythm section, but he played better with a hand-picked trio of accompanists. Parker, incidentally, made few pronouncements about jazz and was opposed to labelling. 'They teach you there's a boundary line to music, but man, there's no boundary line to art,' he said. Another of his oft-repeated sayings was: 'Bop is no love-child of jazz. It is something entirely separate and apart. It's just music. It's trying to play clean and looking for the pretty notes.' Parker was open-minded and relished the music of Stravinsky, Prokofiev, Hindemith, Ravel, Debussy, Wagner and Bach. About a year before his death, Parker mused: 'Music isn't a joke any more. Everyone is serious now. There was a time they called it jazz. Now it's definitely music. I'd call it that. It's something in the baby stage now. The youngsters will pull it up. Everyone is striving for a meaning that will reach the people.'

Parker, much as he disliked the compartmentalizing and naming of jazz styles, was forced to use those designations; but he didn't like it. Neither does his protégé Jackie McLean, also an alto saxophonist. 'It should just be music for the sake of music, and people listening to whatever music they thought was worthwhile listening to,' he says, echoing his idol. 'Cats talk about the "New Thing" so much, but the new thing comes out of the old thing, and in a way they're part of the same thing.'

McLean believes that sound is the foundation of jazz. As he explains: 'It's not about notation, really. I imagine someone could take a chart and write down every chord or every dissonance that Monk plays, but if you played it back from the chart, then it wouldn't be Monk. It wouldn't sound anything like him. So when you start dealing with sounds, you either have to go by your ear, like I'm going, or you have to become a scientist and start measuring all the vibrations and all that kind of stuff.' McLean explains perfectly in that statement one reason why jazz is impossible to satisfactorily define. Perhaps somewhere in the world, at this very moment, a scientist is attempting to analyse a Coleman Hawkins solo, but he could never explain it. He would lack the information even if he knew Hawkins' entire life history, the conscious and unconscious thoughts of the man and all his physical characteristics. No instrument yet devised can assess or measure a human being's

Tommy Flanagan 'd Maivaart' 19 aug '87

Tommy Flanagan

Tommy Lee Flanagan. Piano/Electric Piano/Composer. Detroit, Michigan, March 16 1930.

Took up piano aged 11, also plays clarinet, alto and tenor saxophones, bass and vibes. Made his professional debut with **Dexter Gordon** in 1945. Worked with many top musicians around Detroit, but gained international attention after moving to New York early in 1956. Identified with a group of young Detroit musicians – Donald Byrd, Pepper Adams, Kenny Burrell, Paul Chambers, Doug Watkins, Louis Hayes – who quickly made New York their own.

Flanagan spent a year in the quintet of J.J. Johnson (1956-'57), and also worked with **Miles Davis, Sonny Rollins**. Oscar Pettiford, **John Coltrane**, Tyree Glenn, Harry Edison, **Coleman Hawkins** and Kenny Burrell. Much in demand as accompanist for top singers, he backed **Ella Fitzgerald**, off and on, for more that a decade, and was also a keyboard favourite of Tony Bennett.

Flanagan has recorded prolifically since 1956, making the first album under his own name in 1957. He was the pianist on two of the classic tenor sax-and-rhythm LPs of the 1950s – John Coltrane's *Giant Steps* and Sonny Rollins' *Saxophone Colossus*. It wasn't until the mid-1970s that Flanagan began to regularly record a series of outstanding trio records for a variety of labels in the USA, Germany and Japan. His inventive playing on these sessions earned him, albeit rather tardily, recognition as a top soloist. A quiet, unprepossessing, balding man, Flanagan is a subtle, melodic, lyrical soloist with a wonderful pianistic touch and a superb sense of improvisational organization, good taste and swing. As critic Benny Green has written, Flanagan presents a mild, unruffled, scholarly appearance, but this gentle demeanour should not be misread. Flanagan has a deep love for making music, and the beauty of his conception is apparent immediately he sets his long fingers dancing across the keyboard.

His Detroit contemporary and fellow pianist Barry Harris respectfully calls him 'Father Flanagan', and indeed he occupies the position of a youngish patriarch within his stylistic area. Flanagan is one of the finest of the second wave of bebop pianists, closer to Hank Jones and the late Al Haig rather than Bud Powell or Thelonious Monk.

After so many years of providing discreet assistance for singers, Tommy emerged from his shell to revel in the challenge of freelancing, between touring the world with his trio. He was much admired by the late Coleman Hawkins, and undertook several overseas trips as Hawk's pianist in the twilight of the great tenor player's career. There is an effortless flow to Flanagan's work, he has a rare capacity for self-editing and never turns in a less than professional performance.

Ira Gitler put it well when he suggested that Flanagan 'communicates directly and warmly in a manner which puts him ahead of many pianists erroneously considered to be his peers'. Flanagan formed a logical stylistic link between Al Haig's refined bop style and the impressionism of Bill Evans. *His playing bespeaks a sensitive mind and a nimble imagination.* And there is an enduring quality about his music. There is nothing in the innumerable solos he committed to tape 25 years ago to date them. Flanagan has never been one to trot out the fashionable cliché that might live for a year. The entire 'soul' jazz fad left him untouched.

Drummer Elvin Jones, who worked with Tommy in the J.J. Johnson combo, once said of Flanagan: 'He's so compassionate. You can always hear the lyrics when he plays.' The mainstream of jazz would simply not be the same without 'Father Flanagan' and his stylish 'sermons'.

Flanagan took up the electric piano in the 1970s but uses the instrument sparingly and intelligently. He is among the few pianists who has managed to retain his *sound* and identity on the electric piano which is inclined to remove most players' trademarks.

Tommy Flanagan is the composer of some delightful songs which reflect his melodic bent, including *Eclypso, Minor Mishap, Something Borrowed, Something Blue, Delarna* and *Verdandi.* We could do with more of his writing, and it would be fruitful to hear other groups performing his works. Flanagan is highly regarded by his contemporaries who think of him as 'Mr Reliable' and 'Mr Inspiration' rolled into one.

Recommended records:
The Tommy Flanagan Trio Overseas
Prestige PRST 7632
Tommy Flanagan/The Cats
Prestige/New Jazz LP 8217

Sonny Rollins/Saxophone Collosus
Prestige PR 7326
John Coltrane/Giant Steps
Atlantic LP 1311
Tommy Flanagan/Lonely Town
Japanese Blue Note GP 3186
Tommy Flanagan/Trio And Sextet
Onyx ORI 206
The Tommy Flanagan Tokyo Recital
Pablo 2310 724
Tommy Flanagan 3/Montreux '77
Pablo 2308 202
Tommy Flanagan/Something Borrowed, Something Blue
Galaxy GXY-5110
Tommy Flanagan Plays The Music Of Harold Arlen
Inner City IC 1071
The Magnificent Tommy Flanagan
Progressive PRO 7059

Ornette Coleman

Ornette Coleman. Alto/Tenor & Soprano Saxophones/Trumpet/Violin/Shenai/ Composer. Fort Worth, Texas, March 19 1930.

Mother a seamstress, father a singer and baseball player. Mother bought him alto saxophone at age 14. Mainly self-taught but received some help from a cousin. Played alto for a year, then broke collar-bone in a football game and had to put aside the instrument for a year. Joined school band as a tenor saxophonist. Worked around Forth Worth, playing R&B jobs that called for honking tenor. Coleman modelled himself on saxophonists Big Jay McNeely, Arnett Cobb, Gene Ammons and Louis Jordan. Later imitated Charlie Parker and Allen Eager. Gigged in Forth Worth 1946-'49, had own band for awhile and also worked in large ensemble led by saxophonist Red Connors who introduced Coleman to bebop.

Left Fort Worth to work with a touring carnival minstrel troupe, playing tenor sax in the band that accompanied acts. Quit the show in Natchez and got a job with Clarence Samuels' rhythm and blues group. Played in New Orleans for a spell and toured with Pee Wee Crayton before settling in Los Angeles for nine years (1950-'58). Struggled for many months to find work, sat in with Teddy Edwards, Hampton Hawes, Sonny Criss. Took a job as an elevator operator and studied

71

Ornette Coleman
9-7-'83

harmony and theory. Suffered many rebuffs from established musicians who would not play with him. Persevered and worked in rehearsals with Ed Blackwell, James Clay, Bobby Bradford, George Newman and **Don Cherry**.

Coleman and Cherry struck up a good understanding and formed a partnership. Blackwell was tutoring a young drummer called Billy Higgins. Bassist Red Mitchell was impressed by Coleman's compositional ability and introduced him to Lester Koenig, of Contemporary Records, who decided to record Ornette and his cohorts. The first album, Something Else! The Music Of Ornette Coleman, was recorded and released in 1958 and caused a sensation.

At this stage Coleman was still influenced by Charlie Parker. He was playing a white plastic alto and his music was moving towards atonality, removed from the standard idea of improvisation based on chord patterns. For their second LP, Coleman and Cherry dispensed with piano and used Percy Heath on bass. Critics felt this instrumentation was more suited to Coleman's aims.

In 1959 Ornette and his band moved to New York where Coleman signed for Atlantic Records which sponsored his attendance at the Lenox School of Jazz. The band's opening at the Five Spot in NYC became a focal point for argument among musicians and critics. John Lewis and Julian 'Cannonball' Adderley were enthusiastic about Coleman. John Coltrane also admired the newcomer, as did Eric Dolphy. Coleman caused most of his contemporaries to re-examine their position. The hide-bound rejected his innovations, but others like Jackie McLean, saw the need for revision.

From 1960-'62 Coleman made a series of LPs with Don Cherry for Atlantic. The group also played the Monterey and Newport Jazz Festivals. Coleman formed a trio (with bassist David Izenzon and drummer **Charles Moffett**) in '62 that played the Jazz Gallery. With club work in short supply Coleman promoted his own concert at New York's Town Hall in the winter of 1962. The music was subsequently issued on an ESP-Disk album

Coleman retired from public performance for three years, using the time to compose and study new instruments. He had already added trumpet and violin to his accomplishments, and would later also play the shenai and soprano saxophone.

Resumed club work with an engagement at the Village Vanguard in 1965 where he used both trumpet and violin – and fueled yet more controversy about his abilities. He left for Europe in the late summer of 1965, and gave a concert at the Fairfield Hall, Croydon. Spent several months on the Continent and recorded two LPs for Blue Note Records in Stockholm. On returning to the USA, Ornette later formed a quartet with **Dewey Redman** (saxophones), **Charlie Haden** (bass) and either Ed Blackwell or Ornette's son **Denardo Coleman** on drums. The Coleman LP Science Fiction was a reunion of his Los Angeles clique of the 1950s with Don Cherry, Bobby Bradford and Billy Higgins among others.

Less was heard from Coleman in the 1970s. He tended to concentrate on composing, but would sometimes appear at his Artist House in the Soho neighbourhood of Manhattan. Coleman resumed touring in the 1980s and made a number of trips to Europe for concert appearances.

Now in his mid-fifties, Ornette Coleman is rightly regarded as the key figure in the free jazz movement. Many people who found his approach too radical initially, now accept that he was an important innovator whose ideas influenced and inspired an entire generation of jazz players. Yet his music remains difficult and an enigma to large numbers of listeners who are receptive to most jazz. And it must be said that the styles of Coleman and his followers have failed to penetrate other music to the degree that the efforts of Charlie Parker and Dizzy Gillespie did 20 and more years earlier. Gillespie made no secret of his dislike of Coleman's music when he first heard him. 'I didn't dig Ornette Coleman at the beginning. I imagine I was just like the older guys, how they treated me when they first listened to me,' he says. But later he realized that Coleman had something, 'but it wasn't as strong as Charlie Parker's'. However, he acknowledges that Coleman has enriched the music by his creativity. Coleman was a shaping force on the so-called avant garde, and his musical procedures were rapidly taken up by many other groups in the 1960s.

In the light of all the critical in-fighting over his music, and the sniping by fellow musicians, it is hardly surprising that Ornette Coleman has a sense of bitterness. As he told A.B. Spellman (in

Four Lives In The Bebop Business, New York, 1966): '...I'm not loved because nobody is interested in what I'm doing; they're only interested in writing and talking about it, not the music itself.' Yet Coleman does have numerous devotees who hold him in the highest regard. Richard B. Hadlock described his music as 'emotionally direct, uncluttered and essentially simple', while Whitney Balliett considered that Coleman's 'feet remain firmly in the old blues and his head is full of celestial things'.

In the late 1970s Coleman had a new band with **James 'Blood' Ulmer** (guitar), Charlie Haden (bass), Denardo Coleman (drums) and Barbara Huey (percussion). They played together on the West Coast, in New York and France. 'I think one day music will be a lot freer. Then the pattern for a tune, for instance, will be forgotten and the tune itself will be the pattern, and won't have to be forced into conventional patterns,' Coleman said in 1958. His prediction was correct and he, more than anyone else, made it happen. Ornette Coleman is the composer of many melodies including: Invisible, The Blessing, Chippie, Angel Voice, The Sphinx, Broken Shadows, Trouble In The East, Rock The Clock, Law Years, Street Woman, Love And Sex, Una May Bonita, Change Of The Century, Tomorrow Is The Question, Dough-nut, The Riddle, Space Jungle, The Ark, Sadness and Atavism.

Recommended records:
Ornette Coleman/Something Else
Contemporary C3551
Ornette Coleman/Tomorrow Is The Question
Contemporary M3569
Ornette Coleman/The Shape Of Jazz To Come
Atlantic SD131
Ornette Coleman/Change Of The Century
Atlantic SD1327
Ornette Coleman/This Is Our Music
Atlantic SD1353
Ornette Coleman/Free Jazz
Atlantic SD1364
Ornette Coleman/Ornette!
Atlantic SD1378
Ornette Coleman/Ornette On Tenor
Atlantic SD1394
Ornette Coleman/At The Golden Circle Vols 1 & 2
Blue Note BST 84224/5
Ornette Coleman/The Empty Foxhole
Blue Note BST 84246

Ornette Coleman. An angry man, angry music, a really angry manager. So I did it real fast. Later I showed it to Ornette. Without looking or saying a word he initialled it.

An Evening With Ornette Coleman
Polydor 623.246/7
Ornette Coleman/Ornette At 12
Impulse SIPL 518

Warne Marsh

Warne Marion Marsh. Tenor/Alto Saxophones/Clarinet/Piano/Piano-Accordion/Flute/Composer/Arranger. Los Angeles, California, October 26 1927.

Began on piano but switched to piano-accordion at school. Next took up clarinet, followed by alto saxophone before finally settling on his main instrument, tenor saxophone. Received help with tenor studies from the late Corky Corcoran, saxophonist with Harry James Orchestra. In the mid-1940s his main influences were Lester Young and Charlie Parker.

His first professional job was with the Hollywood Canteen Kids in 1944, then spent 18 months with Hoagy Carmichael's Teenagers. Army service (1946-'47) afforded him the opportunity to meet, through trumpeter Don Ferrara, the pianist and teacher **Lennie Tristano**. Marsh was immediately won over by Tristano's original and purist approach to jazz improvisation and, like other students of Lennie's, learned to *sing* entire solos by Parker, Young, Roy Eldridge and Coleman Hawkins.

Following his Army stint, Marsh freelanced in Los Angeles before joining Buddy Rich Big Band for four months of touring. Settled in New York in the autumn of 1948 and for more than 12 years played and studied with Tristano almost exclusively. He held all manner of non-music jobs rather than compromise his highly personal style. In alto saxophonist **Lee Konitz** he found a kindred spirit; together they evinced an uncanny rapport. Both were present on Tristano's significant records for *Capitol* in 1949.

He and Konitz occasionally teamed up for club and concert jobs and a handful of record dates in the 1950s. Marsh also turned up on a 1953 Metronome All Stars date which gave him the chance to play alongside his idol Lester Young. Marsh says the main quality he got from Tristano was integrity.

'The big thing I got from Lennie was the feeling that if music was worth that much

to him, it could mean that much to me to play only what I wanted to play.' Down the years Marsh has adhered to this philosophy, despite the sniping of critics who branded his music as being flat and cold. In truth, Marsh is an emotional player, but in a subtle way.

The idea patterns that Warne follows are wholly personal, so is his distinctive, closed and slightly choked sound, and his eccentric approach to the beat. *At the heart of his music lies the perception that ego should come second to art.*

Warne appeared with Tristano for a famous reunion engagement at the Half Note in the mid-1960s, but in 1966 he returned to California, and for several years sustained himself by teaching music. However, in 1969, through the efforts of *Revelation Records'* producer John William Hardy, Marsh resumed recording, making a series of splendid albums for the small, independent label. New interest in Warne's work was also further kindled by the release of a number of previously unissued 1950s sessions on English bassist Peter Ind's *Wave* label. In England, where Ind had gathered a coterie of musicians who adhered to the Tristano principles, it became apparent that tenormen like Gray Allard and Chas Burchell were heavily influenced by Marsh. Bobby Wellins, the Scottish tenorist, also reflected his admiration for Warne. Marsh worked with a quartet of his own, and also with pianist Clare Fischer. Marsh was a founder-member of Supersax, the band dedicated to recreating the classic solos of Charlie Parker in ensemble performances, in 1972, appearing on all their early records. Made his first trip to Europe in 1975, touring England and recording again with Lee Konitz. His playing impressed everyone with its strength and beauty. During that visit, Marsh told journalist Brian Case: 'There is nothing that has happened since 1950 to improve my understanding of music or to raise my standards. They were raised as high as they would go by the time I was 20 years old. My growth has been a steady and consistent evolution.'

Certainly Marsh has never wavered in his adherence to a musical approach that was set out on his first jazz recording with Tristano more than 33 years ago.

Hearing Warne Marsh's resilient, timeless music, it is hard to rationalize why this splendid saxophonist had to resort to cleaning out swimming pools for a living in

one bleak period. But then, even if he hadn't been doing that you can be sure the thought of playing commercial trash would never have entered his mind.

As Bill Hardy so accurately put it in his 1970 statement about Marsh: 'Of course he is one of the greatest jazz saxophonists of all time, one of the finest improvisors, and one of the most distinctive, easy to recognize voices on his horn.'

His compositions include *Background Music, I Have A Good One For You, Dixie's Dilemma, Marshlight, Happening, A New Kind of Blues* and *Foreground Music*. A number of these are melodies written on standard tune progressions. Marsh has also demonstrated his ability as an arranger with charts of *Salt Peanuts* and *Ornithology* for Supersax. On several of the albums listed here, performances have been edited to include only Marsh's tenor solos, a procedure of which Mr Marsh approves when it is conducted to capture the *essence* of improvising.

Recommended records:
Warne Marsh/Live In Hollywood
Xanadu 151
Warne Marsh/Release Record.
Send Tape
Wave LP6
Warne Marsh/The Art Of Improvising, Vols 1 & 2
Revelation 22 & 27
Warne Marsh/Jazz From The East Village
Wave LP10
Warne Marsh Quintet, Vol 1
Storyville SLP-1017
Warne Marsh/All Music
Nessa N-7
Star Highs
Criss Cross Jazz 1002

Warne Marsh. You can see the enormous attention he pays to developing his solos. He just doesn't sit around and blow.

Warne Marsh

'soul' — the spirit essence — and that is where our researcher would fail.

A forum for inquiring minds

The late Mary Lou Williams, revered pianist/composer/arranger, felt strongly about the nature of jazz and believed it was being placed in jeopardy by over-education and an obsession with formal training. She told Len Lyons (in *The Great Jazz Pianists,* New York, 1983): 'The music we're trying to save by getting back into the ears of the public cannot be taught. I'm glad I didn't have any formal training. It's the type of music where you need only a few lessons to help you learn the instrument so you can execute your ideas. The music comes from the mind, the heart, and the fingertips. It comes faster than lightning. The music is spiritual. It came from spirituals, ragtime, Kansas City swing, and bop, which is when we lost our creative artists. After bop they began going to school. This destroyed that healthy feeling in jazz.'

Had Dizzy Gillespie followed the formal 'rules' he would not play the trumpet with his cheeks expanded, the late Carl Perkins would not have manipulated the piano keys with his *left* arm parallel to the keyboard, Slide Hampton would not ease the trombone slide with his *left* hand. These players use the wrong technique but it is the right one for them. How would the music teachers have assessed Rahsaan Roland Kirk's phenomenal ability which enabled him to play three different instruments at the same time? Or the unique vocal effects that trumpeters such as Cootie Williams and Clark Terry coax from their horns? In the formal music world such sounds do not exist. Jazz is ceaseless experimentation, a forum for inquiring minds. The investigative musician who questions every procedure may find he can improve on textbook methods. To paraphrase Duke Ellington, if it sounds good it must be good. And that is the measure jazz musicians tend to use.

Classical music and jazz

Enough jazz musicians have demonstrated that they are able to deliver a tricky 'straight' score as written, but none more impressively of late than Wynton Marsalis, the brilliant young trumpeter from New Orleans.

Though Marsalis' formal training might have been anathema to Miss Williams, his father also taught him the importance of expressing *himself.* Aside from his jazz development Marsalis set out to prove that (a) a trumpeter could win classical solo awards and (b) a *black* trumpeter could play *white* classical music with complete authority and conviction. 'I studied classical music because so many black musicians were scared of this big monster on the other side of the mountain called classical music. I wanted to know what it was that scared everybody so bad. I went into it and found out it wasn't anything but some more music.' After receiving a citation for outstanding brass player at Berkshire Music Center summer programme, Wynton remarked: 'It was funny being up there because I could always tell how shocked they were that a black kid my age could play their music so well. I remember how much I shocked Gunther Schuller, who was on the staff, when he found out I could play jazz. You see, I knew they couldn't believe that a seventeen-year-old who could play the hell out of classical music, also knew a lot about jazz.'

Marsalis made his point, and showed himself to be an exceptional interpreter of 'classical' music, blowing away another misconception, destroying the stereotype — the jazz musician who can't and won't play straight. Wynton's stand — subsequently emphasized on his recorded collection of Haydn, Hummel and Mozart trumpet concertos, would have delighted the late pianist Hampton Hawes. In his autobiography *Raise Up Off Me,* with Don Asher, New York, 1974, Hawes wrote: 'In the late forties and fifties our music was called "bebop" or "cool jazz" or "funk", and we were neatly ticked into one of those compartments. I don't know why the people who write about music feel they have to slap labels on everything. It's the same watermelon mentality that says niggers can fuck and play boogie-woogie better than whites. Jews are rich, Irish are drunkards, Germans are mean, Japanese are mysterious and Chinese smoke opium. Who cares? There are only two kinds of music — good and bad. The worst thing that can happen to old good music is that it might become dated for a while, but watch out, in ten to twenty years it will come drifting back like bell-bottoms and W.C. Fields movies.'

Collective individualism

Jazz being a music of specifics, loose generalities will never explain it. Yet in particular comments by writers about certain artists we will gain insights into a whole stylistic area. For example, Whitney Balliet in his eminently readable volume of criticism, *Such Sweet Thunder* (London, 1968), summed up the dichotomy of the prevelant 1960s avant garde style. 'At its worst... the new thing is long-winded, dull and almost physically abrasive. At its best – in the hands of Ornette Coleman and (Cecil) Taylor – it howls through the mind and heart, filling them with an honest ferocity that is new in jazz and perhaps in any music.' Noting that the 'new thing' had suddenly found its audience (this was in 1965), Balliet ventured: 'This revolution is an attempt to free jazz of its metronomic rhythms and its reliance on chordal or melodic improvisation, set keys and choruses of specific length. At its loosest, the new thing is semi-atonal and almost wholly free rhythmically.' A master of the throw-away comment, often in parenthesis, Mr Balliett inserted one of his pithy pearls in his 'New Thing' essay: 'Good jazz rests on collective invidualism.' And in a group context that truth is indisputable.

Jazz is about selection and discrimination – discriminating against the *bad* music. The real individualists know what to absorb and reject, and this is a matter of instinctive taste.

Louis Armstrong, the first jazz genius, was never a man to waste words on analysis when he could prove a point in a few well-chosen bars of music, steered clear of dissecting *his* music. He would offer little insights such as: 'That horn is my boss because it is my life.' This reference to his trumpet indicates the way musicians feel about the instrument that is the key to the door of self-expression. When a colleague asked Armstrong what he thought about and how he achieved his special feeling when improvising, Louis replied: 'Just close your eyes and remember the good times you had when you were a kid. Then you'll find music will just come out.' No two musicians would have the same thought process, and it is impossible to conceive that young players of today concerned with projecting emotions other than love would have employed Armstrong's method. Louis' remark tells us more about the man, essentially genial, humorous, honest and direct, than his music which is beyond words. As Max Kaminsky said: 'That purity that came out of him, that great classical playing; how many could have done that? It's pure genius.'

Louis Armstrong claimed, with total justification, that music was his language in which he could speak to people of every country. Above all, he wanted to make people happy through his music. Not such a bad objective, and one he undoubtedly reached to the delight of literally millions of listeners. Armstrong's significance and unassailable status in the jazz pantheon were expertly summarized by his fellow trumpeter and writer John Chilton: 'The man was undoubtedly the most important and influential figure in jazz. There can be few areas of human acitivity where an individual has had such a dominating role. His playing more than revolutionized jazz, it virtually established the whole structure and technique of jazz improvisation. Staccato solos, harmonically naive, and full of simple, jerky syncopations were the hallmarks of early 'hot' improvisations. They were superseded by the creative majesty of Louis' phrasing. Solos with undreamed – of emotional and technical range flowed effortlessly from his horn. His creativity and harmonic sense revealed new potentials to arrangers; his rhythmic phrasing influenced every jazz instrumentalist.'

The competitive element

Composer Teddy Charles discovered in a 1953 discussion with trumpeter Miles Davis that, independently, they had reached the same conclusions about jazz. As Charles recalled to Ira Gitler a few years later: 'A jazz performance should have unity from beginning to end and the musicians should play within the ideas, structures and moods of the piece – not one soloist after another superimposing their own styles on a basic chord pattern usually in an egoistic display of virtuosity. What you hear many young jazz musicians say is: "I just want to express myself," and that's contrary to aesthetic principles of unity.'

Charles' conclusions may have been fine for him, and propose one method (very successfully realized by Miles Davis, Thelonious Monk, the Modern Jazz Quartet and other groups) but not the *only* way. To hear a variety of soloists superimposing their own styles on a chord sequence can be very stimulating and most exciting. One of many alternatives. It is no good dictating that every jazz performance *should* be played within the rules set down by Teddy Charles, Miles Davis or anyone else. Such an attitude precludes other approaches. Hearing egoistic displays *can* be provocative and instructive. There will always be room for assertive, off-the-cuff blowing, and some of it will be egoistic. The competitive element is very strong, a motivating force, with some musicians, and Jazz would be the poorer for losing their drive.

Letting go and follow your ideas

Earlier the matter of musicians inventing their own technique was touched upon, the conscious and unconscious rule-breaking that jazz musicians indulge in. Those self-taught players – and there are many im-

77

Sarah Vaughan *Pittsburgh* 12 July 81 North Sea

Sarah Vaughan

Sarah Lois Vaughan (known as Sassy, The Divine One). Singer/Piano/Organ. Newark, New Jersey, March 27 1924.

From a working-class background — father was a carpenter and mother a laundress — Sarah as a child sang at Newark's Mount Zion Baptist Church. She studied both piano and organ from 1931-'39. Her big break came when she won an amateur hour contest at the famed Apollo Theatre where the audience was both knowledgeable and critical.
Billy Eckstine persuaded **Earl Hines** to add Sarah to his big band which already included **Dizzy Gillespie** and **Charlie Parker**. She sang and played piano with the band after making her début in the outfit at the Apollo during April 1943. Unfortunately the recording ban was on at that time so Sarah made no sides with Hines. But she was regularly featured on *Body And Soul, East Of The Sun* and *You Are My First Love.* On the latter, with obligatos from Charlie Parker, Sarah stopped the show at theatres across the country.
In 1944 fellow singer **Eckstine** formed a new band using the best young players from the Hines orchestra and of course including Sarah. It was the first large ensemble that fully reflected the bebop revolution. Sarah's speciality was a stunning *I'll Wait And Pray,* again accompanied by Parker's alto saxophone. According to Miss Vaughan: 'It was a very rough band. They kept me in order. I'm telling you they used to beat me to death if I got out of line. I mean literally, kicked my what's-its-name. Oh, my Lord, my arm used to be so sore. But I would never do that again, whatever that was.'
Miss Vaughan regarded her stints in the Hines and Eckstine bands as 'going to school', but she doesn't feel that the playing of Parker and Gillespie affected her style, although she learned a great deal. Her earliest recordings, from 1944, included the first vocal version of Gillespie's *A Night In Tunisia,* re-titled *(Love Is Just An) Interlude,* and Dizzy was a key member of the small backing-group. At this session she also sang a rare blues, *No Smokes,* and her easy swing allied to Gillespie's crackling trumpet made an irresistible combination.
The following year she cut four important sides — *Loverman, What More Can A Woman Do, I'd Rather Have A Memory*

Than A Dream and *Mean To Me* with Gillespie *and* Parker. Many listeners regret that with Parker present the opportunity was not taken to record their earlier collaborations, *You Are My First Love* and *I'll Wait And Pray.*
In 1945-'46 Sarah worked for a few months with John Kirby's Sextet, but after that was a solo attraction who gradually became a headliner. Her first label affiliation was with *Musicraft* and the association showed how her career would be compartmented between jazz and commercial offerings. There were jazz sides with modernists like **Tadd Dameron**, Bud Powell and Cecil Payne, and sessions with strings and other paraphernalia aimed at a wider audience. During the 1948 recording ban she even cut some spirituals, accompanied by a choir.
She moved into the big league with a contract for *Columbia Records* and registered her share of hits, including the wordless *Pinky.* But most of the Columbia output was disappointing, the exception being a beautiful 1950 session in which her now fully matured voice was set off by a small jazz ensemble including trumpeter **Miles Davis** and trombonist Bennie Green. For most of the 1950s and into the early 1960s, Sarah was contracted to *Mercury* Records and her output veered from straight jazz to popular material. She usually toured the USA and internationally with her own trio which in the 1950s comprised either John Malachi or Jimmy Jones (piano), Joe Benjamin (bass) and Roy Haynes (drums). There was an outstanding album with trumpeter **Clifford Brown** (1954) and a fine big band set arranged by Ernie Wilkins and featuring Cannonball Adderley, along with a couple of notable LPs on which her support came from the regular trio.
A spell with *Roulette Records* yielded a nice date with **Count Basie** and another arranged by Gerald Wilson. Then for five years she had no record contract until she signed with *Mainstream* in 1972.
Sarah Vaughan forged a completely new vocal style which owed nothing to Billie Holiday, Ella Fitzgerald, Mildred Bailey or other earlier song stylists. She has an enormous vocal range, perfect pitch and incredible control. She can sound sophisticated or waif-like. *Her great harmonic awareness enables her to take liberties with a melody and often improve on the original.*
However, her self-consciously 'little girl'

manner can be tiresome on occasion. Certain singers have been critical of her jazz work, accusing her of being premeditated, not an improvisor and a non-swinger. One suspects that there is more than an element of professional jealousy involved in these attacks because she can give a brilliant off-the-cuff performance as was demonstrated on her 'live' *At Mister Kelly's* album.
Her popularity in the jazz and popular camps remains undiminished. She has appeared in more than 60 countries, in locations ranging from small clubs to huge stadia, and seems at home in front of a symphony orchestra or with the most intimate assistance of guitar and bass. She has sung for several American presidents, at festivals all over the world, and in many television shows. She appeared in the movie *Harlem Jazz Festival,* filmed on location at the Apollo Theatre.
Sarah has been a potent influence on scores of vocalists, few of whom possess her musicality, dynamics, sense of phrasing and harmonic knowledge. She uses vibrato exactly as the great saxophonists do. She is, at her best, truly incomparable, and given such talent one can tolerate a few irritating mannerisms.

Recommended records:
Sarah Vaughan/Sweet, Sultry And Swinging
Spinorama M-73
Georgie Auld & His Orchestra, Vol 2
Musicraft MVS 509
Sarah Vaughan
Everest FS-250
Sarah Vaughan In Hi-Fi
Columbia CL-745
Sarah Vaughan/Swingin' Easy
EmArcy MG 36109
Sarah Vaughan/At Mister Kelly's
Mercury MG 20326
Sarah Vaughan/With Clifford Brown
EmArcy MG 36004
Sarah Vaughan/In The Land Of Hi-Fi
EmArcy MG 36058
Sarah Vaughan/Sassy Swings The Tivoli
Mercury MG 20831
The Intimate Sarah Vaughan
Roulette 2682 032
Sarah Vaughan/With Michel Legrand
Mainstream MRL 361
Sarah Vaughan & The Jimmy Rowles Quintet
Mainstream MSL 1033

Sarah Vaughan. She puts a lot of humour into her show. But precisely because of this she was so unpredictable. I was virtually too slow. I blew a lot of drawings this way.

portant ones in jazz history — break nearly all the rules. Pianist Hampton Hawes was one such; Erroll Garner, Charlie Parker and Wes Montgomery were others. As Hawes, who died in 1977, said: 'The reason I might sound different to anybody else is because the majority of other pianists playing are trained. They all studied, they all can read, they all know all the rules. I have to hear the rules. I only go by my ear. I depend on my ear and just my heart and my determination, and maybe that's the difference that you hear. The people that are self-taught are the people that have to start from scratch, without no help, not knowing what they are doing, and just soul up on it. I think up on it, and it always comes out unique.'

English bassist Peter Ind believes that one of the essential characteristics of jazz is the sense of letting go — opening up and exposing deep, inner feelings. In a series of lengthy conversations I had with Ind, who is a serious philosopher as well as being a dedicated musician, he commented: 'The evolution of jazz in America was not an accident. Neither was it an accident that it evolved amongst the Negro population but I don't think it was a heritage. I've yet to see an African Negro with that particular and peculiar quality of letting go that the great American jazz musicians have. Where it started and so on was all part of a coming together but the flow of it continues.'

Ind is depressed by displays of 'fake virtuosity' by musicians who practise licks that sound superficially very clever and inspired. 'One of the things I'm sad about is that not more musicians and jazz listeners realize when there is real virtuosity and real musicianship. Not enough of them can distinguish. It's comparatively easy to go up and down an instrument and sound like you've got complete mastery but it's something else to develop a musical line and let it take you, and have the facility, the musicality to follow it through and not lose it. Because what often happens with the jazz musician is that he gets an idea and it's beautiful but it gets out of hand; he can't hold it. His musicality or technique is not enough and he has to let it go. *But being able to follow your ideas through — that's what jazz is really about.* And it's not this flamboyance that passes for it.'

Freedom and limitations

With each new phase of development in the music,

there are judgments that 'this is not real jazz' or more emphatically 'this is *not* jazz'. The bitter attacks on bebop were only surpassed by the strong feelings engendered by the avant garde/new thing in the late sixties. Saxophonist Phil Woods, who many would classify as an archetypal bebopper, was surprisingly open-minded about the new order. But he recognized some of the defects of the so-called free style. 'There's a lot of charlatanism, I find, in anything for the sake of freedom. A funny word freedom, because they think they're not free to swing! If you're really free, why can't you play in time *sometimes.* I like to have the music become fragmented, disintegrated, pulseless if you like, but if something is pulseless it's dead. If your heart stops too long, you die. I like to hear some swing, some time occasionally. But some of the cats *can't* swing. They're too busy expressing themselves.'

Since he made those remarks more than a decade ago, Woods has revised his vocabulary to take on board innovations by the avant garde; he has recorded many 'free' performances, but he is essentially a chordal player. 'Every movement has its charlatans,' he says. 'We surely had enough of them in the bebop times. People would get a few licks together... but I think it was easier to expose them then because the format was fairly rigid as far as playing went. You had to improvise on a series of changes, so maybe you were limited, but when you heard somebody at least you could tell what they were about. And you can still tell something of what they're about, even with the primitive thing. I don't mind if somebody doesn't have techniques the way I'm used to technique as such. I don't care *how* a person plays, it's the musical result that comes out. It doesn't have to be a lovely, singing tone to say a person is a good musician. If he feels like playing that way, then okay, but there has to be something a little deeper than just what appears on the surface. Sometimes I miss the sense of depth in those cats' playing. But the great players always sound great — Ornette, Pharoah, Archie Shepp, Gato Barbieri.'

Woods recognizes the need of all musicians, especially young ones, to experiment and grow. 'Well, you have to. Once you settle for something, you might as well forget it. Just keep selling the old records because they are the same as the new ones. You've got to try to change, for good or worse. Once you become pleased with something and say ''that's it'', then you're in severe artistic trouble.'

Cleanhead Vinson

Eddie 'Mr Cleanhead' Vinson. Singer/Alto Saxophone. Houston, Texas, December 18 1917.

Professional début with Milton Larkins Band; toured with blues singers **Big Bill Broonzy** and **Lil Green** in 1941. Moved to New York the following year and joined trumpeter **Cootie Williams'** large orchestra. Eddie was employed by Williams as a singer. Registered large hits for the band with his vocals on *Cherry Red* and *Somebody's Got To Go*. These successes inevitably led him to form his own group which made a sizeable hit with *Kidney Stew Blues* in 1945.

His big band lasted several years but fell victim to economic pressures in 1949. From then on he headed a sextet for a time, but then worked as a single. Was reunited with Cootie Williams for a few months in '54 and jobbed around Chicago for awhile before resettling in Houston where much of his employment from 1954-'60 was outside music. Resumed travelling and club work in the early 1960s and recorded with fellow altoman **Cannonball Adderley** for Riverside. Also teamed up with another booting saxophonist **Arnett Cobb** for gigs. Joined pianist **Jay McShann** for extensive European tours (1968-'70) and was recorded by the *Black and Blue* label in France.

As Vinson's stock rose again, through the blues boom, he was based in Los Angeles but spent much of the 1970s travelling to many countries to play at the leading jazz festivals. Was with **Count Basie** for a spell and gigged with **Johnny Otis**.

Vinson's singing and playing are full of humour, and exhibit a robust, forthright musical perspective. His nickname stems from premature baldness. As he heads towards old age, Vinson shows no sign of losing energy or enthusiasm for music-making. His influences range from the Broonzy/Leroy Carr/Joe Turner blues spectrum to mainstream altoman Johnny Hodges and the bebop boss, Charlie Parker. *Although he has tended to recycle a limited repertoire, Vinson never fails to inject excitement and a sense of comedy into his performances.* His recordings with Williams, not in the least a recently released broadcast from 1944, remain among the highlights of a still productive and singular career in which Eddie Vinson has put his personal stamp on jazz, the blues and r&b.

Recommended records:
Cootie Williams Sextet/Orchestra
Phoenix LP 1
Eddie Vinson/Cleanhead's Back In Town
Bethlehem LP 5005
Eddie Vinson/Back Door Blues
Riverside RLP 3502

Best Wishes Cleanbury
Elvis Jackson

Jazz styles

Here the purpose is to briefly describe the principal styles of jazz, from 1900 to the present. It would be impossible to do this without reference to the originators of each development, and the geographical areas where these advances were made — New Orleans, Chicago, Kansas City, Harlem and so forth. As jazz became international, the place of discovery was almost immaterial, but the city of origin did loom large in the early history of the music.

Ragtime

A formal and formulized syncopated music, generally for the piano and usually played in 2/4 time. Like the blues it added an important ingredient to jazz. Many of the early jazz pianists, such as Jelly Roll Morton, also played ragtime, and the word rag was used in numerous jazz compositions. Ragtime was centred on Sedalia, Missouri, in the 1890s, with a number of its best practitioners coming from St Louis. Leading ragtime pianists/composers included Louis Chauvin, Tom Turpin, Tom Scott, Joseph Lamb and Scott Joplin, the most famous of them all, a prolific and serious composer. Joplin's music enjoyed an enthusiastic resurgence in the 1970s, more than 50 years after his death, and modern pianists attempted the special intricacies of a stilted but attractive style.

Ragtime greatly influenced the Original Dixieland Jazz Band, and jazz pianists as disparate as Duke Ellington, Fats Waller, James P. Johnson, Willie 'The Lion' Smith and Eubie Blake all reflected in differing degrees an appreciation of ragtime. A commercial version of ragtime, 'honky-tonk piano', is still popular, but the classic rags of Joplin and others had to wait for pianist Joshua Rifkin to return them to a dignified, concert-hall setting. Ragtime is an archaic music which combined march and dance rhythms, but exhibited a sense of swing (momentum), albeit in a rather stiff, conservative manner.

Rags were *written* music, published and widely distributed and played on the parlour pianos of America. But the finest rags also served as vehicles for improvisation. The blues, ragtime and jazz shared a fascination for extemporization; and the three idioms were the inventions of black culture. The ragtime era spanned the years from about 1890 to 1915. When the dance crazes like the cakewalk were spent, the social need for ragtime disappeared. Jazz was the new dance music of the 1920s, and rags were quickly forgotten as feet moved to the steps of the Charleston and Black Bottom.

New Orleans

Both a place and a style, the so-called cradle of jazz. It was in this cosmopolitan Southern city with its French and Spanish influences that black musicians formed the first individual jazz style in the early part of this century. Trumpeter Buddy Bolden is said to have been one of the first distinctive jazz soloists, but his reputation stands on legend and hearsay. Because New Orleans was on the river, had a large black population, a taste for lively music, a ready supply of musical instruments from Europe and a tradition of marching bands, it was the obvious spot for jazz to germinate. And it had a thriving red-light district where music was much in demand.

New Orleans style was improvised ensemble music which sprang directly from the blues and the marching bands. The favoured instrumentation was trumpet, trombone, clarinet, piano, guitar, bass and drums — a classic septet line-up favoured by such leaders as Louis Armstrong and Jelly Roll Morton. Bunk Johnson and Joe 'King' Oliver were the trumpeters who preceded Armstrong. Both helped him and Oliver employed the young Louis in his band.

Besides playing in brothels, sleazy clubs and on riverboats, the New Orleans jazzmen worked together in street parades and at funerals. They learned to combine their syncopated lines in the most difficult of circumstances. Some were self-taught, others knew the basics of music, a few could read and write down the notes they played.

Strangely enough, the full realization of the New Orleans style — its super-charged intertwining ensembles and effervescent, improvised solos — did not happen until some of the most talented young players moved to Chicago in the early 1920s. Among their number

Cleanhead Vinson. What he's got may not be such great shakes, but what he's got comes from way down deep, is completely authentic.

were clarinettist Johnny Dodds and his brother Baby (drums), trumpeters King Oliver and Louis Armstrong, pianist Jelly Roll Morton, trombonist Kid Ory, clarinettists Sidney Bechet and Jimmie Noone. Most of these men, and Henry 'Red' Allen (trumpet), a later arrival, worked in King Oliver's band at some stage. Oliver was the father figure. Chicago gave them the chance to record and show their prowess as soloists. Practically all the New Orleans veterans are now deceased, but the style continues in the city of its birth and in the playing of many 'revivalist' bands in Europe. The blues figured prominently within the style which was relatively undemanding, ideal for dancing and, at its best, classically beautiful (as in the Louis Armstrong Hot Five and Hot Seven recordings).

Dixieland

The white man's adaptation of New Orleans, as epitomized in the first jazz recordings by the Original Dixieland Jazz Band. Cornet player Nick La Rocca was the leader. He had been heavily influenced by King Oliver. The ODJB cut its first records in 1917. They had a head start because they were white. At that time the record companies would not consider 'taking a chance' on black artists. Another white band from New Orleans were the New Orleans Rhythm Kings who also favoured the bright and breezy Dixieland style. The Wolverines, a group of young, white mid-Westerners, played in a similar vein, only they had a genuine original in their ranks in the shape of the brilliant cornet player Bix Beiderbecke, admired by Armstrong and other black trumpeters.

Chicago was where Louis met Bix; where Louis got together with pianist Earl Hines; where the Austin High School Gang had a jumping little band. The High School crowd included two men who would soon be part of the lucrative Swing Era — Benny Goodman (clarinet) and Gene Krupa (drums).

Dixieland was basically light-weight music, regarded as entertainment by the gangsters who manipulated the Chicago speakeasies. In New Orleans too, jazz was always viewed as part of entertainment. Years later, Dixieland was slickly packaged by Bob Crosby in a small group within his big band. It struck familiar chords in the late 1930s with listeners who had been teenagers during the Roaring Twenties. Crosby's main outfit also specialized in orchestrated big band Dixieland.

Commercial Dixieland has been popular in England since the end of World War II, and also has adherents in Germany, France, Holland and Belgium. It is a music rarely, if ever, played by black musicians. Dixieland groups have the conventional trumpet/trombone/clarinet ensemble, but invariably use a banjo which tends to give the rhythm section a leaden quality. The trumpeters usually double as out-of-tune vocalists!

Swing

Swing is both a style and a feeling. The style is that which was propounded by shoals of big bands that played orchestrated jazz in the 1930s. Fletcher Henderson was one of the earliest jazz arrangers who could think in terms of large ensembles and writing complementary parts for the different sections within the conventional big band of 16 of 17 pieces. Don Redman was another respected writer, years ahead of his time, who collaborated with Henderson. By 1930 there were more than a few large ensembles, such as the Bennie Moten Band (eventually taken over by Count Basie) and the Andy Kirk Orchestra in Kansas City; the Duke Ellington Orchestra, operating out of New York; the Casa Loma Band and the aggregation co-led by the feuding and fighting Dorsey Brothers, Tommy and Jimmy.

Swing was generally disciplined, packaged jazz which emphasized the need for a steady flow of new 'charts' (arrangements) to give the band a distinctive sound and repertoire. Swing tended to relegate the improvising jazz musician to short solos of one or two choruses. Bands still required a handful of sparkling soloists, but this was the era of the section craftsman who, along with the star improviser, was subservient to the composer/arranger. Musicians were apparently willing to sacrifice their individuality in exchange for regular employment, but it was a frustrating time for players who wanted to express themselves. On the credit side, these bands were wonderful training grounds for youngsters, providing a thorough musical base and teaching the value of discipline.

Duke Ellington, who led a large orchestra for almost 50 years, was a part of, yet apart from, the Swing Era. He wrote his own music and used the orchestra as his 'instrument'. He composed with particular soloists in mind and by regularly sharing out the solo spotlight managed to keep all his employees happy and satisfied. Ellington's music reflected a breadth of vision not evident in the efforts of the run-of-the-mill stock arrangers.

Count Basie placed great emphasis on the swinging aspect. From the keyboard he directed a smooth, surg-

Buddy Tate, Lou Donaldson, Sal Nistico, Ornette Coleman: four styles.

To Pete
Thanks
Buddy Tate

Dick Vollwerff's Jazzlife   Lou Donaldson

Pete,
Wonderful
Work w/ Soul,
Sal Nistico's

Ornette Coleman Kool Jazz 1-7-83

Dexter Gordon

Dexter Keith Gordon. Tenor & Soprano Saxophone/Composer. Los Angeles, California, February 27 1923.

Came from a comfortable background (rather like Miles Davis). His father was a doctor whose patients included Duke Ellington and Lionel Hampton. At the age of 13 Gordon studied clarinet having acquired the basics of theory and harmony. Started on alto sax at 15 and after the death of his father and on leaving school in 1940 switched to tenor sax, joining **Lionel Hampton**'s saxophone section that also included **Illinois Jacquet, Marshall Royal** and **Jack McVea**. Stayed with **Hampton** for three years. Then gigged around Los Angeles with **Lee Young, Jessie Price** and others. Spent six months with the **Louis Armstrong** Orchestra in 1944; Louis called him 'Brother Dexter' and made him a featured soloist. Also worked with **Fletcher Henderson**. Earned recognition with the **Billy Eckstine** Orchestra (1944-'45) and through his solos on *Blowin' The Blues Away* and *Lonesome Lover Blues*.

He rapidly became one of the most influential bebop tenor saxophonists and worked with a multiplicity of small groups in New York's 52nd Street just after World War II. Recorded *Blue 'n' Boogie* with **Dizzy Gillespie** (1945) and was also on an early session with **Charlie Parker** under Sir Charles Thompson's name. Gordon's first records as leader were for *Savoy,* and many had his name in the titles – *Blow Mr Dexter, Dexter's Deck, Long Tall Dexter, Dexter's Riff, Dexter's Mood* etc.

In California, Gordon teamed with fellow tenorman **Wardell Gray** for gigs and records. The pair brought out the best in each other's playing. Dexter was off the scene for much of the 1950s with drug problems and was incarcerated for several years. He appeared in the West Coast company of Jack Gelber's stage play *The Connection* in 1960, and recorded the original music for *Jazzland.* In 1961 he signed for *Blue Note* and with an LP entitled *Doin' Allright* commenced a series of splendid albums for that label. In 1962 he moved to Europe and after a stay in Paris made Copenhagen his headquarters, although he often returned to the USA for tours. Gordon had appeared at virtually all the major festivals

in Europe, and continued to record for *Prestige, Black Lion, SteepleChase* and *Columbia.* In the 1970s Dexter suffered from over-exposure on records. Too many of the albums were routine and uninspired. Particularly disappointing were Gordon's sessions for *Columbia,* as this was the first time he had been signed with a major label.

Dexter started out as a firm disciple of Lester Young, but later drew inspiration from Charlie Parker. His tone hardened as the 1940s wore on, and his mature work made a great impact on John Coltrane and Sonny Rollins, the tenor titans of the 1950s. Later, Gordon was to absorb aspects of Coltrane's approach, illustrating the circle of influences in jazz. A tall, handsome, friendly and easy-going man, Dexter is always master of the musical situation, unflappable and slightly extrovert. His solos are peppered with amusing quotations, he is an excellent blues player, and has a tender, but unsentimental way with a ballad. His solos unfold with a relentless swing and sure logic. He knows how to build an improvisation to a climax, and relishes the prospect of a musical brush with fellow saxophonists. In the Eckstine band, Dexter was a member of what he termed the 'Unholy Four' – the others were fellow saxophonists **Sonny Stitt, John Jackson** and **Leo Parker**. They were friends as well as section mates but as tempestuous youngsters they got up to all sorts of capers.

With the death of Sonny Stitt in 1983, Dexter is the last of the 'Four' to survive. He is still a riveting improvisor, capable of transporting an audience into an ecstatic state with his long, expressive lines. Gordon has also composed more than his share of interesting melodies including *The Panther, Mrs Miniver, Valse Robin, Stanley The Steamer, Fried Bananas, All Clean, Evergreenish, Hanky Panky, Clubhouse, Jodi, For Regulars Only, Society Red, Landslide* and *So Easy.* Dexter's style was described by Ross Russell as 'heavy, authoritarian, macho'. Dan Morgenstern has written of Gordon's 'Wonderful, firmly swinging time; the authority of his presence; the harmonic sophistication and audacity; the big, bold sound; the masterly tonguing; the drive and energy; *the humour, tinged with irony and touched with sarcasm.'* Alto saxophonist **Jackie McLean** cites Gordon as the influence who made him want to become a musician; he heard

Dexter before Charlie Parker, and describes a gig with Gordon in Copenhagen, during which they made two albums together, as 'the highspot of my musical career'.

Such has been the potent, inspirational influence of 'Dex'; hear a certain Stan Getz session for Savoy from 1946 and it's Gordon's sound and licks. He was *the* man on tenor then; Dexter remains like *an Everest on the tenor scene.* Most saxophonists literally have to look up to him, knowing that his huge strides down the jazz road carried them forward too. To Gordon must belong the credit for amalgamating the conceptions of Parker and Young, and transcending those potentially overpowering influences. After four decades as a professional, Dexter's invention shows no sign of flagging. His tutor in the early days, Lloyd Reese, taught him well, but even he could not have foreseen the heights to which his able pupil would aspire. He is, as Morgenstern placed him, 'the man who first created an authentic bebop style on the tenor saxophone'. Some first and some style!

Recommended records:
Dexter Gordon/The Savoy Sessions
Savoy SJL 2211
Dexter Gordon/The Dial Masters
Spotlite SPJ 130/133
Dexter Gordon/Doin' Allright
Blue Note BST 84077
Dexter Gordon/Landslide
Blue Note LT-1051
Dexter Gordon/Clubhouse
Blue Note LT-989
Dexter Gordon/The Panther!
Prestige PRST 7829
Dexter Gordon/The Jumpin' Blues
Prestige PR 10020
Dexter Gordon/Jackie McLean/The Meeting
SteepleChase SCS-1006
Dexter Gordon/Jackie McLean/The Source
SteepleChase SCS-1020

Dexter Gordon. He started a bit shaky but during the second set I suddenly heard that magnificent tone of his. After the show he wrote a different dedication on each of the drawings. He was amazed at how I could do so many in so short a time.

ing rhythm section. He had an ear for potent soloists and recognized the offbeat appeal of Lester Young's laconic tenor saxophone. Basie was shrewd in his employment of arrangers, demanding from them simple, uncluttered writing that would allow the band to groove.

Swing took off in 1935 when Benny Goodman and his orchestra became an overnight sensation. His success was followed by other white leaders — Artie Shaw, Glenn Miller, the Dorsey Brothers (leading separate bands), Charlie Barnet, Bunny Berigan, Harry James, Gene Krupa, Woody Herman and others.

Ironically, much of the music that kept Goodman to the fore was supplied by black composers and arrangers — Fletcher and Horace Henderson, Benny Carter and Edgar Sampson. This was not appreciated by the public in those years. However, Goodman was the first white bandleader to employ black players — pianist Teddy Wilson and vibraphonist Lionel Hampton — and thus dent the so-called 'colour line'.

Musically, the black bands of Jimmie Lunceford, Cab Calloway and Chuck Webb were superior to Goodman's orchestra, but lacked the commercial clout. There was no big publicity machine behind them. During this period, even Louis Armstrong, the darling of the small group and improvised jazz, appeared with a big band, led by Luis Russell.

Although big bands abounded, like so many dinosaurs, the small combination still flourished in little clubs and for recording sessions. Fats Waller fronted an ever popular combo. The maverick piano genius Art Tatum, whose style was unclassifiable, had no use for big bands. And when not paying dues with Goodman, Teddy Wilson was regularly recording with hand-picked six-, seven- or eight-piece groups.

A host of outstanding soloists was spawned by the Swing Era — saxophonists Coleman Hawkins, Lester Young, Ben Webster, Johnny Hodges, Chu Berry, trumpeters Rex Stewart, Roy Eldridge, Cootie Williams, Buck Clayton, Harry Edison, Oran 'Hot Lips' Page, trombonists Dicky Wells, J.C. Higginbotham, James 'Trummy' Young, Vic Dickenson, Lawrence Brown, Fred Beckett. But it was the clarinet that proved to be supreme in popularity through the efforts of Goodman, Shaw and Herman. Of the drummers, Gene Krupa was idolized by fans, but the influential men were Jo Jones (with Basie), the crippled Chick Webb and Big Sid Catlett.

As a fad, swing lasted considerably longer than anyone had a right to expect. The music became too constricted, predictable and formulized. The addition of string sections, vocal groups and glamorous singers could not disguise its loss of energy and inspiration. The Glenn Miller Orchestra, wherein the musicianship was matchless and the music empty, illustrated the problem of the composer/arranger taking over and suffocating creative expression. The wartime recording ban in the USA signalled the beginning of the end of the era. By then, a group of young black musicians were already shaping the next jazz revolution in the after-hours clubs of Harlem.

Bop, bebop, rebop

The new style which was known by these undignified names was hatched in the early 1940s by a clique of superior players who had resolutely emerged from their apprenticeships with big bands — Dizzy Gillespie (trumpet), Charlie Parker (alto saxophone), Thelonious Monk and Bud Powell (piano), Charlie Christian (guitar), Jimmy Blanton (bass), Kenny Clarke and Max Roach (drums), and Tadd Dameron (piano/composer/arranger). All these men were born between 1914 and 1925. They were bored with the routines of swing and sought a more challenging style which would also restore the importance of the soloist.

These musicians had met during barn-storming band tours when their routes and schedules crossed in Kansas City or Chicago. Charlie Christian and Jimmy Blanton both died in 1942, but their innovations were critical on their respective instruments. Blanton was the first bassist to phrase his lines like a saxophone or trumpet soloist. Christian experimented with altered chords and his rhythmic approach was definitely bop-flavoured.

But Charlie Parker and Dizzy Gillespie were the twin figures who did most to crystallize what came to be called 'modern jazz'. They were harmonically more sophisticated than the swing stylists, they played at faster tempo, they used the chord sequences of familiar standards but wrote new melodies on them. The music was fast, tense, bristling with ideas and energy and 'difficult' for listeners at first acquaintance. Gillespie and Parker were like two perfectly fitting pieces of a jig-saw. They inspired each other, and effectively carried through an incredible musical transition. They were as hard-swinging in their way as the revered swing soloists. By the end of 1945 their personal appraisals of jazz were complete, and the music emerged as a definite and lasting idiom. They were also the finest soloists in the style, closely followed by Bud Powell, trumpeter Fats Navarro and tenor saxophonists Wardell Gray and Dexter Gordon. Monk's contribution was in the sphere of composition, while Dameron, known as 'The Prophet', shone as an arranger able to make a six-piece group sound like ten, and to chart feasible, written courses for big band boppers. Bebop was the first jazz style to be fully realized in New York, the city to which all jazz musicians seeking recognition gravitated from the mid-1930s onwards. The specific clubs where the new 'rules' were devised were Minton's and Monroe's. Drummer Kenny Clarke had begun to amend his style as early as 1937. He disliked the old style of emphasizing the rhythm on the bass drum. Clarke switched it to the top cymbal, employing the bass drum sparingly for what came to be known as 'bomb dropping' (it was wartime!) effects. Between the innovations of Clarke (elaborated by Max Roach), Powell and Blanton a new conception of a supportive rhythm section was devised. Neither bop nor its leaders made audience concessions. They offered the music on a 'take it or leave it' basis, seldom bothering to explain their aims or procedures, never mind announce tune titles. Not that names meant much. If somebody requested *Whispering,* the bop group would play *Groovin' High,* a line based on the *Whispering* chord progression.

The boppers (Dizzy Gillespie apart) tended to be uncommunicative introverts who hid their feelings and identities behind a mysterious facade which encompassed dark glasses, a far-out, monosyllabic language, all deliberately constructed to keep out the squares and hippies.

Consequently the music was misunderstood and the musicians bitterly attacked by older colleagues and certain critics. Fortunately there were exceptions. Saxophonist Coleman Hawkins, though not a modernist, recognized the validity of the new music and employed many of the players in his bands and on record dates. Commentators like Leonard Feather and Ross Russell went to bat for bebop, and their serious writings on the subject were influential and counterbalanced a welter of idiotic statements from leading musical personalities.

By 1947 when Dizzy Gillespie had launched his second large orchestra and Charlie Parker was leading his best quintet the durability of bop was being contested only by those who refused to accept reality. The style held greatest sway from 1945-'55, reaching a creative zenith from about '47-'50.

An unfortunate aspect of the bop cult and lifestyle was the widespread use of dangerous narcotics by a large number of its leading and following figures. Heroin claimed some of the outstanding talents including Parker, Navarro and Gray. Others were able to overcome their addiction, but had disturbed personalities. Bud Powell suffered severe bouts of mental illness while Thelonious Monk's eccentric behaviour certainly held back the recognition that he eventually gained in the late 1950s. Dizzy Gillespie differed from so many of his contemporaries in that he was a well-adjusted realist. He 'took care of business' and never messed with hard drugs. Although Dizzy paraded the symbols of the cult (beret, dark glasses and goatee), he out-distanced the trivialities by his charisma and musicality.

A thin, serious young man who stood shoulder-to-shoulder with Charlie Parker in those years effected the next stylistic departure before the 1940s were played out. His name was Miles Davis.

Cool jazz

Davis had been closely connected with bop since 1944 when he sat in with the Billy Eckstine Orchestra in his hometown of St Louis. The Eckstine band was one of the hotbeds of the music, containing such alumni as Gillespie, Parker and Gordon. Miles learned his craft and soon discovered a way of playing that differed markedly from Dizzy Gillespie's trumpet style. Davis liked to play in the middle register and shunned the pyrotechnics which were Dizzy's hallmark. He played 'cool' long before the phrase was coined.

Cool jazz was more restrained than bop and, just as swing did, it gave full deployment to arrangers' skills. Davis discovered a soul brother in Gil Evans whose orchestral expertise, using French-horns, tuba and clarinets to produce an unusually dense sound, had been evident in the Claude Thornhill Orchestra's recordings of the 1940s.

In 1948 Davis formed a nine-piece band which played a couple of brief engagements. It was like a scaled-down version of the Thornhill ensemble, and in addition to Evans, Gerry Mulligan, Johnny Carisi and John Lewis supplied arrangements. The band recorded in 1949 and '50, and the 12 tracks they made were packaged as *The Birth of the Cool.*

The music tended to be more restrained than bebop, and the instrumentalists were less fiery than the conventional bop players. The Davis recordings were extremely influential on many Hollywood musicians, notably Shorty Rogers, whose Giants were patterned on the Davis nonet, Bud Shank, Chet Baker, John Graas and Bob Cooper. Gerry Mulligan actually moved to the West Coast and continued to preach the cool message

Jimmy Witherspoon

10-5-'83

Jimmy Witherspoon

James (Jimmy) Witherspoon.
Singer/Bass. Gurdon, Arkansas, August 8
1923.

Father sang in a local church choir and
mother was a pianist. As a child 'Spoon',
as he is known, won first prize in a singing
contest. Ran away from home in early
teens and settled in California. Served in
the Merchant Marine in the Pacific
1941-'43, and sang with a number of
bands, including pianist Teddy
Weatherford, in India. Depped for and
eventually replaced Walter Brown in the
Jay McShann Orchestra, last of the great
Kansas City bands, in 1944, staying for
four years. On the West Coast for much of
the late 1940s but played the Apollo
Theatre, New York, in 1950.
First big hit was *'Tain't Nobody's*
Business in 1952. Toured widely as a
single in 1950s, appearing in Detroit, New
Orleans and Chicago. Many recordings
with Jessie Stone, Jay McShann, **Slide**
Hampton, Gerry Mulligan and **Ben**
Webster, **Coleman Hawkins** and **Roy**
Eldridge. First European tour with Buck
Clayton All-Stars in 1961. Also toured
with **Count Basie** (1963) including a trip
to Japan. Appeared at several Monterey
festivals, and was a frequent visitor to
England for club and concert, radio and
TV dates in the 1960s.
Stayed busy in 1970s, working for awhile
as a DJ in Los Angeles. Appeared in film
The Black Godfather (1974) and featured
in many TV jazz programmes.
Witherspoon is *an accomplished and*
convincing blues singer who, because of
his route into music, sounds more at
home when surrounded by jazz musicians
as in his early work with McShann's small
group.
Witherspoon is classified as a 'blues
shouter' because of his band background.
Fair enough, but he can be sensitive and
restrained if that's the mood demanded.
As Paul Oliver has written, Witherspoon
has respect for blues singers of older
generations and his repertoire includes
classics associated with Leroy Carr,
Bessie Smith, Ma Rainey and W.C.
Handy. In the mid-1970s his recording of
Love Is A Five Letter Word was another
very big hit for this likeable singer who is
always the first to acknowledge the
contributions of his supporting musicians.
His compositions include *Times Getting*
Tougher Than Tough, Bags Under My
Eyes, Money's Getting Cheaper,
Part-Time Woman and the poetically titled
Rain Is Such A Lonesome Sound. Some
1959 recordings by Witherspoon with the
empathetic Ben Webster are especially
memorable.
Spoon's main influences were Bill
Broonzy, Doc Clayton, Joe Turner and
Jimmy Rushing. As pianist Billy Taylor
commented in his notes for a
Witherspoon album, every great blues
singer is a great story teller and Jimmy 'is
one of the very best'. His stature in jazz,
blues, and rhythm and blues is as tall
today as it was 30 years ago, and
whenever he picks up a microphone there
will be an involved and uninhibited
audience to cheer him on; he is a truly
charismatic figure.

Recommended records:
Jimmy Witherspoon With Jay
McShann's Band/Spoon Calls Hootie
Polydor 423241
Jimmy Witherspoon/Sings The Blues
Ember CJS 820
1959 Monterey Jazz Festival
Ember CJS 834

Duke Jordan

Irving Sidney Jordan. Piano/Composer.
Brooklyn, New York City, April 1 1922.

Studied piano from ages of eight to 16.
Played in the school band at Brooklyn
Automotive High School and after
graduating in 1939, joined Steve Pulliam's
Manhattan Sextet (Jimmy Nottingham was
on trumpet) which won the 'most
promising amateur combo' prize at 1939
New York World's Fair.
Left Pulliam in 1941 to join Clarke Monroe
in the sextet that later worked under
Coleman Hawkins' leadership at Kelly's
Stables on 52nd Street. Spent a year with
Al Cooper's Savoy Sultans, then returned
to 52nd Street with trombonist J.J.
Johnson and other groups. Also worked
with Roy Eldridge big band and the trio of
guitarist Teddy Walters. While with
Walters at the Three Deuces, Jordan was
heard and recruited by alto saxophonist
Charlie Parker in the spring of 1947.
He was a member of Parker's best quintet
for 18 productive months. The group, also
including Miles Davis, Tommy Potter and
Max Roach, made many recordings for
Dial and *Savoy.* Jordan's impeccable
accompaniment, his beautiful
introductions to masterpieces like
Scrapple From The Apple, Embraceable
You, Out Of Nowhere and *My Old Flame,*
his exquisite solo miniatures, models of
compactness, are non-pareil in the idiom.
On leaving Parker, Jordan worked off and
on with tenor saxophonist **Stan Getz** for a
couple of years and occasionally gigged
with Parker when either Al Haig or Walter
Bishop Jr were unavailable. In 1950 he
was a member of the Gene Ammons/
Sonny Stitt Band, and in 1951 he played
with **Coleman Hawkins** for awhile. Later
associations included Eddie Bert, Oscar
Pettiford, Art Farmer and Gigi Gryce,
Howard McGhee and Rolf Ericson.
Toured Scandinavia with trumpeter
Ericson's group in 1956 and returned to
Europe three years later to make two film
soundtracks, composing the score for the
French movie *Les Liaisons Dangereuses.*
Jordan made the first trio recordings
under his own name in 1954, at which
time he could not earn a living from jazz
and was giving piano lessons. Although
he subsequently recorded albums for
Signal, Blue Note and *Charlie Parker*
Records, the 1960s were a bleak time for
Duke, and work was so scarce he was
forced to take a job outside music, driving
a New York taxi cab for many years. The
picture started to change for the better in
1973 when he was invited to Denmark
and made his first trio sides for 18 years
for the *Spotlite* and *SteepleChase* labels.
For the past decade he has been a busy
man, playing in most European countries
and Japan, with occasional residencies in
New York. His recorded output has
burgeoned and many new Jordan
compositions have been heard. Originally
influenced by Teddy Wilson and Art
Tatum, Jordan also liked Duke Ellington —
hence his nickname. Jordan's playing,
unlike that of many bebop pianists is
neither tense nor staccato. He spins long,
lyrical and melodic lines, and his
improvisations are well-shaped and
economical. Consistency and
conciseness are his watchwords.
Jordan is the composer of a long list of
original melodies. Two of the earliest and
best-known are *Jordu* (a jazz standard
recorded by many groups) and *Flight To*
Jordan. Other notable Jordan tunes
include *Forecast, Vacker Flicka, Starbrite,*
Split Quick, Tall Grass, Love Train, No
Problem, Misty Thursday, Flight To
Denmark, Flight To Japan, Night Train To
Snekkersten, I'm Gonna Learn Your

Style, Two Loves, Jazz Vendor and
Scotch Blues. Duke Jordan epitomizes
the dedicated jazz musician, totally
committed to a style and resolutely
improving his interpretation of it.

Recommended records:
Charlie Parker On Dial, Vols 4-6
Spotlite 104/5/6
**Charlie Parker/The Complete Savoy
Studio Sessions**
Savoy S5J 5500

Duke Jordan/Jordu
Prestige PRST 7849
Duke Jordan/Trio & Quintet
Signal S 1202
Rolf Ericson/Transatlantic Wail
Pye Nixa NJL 5
Duke Jordan/Flight To Jordan
Blue Note BLP 4046
Duke Jordan/The Murray Hill Caper
Spotlite DJ5
**Cecil Payne & Duke Jordan/Brooklyn
Brothers**

Muse MR 5015
Duke Jordan/Flight To Denmark
SteepleChase SCS-1011
Duke Jordan Quartet/Misty Thursday
SteepleChase SCS-1053
Duke Jordan Trio/Live In Japan
SteepleChase SCS-1063/4

*Duke Jordan. There were twelve people in the
audience. He gave a running commentary
between each number as if he was explaining
to a bunch of boarding-school girls what he
was doing. I thought: this jazzman ain't spoiled.*

through his quartet with Chet Baker, and a tentet that echoed the Miles group in many respects.

Alto saxophonist Lee Konitz, a member of the Capitol band experiments, was also closely identified with cool jazz, as was his mentor Lennie Tristano and other members of the so-called Tristano School. Lennie had an astounding appreciation of jazz history. One of his tutorial techniques was to get students to sing the solos of Louis Armstrong, Roy Eldridge and Charlie Parker to heighten their awareness of the components of jazz improvisation.

Tristano was never really a part of the 'cool' except in the minds of the public who, not for the first time, had been fed mis-information about jazz.

The cool approach gathered a clutch of adherents in Europe, especially among a group of Swedish musicians. Arne Domnerus could out-Konitz the man himself. Bengt Hallberg was a very cool pianist. The style seemed to fit the Scandinavian temperament. Stan Getz, who never played with the Davis ensemble, was nevertheless the epitome of the cool tenor saxophonist, somewhat detached and carefully melodic, at least during that phase of his development. When Getz settled in Sweden in the early 1950s he converted many to his distinctive tone. Getz was known as 'The Sound'. Cool jazz concerned itself with a low-key sound, a gentle approach. Which is not to say it failed to swing; much of it did, but never in unrestrained fashion.

The cool chapter was fleeting. Once Miles Davis had accomplished his objectives with the nonet he moved on to other preocupations. But 3,000 miles away the cool lingered on in another, more overtly commercial form.

West Coast jazz

White musicians in Hollywood and San Francisco soon scented exploitable possibilities in the 'cool'. They added a pretty veneer and fashioned a music which was easy listening and readily appealing to high school and college youngsters. A number of the musicians involved – Shorty Rogers, Bob Cooper, Shelly Manne, Art Pepper – had worked with the Stan Kenton Orchestra. They were all accomplished studio players.

From San Francisco came Dave Brubeck and his quartet. Gerry Mulligan and Chet Baker achieved rapid success with their pianoless quartet. West Coast jazz, despite its melodic attractions, was gutless music. The rhythm sections rarely sparked, and there was a sameness and predictability about so many of the polished,

yet superficial, performances that were turned out in conveyor-belt quantities. In opting for musicial precision, the instrumentalists too often sacrificed feeling. The glut of West Coast albums also tended to obscure the talented black players who resided in California – Teddy Edwards, Dexter Gordon, Wardell Gray, Hampton Hawes, Sonny Criss, Kenny Drew, Sonny Clark etc. They struggled to exist in those years.

The death of Charlie Parker in 1955 jolted the jazz world out of a trance-like state of complacency. Musicians and listeners were reminded again of the virile sound and unflagging swing of Parker at the peak. The moment was ripe for a bop revival with an emphasis on the driving qualities of that style. The scene once more shifted to New York.

Hardbop

Drummer Art Blakey, more than any other individual, encapsulated the spirit of hardbop, as did the quintet known as the Jazz Messengers. The group, with Kenny Dorham (trumpet), Hank Mobley (tenor sax), Horace Silver (piano) and Doug Watkins (bass), made its recording début at Café Bohemia eight months after Charlie Parker's demise. Blakey was a rhythmic powerhouse who relentlessly drove his young cohorts. If the rhythms were less subtle than in classic bop, they were impelling.

Horace Silver's gospel-tinged piano was also a key element, along with his facility for writing 'funky' (earthy) tunes on which he sometimes employed strutting march tempos. Bobby Timmons continued this pianistic tradition in a later edition of the Messengers. The group re-explored the blues, and the soloists played with passion and fire – qualities conspicuous by their absence from West Coast jazz which had also neglected the blues. Silver went on to form his own quintet which hard-bopped its way into the late 1960s before the leader sought other challenges. Hank Mobley stuck by the style until his disappearance from the scene around 1970.

Mobley also played in the band of Max Roach who, with trumpeter Clifford Brown, had taken hardbop to California in 1954. The Brown/Roach combo was one of the best of its time and would have gone on to greater heights but for the untimely deaths of Brown and pianist Richie Powell in a car crash in 1956.

An infusion of young musicians from Detroit also swelled the forces of hardbop. Donald Byrd, Pepper Adams, Paul Chambers, Tommy Flanagan, Kenny Burrell, Thad and Elvin Jones were all fluent instrumentalists in this

Lionel Hampton
Vredenburg Utrecht 2 mei 82

Lionel Hampton

*Lionel Hampton. Vibraharp/Marimba/
Piano/Drums/Composer/Singer.
Louisville, Kentucky, April 12 1913.*

Family moved to Chicago when 'Hamp'
was seven years old. Started as a
drummer and became a member of the
Chicago Defender Boys' Band. The
Defender was the blacks' own paper in
that city. Hampton left school and with
three Chicago musician friends –
saxophonist Les Hite, trumpeter George
Orendorff and trombonist Louis Taylor –
headed for California in 1928.
In Los Angeles, Lionel took piano lessons
from the late Teddy Weatherford, and then
landed the drummer's spot in saxophonist
Paul Howard's quartet. Howard
encouraged the youngster, and it was in
Culver City that Hampton made his first
records as a member of Paul Howard's
Quality Serenaders. Hampton quit the
Howard group in 1930 to join his old
friend Les Hite whose band was being
fronted by trumpet star **Louis
Armstrong**.
Around this time Hampton started
dabbling with the xylophone, and he was
immediately attracted to vibes when he
found a set in a recording studio. He was
first heard as a solo vibraphonist on
Armstrong's recording of *Memories Of
You,* waxed on October 13, 1930.
Lionel assumed leadership status in 1934
with a group of young musicians, and one
evening **Benny Goodman** heard him and
was impressed. However a couple of
years passed before Lionel was invited to
join the Goodman organization as a
member of the special quartet within the
band. On occasion Hamp also played
drums with the full orchestra, but his
renown stemmed from his mercurial vibes
solos. Hampton made many small group
records with Goodman, and on his own
account also recorded a splendid series of
small combo sides, featuring soloists like
**Dizzy Gillespie, Chu Berry, Benny
Carter, Ben Webster** and **Coleman
Hawkins,** for *Victor* Records.
In September 1940 he was able to launch
his own big band. It was 15 months
before the orchestra was recorded but the
first session produced a hit in *Flyin'
Home.* The outfit was a huge commercial
success throughout the 1940s during
which many talented modernists like
**Dexter Gordon, Fats Navarro, Charles
Mingus** and **Illinois Jacquet** passed

through the ranks.
The Hampton band was a hotbed of
musical excitement, and was quite a
visual spectacle. Hamp would sometimes
dance on top of his drums, and he
encouraged tenor and trumpet battles and
rivalry between the different sections.
*Whether he was behind the drums,
hammering the vibes or plunking at the
piano with one or two fingers of each
hand, Hamp was an inspiration to those
around him.*
The early band records were superb, but
after World War II Lionel tried to jump on
the bebop bandwagon and made some
nonsensical comments about the new
music. Still, he could be relied upon to
bring home the bacon with hit sellers like
Hamp's Boogie Woogie, loud, frenetic and
musically poor. Some of his work
bordered on rhythm and blues, and it is
perhaps no accident that r&b specialists
Joe Morris, Earl Bostic and **Arnett Cobb**
started out as section players with Hamp.
His late wife Gladys was an astute
businesswoman and took care of the
paperwork. Together they founded the
GladHamp record label. Extensive
overseas tours became commonplace for
Lionel from the 1950s onwards, and he
assembled a particularly impressive band
for a 1953 swing through Europe. It
contained trumpeters **Clifford Brown** and
Art Farmer, drummer Alan Dawson,
pianist George Wallington and singer
Annie Ross among others.
In 1955 Hamp participated in *The Benny
Goodman Story,* a loosely biographical
movie. He kept the big band going for
another 10 years, but since the
mid-1960s has been usually heard in
small groups. He occasionally
reassembled bands for special concerts
or festival appearances. He called his
smaller group The Inner Circle.
Hampton's taste has sometimes been
suspect, and rabble-rousing pieces like
Hey! Ba-Ba-Re-Bop did little to enhance
his reputation with critics. Neither has he
always been aware of the abilities of the
musicians in his bands.
In 1964 he took a large orchestra to the
Antibes Jazz Festival. The saxophone
section had two baritone saxophonists,
Pepper Adams and **Cecil Payne.**
Adams was allocated all the solos, until
somebody pointed out to Hamp that
Payne was a bebop veteran of the
Gillespie band and a fine soloist. After that
Hampton had the two baritones playing
chase choruses in front of the band! The

Hampton band frequently sounded
raggedy, but it was a tribute to the
leader's stamina that he was able to
maintain it for more than 25 years.
It is as the first and one of the best
vibraharpists that Hampton has earned his
place in the jazz histories. He is a nimble,
melodic soloist who feels at home with
the modernists, many of whom he
recorded with in the 1950s for the *Verve*
label. His most felicitous records have
been in a small group context. He remains
open-minded about style, and in the
1980s has recorded with pianist **Chick
Corea**.
Even today when the name of Lionel
Hampton is mentioned, it is automatically
linked with those of Benny Goodman,
Teddy Wilson and Gene Krupa, the
quartet of 45 years ago that symbolized
swing in miniature. A number of Hamp's
early records are included in the Benny
Goodman album listing. Those below
represent a cross section of sides under
his own name.

Recommended records:
Lionel Hampton's Best Records, Vol 3
French RCA Victor 731048
**Lionel Hampton/Steppin' Out,
1942-'45**
Decca DL 79244
**Lionel Hampton/All-American Award
Concert**
Brunswick LAT 8086
**Lionel Hampton & The Just Jazz All
Stars**
Vogue VJD 508
Lionel Hampton Concert 1948
Weka WK 12-1
**The Fabulous Lionel Hampton & His
All-Stars**
Concert Hall BJ 1238
Hamp's Big Band
Audio Fidelity AFSD 5913
Lionel Hampton/Newport Uproar!
RCA Victor LSP-3891

vein. They were joined in a burgeoning New York jazz fraternity by the brothers Nat and Julian 'Cannonball' Adderley from Tampa, Florida, and the twins Art and Addison Farmer who also espoused the style.

Miles Davis also found hardbop rhythm sections to his liking and recorded with spirited saxophonists such as Jackie McLean, Sonny Rollins and John Coltrane, who spent several years as a member of the Davis quintet. In this atmosphere, Thelonious Monk was at last accorded the chance to put his work on record with the help of skilled interpreters of his music, like Rollins, Coltrane, Roach and Blakey. Other bop pianists — George Wallington, Walter Bishop, Al Haig and Duke Jordan — were back in demand again.

Hardbop gave rise to expressions like funky, soul and groovy. It was a back-to-the-roots movement, and by 1958 it had all but washed away the insipidness which prevailed in the West Coast years. But, with another of its ironic twists, jazz had discovered a new flavour — in Hollywood!

Free form/Avant garde/New thing

Something else! was the declaration by saxophonist Ornette Coleman as the title of his 1958 Contemporary album recorded in Los Angeles. It sent shock waves through the jazz world and set off a decade of controversy. Who was this man with a white plastic saxophone who could not even play properly? That was the type of question asked.

Today that record sounds relatively conventional, with a totally traditional bebop instrumentation of trumpet, saxophone, piano, bass and drums. Significantly, Coleman would leave out piano from his future groups.

96

The saxophone leaves ample space for the idea 'each musician his own sound'. Here three tenor giants: Eddie Lockjaw Davis, flanked by Arnett Cobb and Johnny Griffin.

Coleman was struggling to cast off the ball and chain of improvising on chord sequences. He was interested in melodic shapes and did not necessarily need a constant, metronomic rhythm. He wanted to be released from the pulse and play 'free'.

Debate raged about Coleman and his trumpeter Don Cherry. When they appeared in New York all the top musicians checked them out, reaching widely different conclusions, just as the swingmen had about Charlie Parker and Dizzy Gillespie 15 years earlier.

The 1960s was a time of musical ferment. John Coltrane and Eric Dolphy were exploring chords as nobody had done before. Cecil Taylor's angular piano style at last began to get full attention. The squawking and squeaking of saxophonists Albert Ayler and Archie Shepp left many listeners feeling battered and bemused. Much of the music was apt to sound ugly, but as its defenders argued it was only reflecting society. It certainly wasn't music to dance to or beat time to. It was for listeners only, and they needed dedication.

One record issued at the time featured a single unedited and cacophonous performance on one side while side two was blank. The joke was that you needed to play side two immediately after side one in order to recover!

Free form became assimilated, as with all other jazz styles. The best survived, and the rest was forgotten. Much of it was incredibly boring, and was responsible for emptying clubs and concert halls. But it could be gripping and exciting. It was essentially a music to be heard 'live', not listened to cold on record.

Established musicians, including Miles Davis and Jackie McLean, revised their approaches in the light of the avant garde's experiments. Davis was at first bitingly cynical about the music, but he changed his opinions later.

The 'New thing' was well received in Europe, and many Continental players adopted the free approach. Americans and Europeans enjoyed playing this music together, and international groups became almost commonplace.

Inevitably, there was a reaction against all this freewheeling stuff which had left too many listeners floundering behind. The basics were beckoning. People wanted to snap their fingers to a beat again.

Jazz rock/Jazz funk/Crossover

These are all labels applied to concerted (and largely commercial) attempts to effect a marriage between improvised jazz and the heavy pulse of rock and roll, given greater prominence and emphasis by amplification. One of the first to try such a merger was hardbop trumpeter Donald Byrd in the late 1960s. He was followed by tenor saxophonist Stanley Turrentine, trumpeter Blue Mitchell, the Buddy Rich Orchestra and others.

Pianist Herbie Hancock, on leaving Miles Davis, easily made the switch to a fusion setting. Hancock, who had already written a catchy bestseller entitled *Watermelon Man,* may have influenced Davis into his first flirtation with rock around 1969. The fact that Miles was intrigued by this possible amalgamation, led many others, including Freddie Hubbard, Chick Corea and George Benson, to try their luck. All achieved considerable commercial success, although the jazz content of much of the music tended to be minimal.

The four-square rock beat left little to the imagination, and did not serve to inspire particularly well jazz musicians used to fluid and responsive rhythm sections. Nevertheless, this uneasy union did introduce to a new generation the jazz form, in however a diluted a measure. Davis, Hubbard, Byrd, Hancock and Benson became household names with teenagers, and it is difficult to see how else these jazz stylists could have gained that kind of popularity.

The jazz-rock affiliation has continued well into the 1980s as jazz funk and has a great following in England where the Dick Morrissey/James Mullen Band, using a vast arsenal of electronic effects, is enormously successful. American drummer Alphonse Mouzon, is another jazz-rock artist who commands adulation among young listeners.

Free-form jazz and jazz rock have between them been responsible for the introduction of electronics into jazz via synthesizers which can conjure up brass and string sections at the touch of a button. This facility enables a well-equipped small group to sound like a big band. There are synthesizers for practically every instrument and even the human voice.

There are electronic attachments for brass and reed instruments to permit amplification or echo effects. Miles Davis, for example, has used a wah-wah foot pedal device for his trumpet. However, these various attachments have not proved to be as acceptable as electric piano and electric bass in the rhythm section. These instruments are easily portable and thus very convenient.

The positive results of the whole 'crossover' movement was that it got musicians of all persuasions, including classical players, working together, swapping ideas and seeing the other stylist's point of view. It fos-

tered understanding, if not particularly special music. When the bebop versus New Orleans argument was still raging in the 1950s, critic Stanley Dance coined a useful word to cover the collective approach of a generation of players who were in danger of being forgotten by a fickle public. The word beautifully summed up where those musicians stood in the jazz story up to that time.

Mainstream

This was the convenient title given to the sort of jazz expounded by musicians who formed their styles in the 1930s and were generally of a swing persuasion. They included Coleman Hawkins, Ben Webster, Don Byas, Harry Edison, Roy Eldridge, Lester Young, and the players associated with the Duke Ellington and Count Basie orchestras. To have called them 'Swingmen' in

1958 would have been the kiss of death. Mainstream epitomized their musical attitude. They were in the middle, falling between traditional jazz and bebop.

With the passage of time the jazz mainstream has broadened, and would now incorporate a group like VSOP II which plays in the style of the Miles Davis Quintet circa 1965! There is far more tolerance today within jazz. A young audience would not consider Buddy Tate and Harry Edison 'old hat' because of their chosen area of expression. Indeed there is a quiet revival afoot for mainstream and the likes of Red Norvo, Billy Butterfield, Slam Stewart and Slim Gaillard.
One of the attractive virtues of these musicians is that they retain a sense of humour which imbues their music. Listening to bassist Slam Stewart or his old compadre Slim Gaillard will provide music of quality but also much hilarity.

Grand Mixer D. St., the exponent of scratching ('playing' records by rythmically shifting them with both hands under the pick-up's arm). It was my turn to 'scratch' him.

99

Horace Parlan

Horace Louis Parlan. Piano/Composer. Pittsburgh, Pennsylvania, January 19 1931.

Piano lessons with private tutors from age 12. Right hand partially paralysed by childhood attack of polio. Teacher Mary Alston and bassist Wyat Ruther encouraged him to persist, and he developed an unusual left-handed style. Worked with local groups in Pittsburgh 1952-'57, played around Washington briefly, then to NYC as pianist with **Charles Mingus**' Jazz Workshop for several years in late 1950s. With Lou Donaldson 1959-'60, and pianist in a co-operative quartet with **Booker Ervin** (tenor sax) known as The Play House Four 1960-'61. Other affiliations included Eddie Davis-Johnny Griffin Quintet, **Roland Kirk**.

Disenchanted with New York, moved to Copenhagen in the spring of 1972, and lived in Europe ever since. Subsequently accompanied many distinguished soloists including Dexter Gordon, Al Cohn-Zoot Sims, Red Rodney, **Archie Shepp**.

In the early 1960s Parlan's regular playing companions were George Tucker (bass) and Al Harewood (drums). Together they comprised one of the most formidable, hard-swinging rhythm sections and were virtually the house trio at *Blue Note* Records, making a series of splendid sides with saxophonists Booker Ervin and **Stanley Turrentine**.

Parlan comes from the Horace Silver 'funky' school of piano playing, but his style is thoroughly personal and recognizable. An honest, unpretentious person and musician, Horace is never happier than when in contact with his beloved keyboard. Then his face really lights up. Parlan left New York because of the unsafe streets and the rising crime rate which made him a victim when he was mugged in Harlem. 'I have not regretted my decision for one moment,' he says. 'Since coming to Europe I feel that I've developed more – both as a musician and a person. It's funny but I've actually had more opportunity to play with American soloists since I've been over here than I did during my last years in New York.'

Horace Parlan's music has both strength and sensitivity, and the fact that he plays *everything* so well is a tribute to his determination to overcome a severe handicap.

Recommended records:
Stanley Turrentine/Look Out!
Blue Note BLP 4039
Horace Parlan Quintet/Speakin' My Piece
Blue Note BLP 4043
Horace Parlan/Up And Down
Blue Note BLP 4082
Booker Ervin/Exultation!
Prestige PRST 7844
Horace Parlan/Blue Parlan
SteepleChase SCS-1124
Horace Parlan Trio/No Blues
SteepleChase SCS-1056
Horace Parlan Trio/Hi-Fly
SteepleChase SCD-17003

Love and peace
Horace Parlan

Kirk Lightsey

Kirk Lightsey. Piano/Electric Piano/Composer. Detroit, Michigan, February 15 1937.

The 'Motor City' has produced a long line of superior pianists (e.g. Hank Jones, Tommy Flanagan, Barry Harris, Hugh Lawson) and Kirk Lightsey, though less well-known than the others, belongs to this tradition. Learned the basics of music and the piano from Johnson Flanagan (Tommy's brother). Attended the renowned Cass Tech School where fellow pupils included Hugh Lawson and Paul Chambers. Pianist Barry Harris was a great influence on Lightsey.
Part of the explanation for Kirk's comparative obscurity, until quite recently, was his decision to opt as accompanist to jazz vocalists like Damita Jo and **Anita O'Day**. Lightsey, of course, played with many top jazz names in his hometown but was not widely known beyond its boundaries. That is until he participated in two marathon recording sessions with trumpeter **Chet Baker** for *Prestige* in August 1965. The dates yielded five albums, and Lightsey earned unstinting praise for his contributions.

A slight McCoy Tyner influence was detected in Lightsey's contributions to the Baker records. Around that time Lightsey also appeared on a couple of *Prestige* dates with **Sonny Stitt** and Bennie Green. After this impressive recording début as a combo pianist, Kirk Lightsey was expected to make a name for himself as a leader in his own right, but it didn't happen.
In the 1970s Kirk moved out to California and there was talk of him making albums under his own name for an independent label, but the plans never materialized. However, towards the end of the decade he became the pianist in the excellent **Harold Land/Blue Mitchell** Quintet which set out to revive the style of earlier Horace Silver groups. The unit made a splendid album for *Concord Jazz,* but the death of Blue Mitchell in 1979 resulted in the outfit's demise.
In the 1980s Kirk Lightsey has at last begun to receive proper attention. He regularly appears in duo or quartet settings with bassist **Ron Carter**; does duo gigs with bassist Gary Peacock, and has toured Europe with **Dexter Gordon**. This work has highlighted Lightsey's abilities as a soloist. He has recorded with Chet Baker and **Jimmy Raney**, and made

a series of solo and trio albums for *Sunnyside Productions, Criss Cross Jazz* and *Timeless Records.*

Recommended records:
Chet Baker Quintet/Smokin'
Prestige PR 7449
Chet Baker Quintet/Groovin'
Prestige PR 7460
Chet Baker Quintet Comin' On
Prestige PR 7478
Chet Baker Quintet/Cool Burnin'
Prestige PR 7496
Harold Land-Blue Mitchell Quintet/Mapenzi
Concord Jazz CJ-44
Anita O'Day/Once Upon A Summertime
Glendale GLS 6000
Rufus Reid/Perpetual Stroll
Theresa TR 111
Kenny Burrell/Sky Street
Fantasy F 9514
Kirk Lightsey/Solo
Lightsey 1
Kirk Lightsey/Solo
Lightsey 2

Horace Parlan. When he finally came in after a long wait I thought: what's the matter with the man. Later in the dressing-room I happened to hear him mention that as a child he'd had polio. It looks as though his fingers are double jointed.

Oscar Peterson

Oscar Emmanuel Peterson.
Piano/Organ/Singer/Composer/Author.
Montreal, Quebec, Canada,
August 15 1925.

Commenced a thorough classical training from the age of six. Was impressing listeners in the late 1930s when as a 14-year-old he scooped a prize in local amateur contest; subsequently offered a spot on a weekly local radio show. At 19, Oscar became the featured pianist with the orchestra of Johnny Holmes, an immensely popular leader in Canada. This exposure made him a nationally known music personality, and soon American band leaders were making him offers, notably Jimmie Lunceford. Peterson resisted these overtures, preferring to remain in Canada until 1949.

In September of that year promoter Norman Granz finally lured Oscar to New York where he was featured in a successful Jazz At The Philharmonic concert at Carnegie Hall. Granz became his manager, and Oscar signed for *Norgran Records* to begin a long and fruitful association with Norman. Leading a trio (no drums) with **Ray Brown** (bass) and **Irving Ashby** (guitar), Oscar toured the USA with JATP, recording with all its stars – **Lester Young**, Coleman Hawkins, Charlie Parker, Roy Eldridge, **Ella Fitzgerald** etc. Apart from changes of guitarist (**Barney Kessel** replaced Ashby; **Herb Ellis** took over from Kessel), the Peterson Trio retained its format for nine years, working as a club unit and in the context of JATP.

From 1952 Oscar was an annual visitor to Europe with Jazz At The Phil, and later under his own name. He also played in Japan and became a truly international jazz star attraction. In the autumn of 1958, when Herb Ellis left the group, Peterson changed the character of the trio, bringing in **Ed Thigpen** on drums. The move was welcomed. The switch gave Peterson even greater solo responsibility and authority. Before Thigpen was finally chosen as the trio's percussionist, Gene Gammage served briefly as the drummer. The Peterson/Brown/Thigpen combination proved to be especially durable during its six-year life.

The next trio featured **Sam Jones** (bass) and Louis Hayes (drums), who had worked with Cannonball Adderley, and maintained Oscar's huge following

through the late 1960s. Peterson temporarily tired of the trio setting, broke it up in 1972 to concentrate on solo and duo recital work, but after this interlude reverted to using bass and drums, his sidemen including drummers **Bobby Durham** and Ray Price and bassists George Mraz and **Niels-Henning Ørsted Pedersen**. With the latter, Oscar formed as close an association as he had enjoyed with Brown for so many years. Whenever he is in Europe, Peterson insists on having NHØP on bass; drummers vary, depending on the country in which Oscar is appearing. Originally inspired by Art Tatum (who greatly admired Peterson's technique and professionalism) and Nat 'King' Cole, Oscar also listened to Earl Hines, Teddy Wilson, Count Basie and Erroll Garner. He was barely touched by the bebop style of Bud Powell in the 1940s. Rather like Tatum in his day, Oscar is lauded by virtually every other jazz pianist for his magnificent technical authority; an ability to play *anything* and make it *something*. His virtuosity has made more than a few critics hostile, and the emotional content of his work has been called into question, and of course there are times when Peterson is uninspired, but even then he will turn in *performances of astonishing clarity and perfect execution*. His almost frightening mastery of the keyboard has not deterred his thousands of admirers one jot. Peterson by the mid-1950s was a great popularizer of modern jazz, and enjoyed a following that only Dave Brubeck, Erroll Garner and George Shearing, among his contemporaries, could match.

Peterson's versatility has been deployed on hundreds of recordings with such diverse soloists as **Lionel Hampton** and Milt Jackson, Louis Armstrong and Dizzy Gillespie, **Ben Webster** and Stan Getz. His touch has also assisted singers like Ella Fitzgerald, **Anita O'Day**, Bill Henderson and Armstrong. This versatility is further demonstrated by his own singing which shows a marked affinity for the style of Nat 'King' Cole. Indeed, Peterson once recorded a vocal tribute to Cole that was good enough to indicate that Oscar could have made a comfortable living as a ballad singer in the Cole tradition. It should be pointed out too, that Peterson is a most proficient organist to judge from his occasional use of this potentially overbearing instrument. Peterson is not a jazz innovator and

neither has he been particularly influential (it's too difficult to play as well as he does!). Yet year in, year out he bewitches audiences and bemuses fellow pianists with his brilliance.

Peterson plays Peterson, and that makes him revered by many and respected by most. Styles wax and wane in jazz, but Oscar's style never goes out of style. It's a constant. Peterson is not generally listed as a composer but he has written many attractive lines and is the author of a number of durable blues. His publications include *Jazz Exercises and Pieces* and *Oscar Peterson New Piano Solos*. Peterson has made scores of albums. This selection offers LPs in chronological order from his early days to more recent offerings.

Recommended records:
Oscar Peterson/Flaming Youth
Japanese RCA RA-5399-400
The Oscar Peterson Trio
Verve MGVV 8024
Oscar Peterson Plays Count Basie
Verve MGVV 8092
The Jazz Soul Of Oscar Peterson
Verve MGV 8351
Swinging Brass With Oscar Peterson
Verve MGV 8364
Oscar Peterson-Milt Jackson/Very Tall
Verve MGV 8429
Oscar Peterson/Canadiana Suite
Mercury 20975
The Great Oscar Peterson On Prestige!
Prestige PRST 7620
Oscar Peterson/Soul-O!
Prestige PRST 7595
Oscar Peterson & Roy Eldridge
Pablo 2310 739
Oscar Peterson & Dizzy Gillespie
Pablo 2310 740
Oscar Peterson & Joe Pass/Porgy & Bess
Pablo 2310 779
Count Basie & Oscar Peterson/Satch & Josh Again
Pablo 2310 802
Oscar Peterson-Joe Pass-Ray Brown/The Giants
Pablo 2310 796
Oscar Peterson & Freddie Hubbard
Pablo 2310 876
Oscar Peterson & Milt Jackson/Two Of The Few
Pablo 2310 881

Oscar Peterson. Here he is displaying his great virtuosity at the North Sea Jazz Festival in 1981.

The Oscar Peterson trio 'seen' from the stage director's booth. It was so extremely dark in there that I could only capture the music's rhythm.

Billy Higgins

Billy Higgins. Drums/Composer.
Los Angeles, California, October 11 1936.

Raised in the Los Angeles ghetto of Watts, Higgins started playing drums at the age of 12. First experience was gained with rhythm and blues groups around LA. Listened to many drummers, but received invaluable instruction from the New Orleans percussionist Edward 'Ed' Blackwell. Both drummers spent much time rehearsing with alto saxophonist Ornette Coleman in the late 1950s. Blackwell generally credited with teaching Higgins the responsibilities of the drummer and especially the use of overtones.

Higgins drummed on **Coleman**'s first controversial album *Something Else!* for *Contemporary* and was subsequently on a number of Coleman LPs. His loose style found favour with many other leaders outside the avant garde. He worked and recorded with **Red Mitchell**, Teddy Edwards, Joe Castro etc in the 1950s. Was with Coleman at the Five Spot Cafe

in 1959 and elected to remain in New York.

In the early 1960s Higgins became part of a magnificent house rhythm section for *Blue Note* Records. His partners were pianist **Sonny Clark** (who died in 1963) and bassist Butch Warren (a great talent who disappeared from the jazz scene). They accompanied Jackie McLean, **Dexter Gordon**, Stanley Turrentine and many others. Higgins also recorded with Herbie Hancock, Hank Mobley and **Sonny Rollins**. Continued to play with Ornette Coleman into the 1970s, as well as Bill Lee Brass Company and Chris Anderson.

But for much of the 1970s was in a quartet with pianist **Cedar Walton** and tenorman **Clifford Jordan**. They toured Europe and Japan and made a series of good records for *Muse* and *SteepleChase*. Higgins also toured and recorded with saxophonist Jimmy Heath, and continued to be in demand for dates by such leaders as **Jimmy Raney**, Barry Harris, Charles McPherson, **Mal Waldron**, Curtis Fuller and Sam Jones. Bassist Jones said of Higgins: 'Billy's like

my right-hand man. When he's in back of you everything's fine.' Jimmy Heath has said of the drummer: 'Billy is always happy and makes me happy also. He listens.' Heath dedicated one of his compositions, *Smilin' Billy,* to Higgins. He wrote it 'for the love of the way Billy Higgins plays and for his love of music and of playing'.

A sensitive, adaptable drummer, *Higgins is considerate of the soloist and always listening to help rather than hinder.* As a youngster he backed a variety of singers including Amos Milburn, **Bo Diddley** and **Jimmy Witherspoon**. All had different requirements which Billy learned to fill. He cites Roy Haynes as an important influence, and also admires Tony Williams, Frank Butler, 'Ed' Blackwell and Elvin Jones.

Higgins, with more than 30 years of drumming under his belt, has firm views on how the kit should be played. He told Valerie Wilmer in her book *Jazz People* (London 1970): 'You're not supposed to *rape* the drums, you make love to them as far as I'm concerned.' In the same interview, Billy stated: 'Music don't *belong*

Billy Higgins

to *nobody*. If they could just realize that music doesn't come *from* you, it comes *through* you, and *if* you don't get the right vibrations you might kill a little bit of *it*. You can't take music for granted.' And neither can you take Billy Higgins for granted; he plays so well, so responsively and so responsibly.

When Higgins sits behind the drums his face fairly beams with pleasure. There will be no 'rape' but musical lovemaking on a high plain. Billy has lived through his quota of problems, and managed to keep them off the bandstand. To him jazz is joy and life is jazz.

Recommended records:
Ornette Coleman/Somethin' Else
Contemporary C 3551
Dexter Gordon/Go!
Blue Note BST 84112
Dexter Gordon/A Swingin' Affair
Blue Note BST 84133
Herbie Hancock/Takin' Off
Blue Note BST 84109
Sam Jones/Cello Again
Xanadu 129
Barry Harris/Bull's Eye!
Prestige PRST 7600
Sonny Rollins/Our Man In Jazz
RCA LSP-2612

Abbey Lincoln

Anna Marie Wooldridge/Aminata Moseka Gaby Lee. Singer/Actress. Chicago, Illinois, August 6 1930.

Born Anna Marie Wooldridge, the tenth of 12 children, she was brought up in Calvin Center, Michigan. During her high school she worked as a housemaid. She used social functions as an oulet for her singing and acting talents. Toured Michigan with a dance band when still a teenager. She moved to California in 1951 to work in local clubs. Also spent two years in Hawaii singing under the name of Gaby Lee. Returned to the USA in 1954 and for the following three years worked with considerable success in Hollywood supper clubs. Changed her name again (in 1956) – to Abbey Lincoln, and recorded her first album, with **Benny Carter**'s Orchestra, for the *Liberty* label in '56. Abbey became more widely known when she appeared in the Hollywood comedy, *The Girl Can't Help It* (1957), about the pop music business. It was an

absurd movie, but Lincoln's appearances were more memorable than much else in the picture. At this time Abbey Lincoln was a glamorous cabaret singer who relied on her looks rather than her voice. She dressed in décolleté gowns, and her advisors cultivated the image of a sexy torch-singer.

Abbey was a newcomer to jazz, and was wrestling with some challenging material, such as Randy Weston's *Little Niles, Strong Man* and *Afro-Blue* on her early *Riverside* albums.

More importantly she met percussionist **Max Roach** who drummed on two of the records for *Riverside*. Roach and Lincoln were married in the early 1960s. Abbey Lincoln gradually switched over to jazz work, becoming involved in the civil rights movement of the early 1960s through her records and performances with Roach. Abbey Lincoln was also well to the fore in arguing for women's equality in music and was an early, but not strident, member of the feminism movement, seeing women's rights in the context of *all* people's rights. In Leonard Feather's 1961 edition of *The Encyclopedia Of Jazz* (Horizon Press, New York) she was described thus: 'A superior pop singer who has earned acceptance in jazz circles.' But in *The Encyclopedia Of Jazz In The Sixties* (Horizon Press, New York, 1966), it was noted that she had developed from a synthetic 'intimate' singer into a 'far more individual performer, proud of her racial heritage'.

In 1960 she was a vital voice in the *Candid* album, *We Insist! (Freedom Now Suite),* composed by Oscar Brown Jr and Max Roach; a strong message for those changing times. She and Roach performed this extended work on a number of subsequent occasions and it later formed the basis for a film.

Abbey, always surrounded by the best jazz musicians of the day, made a series of records with Roach for the *Candid, Mercury* and *Impulse* labels. It was Abbey Lincoln's *Candid* album *Straight Ahead* which caused a critical furore in 1962. After the flurry of albums in the early 1960s Abbey Lincoln (she was given that name by the late Bob Russell, her manager in the 1950s and the lyricist of such songs as *Do Nothing Till You Hear From Me* and *Crazy He Calls Me*) also developed as an actress, landing plum parts and making an exceptionally good job of them in movies like *Nothing But A Man* and *For Love Of Ivy*.

She and Roach were divorced, and Abbey moved to Los Angeles in 1970. She appeared in the disaster movie *A Short Walk To Daylight* and was featured, acting, singing or both in many television programmes. She still made the occasional club appearances in LA and San Francisco, and continued to be active in community and political affairs. She taught drama at a West Coast university in the mid-1970s. Visited Africa on a number of occasions and became a firm friend of Miriam Makeba. Also visited Japan, making two albums there, and Europe. She was given a new name – Aminata Moseka, the first part was coined by the president of Guinea and Moseka by the then Zaire Minister of Information. But in the jazz community she continued to be known as Abbey Lincoln – the name that made such a vivid impact because of the music and the ideals she represented in the early 1960s.

She continues to act, sing, work in clubs and occasionally plays the European music festivals. In middle-age, no longer the militant rebel, Abbey Lincoln nevertheless hews closely to the high musical standard. She is an artist of integrity, still aware that much remains wrong in the world, and the era of equal opportunity for all peoples has yet to arrive. She has plenty to sing and talk about in that world.

Recommended records:
Abbey Lincoln
Liberty LRP-3025
Abbey Lincoln/That's Him
Riverside RLPS 1107
Abbey Lincoln/It's Magic
Riverside RLP-277
Abbey Lincoln/Abbey Is Blue
Riverside RLP-308
Abbey Lincoln/Straight Ahead
Jazzman Records 5043
Max Roach/Moon-Faced & Starry-Eyed
Mercury SR 60215
Max Roach/We Insist! (Freedom Now Suite)
Candid CM 8002 or Amigo AMLP 810
Max Roach/Percussion Bitter Sweet
Impulse AS-8
Abbey Lincoln/People In Me
Inner City IC 6040
Abbey Lincoln/Golden Lady
Inner City 1117
Max Roach & Abbey Lincoln/Sounds As A Roach
Lotus LPPS 11116

Abbey Lincoln. The man in the background is Archie Shepp. I showed her the drawing, then still in an unfinished state; she didn't want to put her name on it. 'You do it,' she said. Women, you always have to make them more beautiful. But she really is.

Abbey Lincoln

Dave Brubeck

David Warren (Dave) Brubeck.
Piano/Composer. Concord, California,
December 6 1920.

A musical background (mother a pianist and two brothers teachers of music) explains why Brubeck started playing piano at the age of four, tutored by his mother. He started studying the cello at the age of nine. Early experience from the age of 13 as pianist with Dixieland, swing and hillbilly bands. Majored in music at College of Pacific where during his stay (1941-'42) he led a twelve-piece band. Brubeck's musical training was largely classical. At Mills College in Oakland, California, he studied composition under **Darius Milhaud**. And while in the Army he continued his composition studies under **Arnold Schoenberg**. After serving in Europe, Brubeck resumed his studies with Milhaud, and polished up his piano technique under the guidance of Fred Saatman.

In 1946 he led his own octet, played with a trio in 1949, and from 1951 fronted a quartet with alto saxophonist **Paul Desmond** prominently featured. The incongruous Brubeck-Desmond partnership lasted for 16 years, although Desmond was on the first octet sides dating from 1949.

The Brubeck quartet first made an impact in San Francisco but its records soon propelled the group to national and international fame. Along with the Modern Jazz Quartet, the Brubeck four were the most successful jazz combo of the 1950s and 1960s. Concerts and festivals were their main outlet, and Brubeck was idolized on the American college circuit. From 1958 the quartet, following a successful appearance at the Newport Jazz Festival, embarked on a series of lucrative world tours, and became extremely popular in Britain and on the Continent. They made an unprecedented *two* national tours of Britain in 1961 and the leader was also there in the summer to work on a movie *All Night Long*. Brubeck became a controversial figure with his heavy-handed piano playing and compositions written in unconventional time signatures. Many critics felt he was incapable of generating swing in his playing, despite the assistance of a skilled rhythm section in Eugene Wright (bass), **Joe Morello** (drums) and the always lilting saxophone of Desmond. A genial

and generous man – and an arch opponent of racialism, Brubeck was nevertheless stung by the reaction against him in the jazz press. 'Most critics who have started out disliking me have only grown in their intensity and bewilderment that I have had any success at all,' Dave wrote to the English musician/commentator Steve Race who had supported his fellow pianist in print and described him in an early article as 'the most important man in new jazz'.

Race was definitely in the minority, but Brubeck did have his defenders back home. Don Demichael pointed out that little had been said by the critics about Dave's 'harmonic concept, his remarkable sense of time, and his ability to construct solos with a beginning, middle, and end'. John Tynan considered that 'Brubeck's piano is strong, assertive and undeniably individualistic'. Even Martin Williams, not among the Brubeck lovers, had to admit: 'His playing has a "nice guy" quality that many people would be pleased to have around the house.'

And certainly for many years thousands of people had a great deal of Brubeck around the house, to judge by the number of records he sold.

The pianist's penchant for unlikely time signatures paid off handsomely in 1959 when an attractive tune in 5/4 metre became an international hit. Few people could have predicted that *Take Five* would find its way on to juke-boxes all over the world, but it did; the public dug the melody and weren't concerned that it had five measures to a bar – the piece sounded right. Brubeck later made a new version of the composition with singer **Carmen McRae**, and the number is still something of an anthem for its creator. Brubeck is proud of his experiments in far-fetched metres, as demonstrated in *Time Out, Time Further Out, Countdown Time In Outer Space* and *Time Changes*, which were interesting if unconvincing. The quartet seemed to be at its most fluid and fluent when dealing with material of more conventional character, the album of Southern songs, *Gone With The Wind* (1959) being particularly engaging. Putting aside the musician's quirky piano style, there can be no argument about his status as a composer. *The Duke*, his heartfelt tribute to Ellington, was recorded by Miles Davis among others. The Brubeck 'book' of good tunes would also include *It's A Raggy Waltz, In Your Own Sweet Way, Blue Rondo A La Turk* and

I'm In A Dancing Mood.
Brubeck went on to write more 'ambitious' works for symphony orchestras following the disbandment of his quartet at the end of 1967. He has never subsequently achieved the balance struck by the Desmond/Wright/Morello combination. **Gerry Mulligan**, Jack Six and Alan Dawson toured with the pianist. Later Brubeck employed his three sons, Chris (trombone/bass), Danny (drums) and David (keyboards/synthesizer). All are talented, but the middle son Chris is the one who has worked most frequently with his father in recent years.

Brubeck was back in England in 1983 and the middle-aged faithful turned out in droves to listen to their hero, but they still missed the presence of the late Paul Desmond who stamped so much of Brubeck's music with a vintage quality. Brubeck has been a *great popularizer for modern jazz, and a friendly and good-natured ambassador.* His piano playing was heard at its best in an unpretentious solo session recorded in 1956. In a group context his baroque approach has often been leaden and lumbering.

But let the last words on Brubeck rest with his longest collaborator, Paul Desmond, who wrote in 1960: 'Dave is amazing harmonically, and he can be a fantastic accompanist. You can play the wrongest note possible in any chord, and he can make it sound like the only right one.'

Recommended records:
Brubeck Plays Brubeck
Columbia CL 878
Dave Brubeck/Gone With The Wind
Columbia CL 1347
Dave Brubeck/Dave Digs Disney
Columbia CL 1059
Dave Brubeck/Time Out
Columbia CL 1397
Dave Brubeck/Time Further Out
Columbia CL 1690
'People seem to think I'm a classical pianist and composer who turned to jazz. It's not true; there's no truth to it at all.'
'The great technique that a jazz musician should have is to play something you never played before and to make it happen.'
(Dave Brubeck)

Dave Brubeck. You can see the difference in expression when he's playing and when he's listening to his fellow musicians. It struck me how intensely they were discussing what they had just played when I went back-stage during the break. No way this band is played out!

Lee Konitz

Lee Konitz. Alto/Tenor/Soprano/Varitone Saxophones/Clarinet/Composer. Chicago, Illinois, October 13 1927.

First experience (on tenor sax and clarinet) gained with dance bands around Chicago at the age of 15. Was with the band of Gay Claridge, and then spent a few months with **Jerry Wald**. After studying at Roosevelt College, he went on the road with the **Claude Thornhill** Orchestra, and was a featured soloist on such records as *Yardbird Suite* and *Ornithology*.

The Thornhill band, with its unusual French-horn section and the modern orchestrations of Gil Evans, was a precursor of the Miles Davis Capitol 'Birth of the Cool' band, of which Konitz became a key member for its two brief public engagements and one LP.

Konitz was working in Chicago, wearing yellow socks and brown shoes with his tuxedo (!), when he met pianist **Lennie Tristano** at the Winkin' Pup ballroom. Tristano, a master pianist of great originality, heard something in Konitz' playing and Lee became almost a founder member of the so-called Tristano School. At the age of 18, Konitz switched to alto, but although Charlie Parker was the most imitated practitioner on this instrument, Lee avoided listening to him. 'I avoided getting familiar with Bird. I think Lennie detected whatever was unique in my approach to the line. Maybe — I don't know for sure — he encouraged me *not* to listen to him or get that close.'

Tristano was wise, for at an impressionable age, Lee was able to develop a completely individual sound that owed nothing to Parker or any other saxophonist of the day. The late Art Pepper followed a similar route and came to conclusions that were accidentally close to Konitz' at times.

As English critic Alun Morgan has written: 'The Konitz sound is clear-toned, light and pure but capable of an incisive knife-edged quality when the tempo increases.'

Besides recording with Thornhill and Davis, Lee was present on Tristano's equally famous *Capitol* recordings which included the first attempts at free improvisation. **Davis** was present on one of the first Konitz-led dates for *Prestige,* but that was the end of their collaboration. It was a surprise to many people when

Lee joined the brassy, bellicose band of **Stan Kenton** in August 1952. What was a cool saxophonist with a 'fragile' tone doing with Kenton? Konitz quickly adapted to this intimidating environment, and hardened his tone. 'It was a difficult band to play with. It's a brass band, essentially, a trumpet-trombone brass band,' Lee recalled to Ira Gitler. 'I did enjoy a lot of it. I got some strength from the experience, because you just had to lay it down or they'd lay you out!'

He stayed for some 16 months and never really worked with a big band again, rejecting many lucrative opportunities in favour of working in an intimate setting — from duo to sextet. There were occasional reunions with Tristano and his tenor counterpart **Warne Marsh**. **Sal Mosca** and Ronnie Ball were the only pianists (Tristano apart) that Lee relished working with in the 1950s. Of all the Tristano devotees, Konitz is the one who achieved the widest recognition and most consistent artistic success.

After a spell of self-imposed inactivity in California during the early 1960s, Lee resurged, toured Europe, and made some astonishingly good records, including a magnificent trio jam session with Sonny Dallas (bass) and Elvin Jones (drums). Through the 1970s Konitz held his rightful place as a respected original. He has been a regular playing visitor to European festivals, recording in London, Copenhagen and Rome for a variety of labels. He has also successfully toured Japan and made a number of film soundtracks.

Konitz is an adventurous, spirited improvisor, unafraid to try something different. He organized four saxophonists in his own *Tribute To Bach and Bird,* a performance which probably triggered the idea of Supersax, taped a series of dazzling duets with various contemporaries in 1967, and in New York during 1975 unveiled a significant nine-piece ensemble.

Years earlier Jimmy Giuffre arranged a record date on which Lee was backed by a full saxophone section. Pianist on the record was **Bill Evans** who said of Konitz: 'He is an original. He has been a significant influence on my musical growth. Besides Lee's originality, I admire his mind, his values, the warmth of his sound, the flexibility. "Thinking" musicians are so often thought of as unable to really swing. But Lee definitely does.'

He also has the ability, as did Lester Young, of being able to play just behind the beat and still be in time. His playing does not overtly drip emotion, but deep feeling is present in all his work. His stance towards playing was well expressed by Konitz himself: 'I find that music is like a great woman; the better you treat her, the happier she is. There's not much for me to say about my music — I play because it's one of the few things that make sense to me.'

To judge from the continued artistic growth of Lee Konitz he has been treating music very well indeed in the 22 years since he wrote those words, for he has maintained his creativity on a very high level. His 1971 album *Spirits,* dedicated to his greatest influence, Lennie Tristano, was a gem. He remains a 'musician's musician' who has blossomed into a great communicator... or maybe it's just that with the passage of time people caught up with Lee Konitz who was too far out for ears in the 1940s and 1950s.

Recommended records:
Lee Konitz/Ezz-thetic
Prestige PRST 7827
Lee Konitz Meets Jimmy Giuffre
Verve MG VS-6073
Lee Konitz/Subconscious-Lee
Prestige PR 7250
Lee Konitz/Motion
Verve V-8399
The Lee Konitz Duets
Milestooe MSP 9013
The Alto Summit
Prestige PRST 7684
Lee Konitz/Spirits
Milestone MSP 9038
Worthwhile Konitz
Japanese Atlantic P-6109
Lee Konitz/Timespan
Wave LP 14
Lee Konitz/Jazz A Confronto
Horo HLL 101-32
Lee Konitz-Warne Marsh/London Concert
Wave LP 16
Lennie Tristano/Crosscurrents
Capitol M-11060
Lennie Tristano
Atlantic 1224

Lee Konitz

Philly Joe Jones

Joseph Rudolph Jones.
Drums/Saxophone/Bass/Piano/
Timbales/Leader. Philadelphia,
Pennsylvania, July 15 1923.

Learned musical basics from his mother, a piano teacher, as a child. Studied drums with Cozy Cole; also helped by Max Roach and Art Blakey. Worked with local bands around Philadelphia, and backed visiting bebop stars like Dexter Gordon and **Fats Navarro**. Worked with Ben Webster, but spent several years in trumpeter Joe Morris' rhythm and blues group which also included Johnny Griffin and **Elmo Hope**. Four years Army service during which he was a military policeman. From 1950 freelanced around New York with **Zoot Sims**, Lee Konitz and Tony Scott. Started working with **Miles Davis** in 1952, and drummed on the famous *The Serpent's Tooth* record session with Davis, **Charlie Parker** and Sonny Rollins (January 1953). Also recorded with Tony Scott and **Tadd Dameron** that year. With Dameron band in Atlantic City. Member of Miles Davis Quintet (1955-'58), Gil Evans Orchestra (1959), then led own small group. Also briefly co-led a unit with bassist Doug Watkins. Rejoined Miles Davis for a short spell in 1962. Worked around Los Angeles and San Francisco 1964-'66, went to Japan for concerts in 1965. Lived in London, England 1967-'68, teaching advanced students and publishing his tutor, *Brush Artistry*. Then played jobs and recorded in Munich and Paris.

Returned to USA in 1972 after working in many European countries. Reunited with pianist **Red Garland** in a trio for awhile, but subsequently formed a jazz/rock group. Regular trips to Europe in 1970s and '80s for tours and concerts, festivals and club appearances. In 1983 formed nine-piece band called Dameronia, dedicated to reviving the music of Tadd Dameron.

Philly Joe Jones (given that name to distinguish him from swing drummer Jo Jones) was influenced by Big Sid Catlett, Max Roach, Art Blakey and Cozy Cole. Developed a highly explosive, propulsive style which kept soloists on their toes. Appeared on scores of important albums for *Blue Note* and *Riverside* in 1950s, and on countless occasions has proved himself a resourceful soloist and driving, attentive accompanist. His grasp of time and timing, and lightning-speed reflexes are fantastic.

Jones influenced many young drummers of the fifties when he had joined Kenny Clarke, Max Roach and Art Blakey as one of the élite percussionists. Jones can be supple, sensitive and supportive when required and his many trio recordings, with pianists such as **Bill Evans**, Red Garland, Kenny Drew and Sonny Clark, illustrate his skill in this context. Jones is also an accomplished impressionist, and his impersonation of Bela Lugosi's Dracula is incredibly accurate. A number of his fellow musicians feel he could have been a splendid actor, if given the opportunities.

Tenor saxophonist Johnny Griffin once observed to drummer Art Taylor in the latter's fine collection of interviews, *Notes And Tones* (New York, 1982): 'Philly is a fantastic cat. He turned out to be one of the world's greatest drummers. Even-handed.' Jones is many other things — a deft arranger, a canny band organizer, a finder and encourager of talent, a patient and understanding teacher. Miles Davis used to tell people that Philly Joe was his favourite percussionist: 'He's got the fire I want... Jazz has got to have *that thing*, and he's got it.' Critic Nat Hentoff suggested in 1960 that Jones was 'the most original drum soloist in jazz as well as an extraordinarily invigorating section man'. He explained why: 'He is a master of creating, balancing and fusing polyrhythms while implying an irresistibly pulsating rhythmic line. He challenges his sidemen, and it's impossible for anyone to coast with Philly Joe behind him.'

Jones reveals his dexterity and imagination most potently in four- and eight-bar exchanges and breaks. Admirers of his work invariably think of Philly Joe's crackling and precise playing on Miles Davis' version of *Gone, Gone, Gone* or his electrifying solo in *Salt Peanuts* (on his own *Atlantic* album) as typifying the extrovert style of PJJ. Now past 60 and having led a hectic and at times fraught life, Philly Joe is still a master of the 'tubs', the personification of the complete and professional drummer who never misses a beat. A true titan of *time*.

Recommended records:
The Clifford Brown Memorial Album
Prestige PRST 7662
Bill Evans Trio/Everybody Digs Bill Evans
Riverside RLP 12-291
Kenny Drew/The Tough Piano Trio
Jazzland JLP 9
Miles Davis/Miles Ahead!
Prestige PRST 7822
Miles Davis/Porgy And Bess
Columbia CL 1274
Sonny Clark Trio
Blue Note BLP 1579
Sonny Rollins/Tenor Madness
Prestige PRST 7657
Clark Terry-Thelonious Monk/In Orbit
Riverside RLP 12-271
Philly Joe Jones/Showcase
Riverside RLP 12-313
Philly Joe Jones/Philly Joe's Beat
Atlantic 1838
Philly Joe Jones/Trailways Express
Polydor 2460 142
Philly Joe Jones/Dameronia
Uptown UP 27.11

'That's where all that kind of music comes from — from black weakness. You get black power from black weakness.' (Philly Joe Jones)

Johnny Griffin

John Arnold (Johnny) Griffin. Tenor
Saxophone. Chicago, Illinois, April 24,
1928.

His father was an ex-cornetist and his mother a singer. Learned the basics of music at DuSable High School from Captain Walter Dyett whose pupils also included Gene Ammons, Nat Cole and Bennie Green.

At 17 Griffin was a good enough tenor player to join the **Lionel Hampton** Orchestra where he stayed for two years (1945-'47). His next job was with the Joe Morris rhythm and blues outfit which numbered pianist **Elmo Hope** among its personnel. Then was featured with **Arnett Cobb** (1950), **Jo Jones** (1951) and various pick-up groups around Chicago for several years.

Went to New York in 1956 and was immediately signed by *Blue Note* Records. Spent eight months as a member of **Art Blakey**'s Jazz Messengers in 1957, and for much of 1958 worked with pianist **Thelonious Monk** with lengthy engagements at the Five Spot Cafe. Returned to Chicago for local work 1958-'60, but then formed a highly successful quintet in which fellow tenorman **Eddie 'Lockjaw' Davis** was the co-leader. The group disbanded in the

summer of 1962 and at the end of that year Griffin moved to Europe, his main base of operations ever since.

Lived in Paris for most of the 1960s, but in the 1970s became a resident of The Netherlands. Has played in virtually every European country, the leading clubs and top festivals, making numerous recordings along the way. Appeared on two of the more impressive later albums by **Bud Powell**, and joined **Dizzy Gillespie** for a pair of fine albums taped in Paris.

Small of stature but possessing a distinctive vocal tone with pronounced vibrato (not too common in men of his generation), Griffin is appropriately known as the 'Little Giant'. *He has a fertile imagination, a bubbling, attacking manner, a fondness for doubling the tempo, and an ability to sustain excitement in extended improvisation.*

'JG' is not a fellow to trifle with at a jam session, as the late **John Coltrane** and **Hank Mobley** discovered when they joined him on one of his earliest records, *A Blowing Session;* Griffin comprehensively demolished his more famous (at that time) contemporaries. The outgoing Griffin's rapid fire delivery impressed critic Ira Gitler who called him one of 'the fastest guns alive'!

Johnny showed he was more than merely a speed merchant during his tenure with Monk. He mastered Monk's difficult music and his fecund flights made an ideal foil to the pianist's ruminative rumblings. There was a haunting quality about the way he delivered on certain Monk compositions, notably *Comin' On The Hudson* and *Light Blue.* Listeners still recall with pleasure a Riverside album, arranged by Norman Simmons, of Griffin's entitled *The Big Soul Band,* as a 1960 example of jazz rediscovering its roots in spirituals. On Griffin's *Studio Jazz Party,* the leader and his colleagues came close to capturing the real feel of a jam session, with food and drink laid on and the studio crowded with friends. Griffin once said: 'They always talk about my being quick but what is "quick"? It's just my way of expressing myself, that's all. To be quite honest, the reason for my playing like I do is because I'm so nervous. I just have to take my horn in my hand and it starts to vibrate. I don't play in order to prove anything, I just play because I enjoy it.'

There is, in any case, a more reflective side to Griffin's art. I remember hearing him play at an English country jazz club in

a pastoral setting with a brook, populated by ducks and moorhens, running past the side exit door. It was here that Johnny drew breath between sets. He was accompanied by the blind English pianist Eddie Thompson whose guide dog lay snoozing beside the piano. The surroundings affected Griffin who played a series of laid-back ballads; he was completely relaxed.

Living in Europe enabled the tenorman to frequently renew a longstanding musical association with pianist **Kenny Drew**, and hy was also a star soloist with the **Francy Boland/Kenny Clarke** Big Band in the late 1960s. Griffin's playing is indicative of his big city roots. In his work will be found the bustle, passion, humour, anger and frustration of Chicago. As he says, no matter where he happens to be living: 'I'm still genuine Chicago!'

Recommended records:
Johnny Griffin/A Blowing Session
Blue Note BLP 1559
Johnny Griffin/The Big Soul Band
Riverside 673025
Johnny Griffin/The Kerry Dancers
Riverside RLP 420
Johnny Griffin/You Leave Me Breathless
Black Lion 2460 178
Johnny Griffin/Blues For Harvey
SteepleChase SCS-1004
Johnny Griffin's Studio Jazz Party
Riverside RLP 338
Johnny Griffin/Foot Patting
Young Blood SSYB 11

Monty Alexander

Montgomery Bernard Alexander. Piano/Composer. Kingston, Jamaica, June 6 1944.

Began playing piano at the age of four, studied with several private teachers between 1950 and '58 to acquire thorough foundation in classical music. Formed own band at school, playing calypso and rhythm and blues. Listened to Louis Armstrong and Nat 'King' Cole and decided to play jazz. An important early influence was West Indian jazz guitarist Ernest Ranglin with whom he played. Moved to USA in '62, working around Miami. Heard by club owner Jilly Rizzo when playing in Las Vegas and that led to appearances in New York. Pianist Les

McCann was impressed by Alexander and persuaded *Pacific Jazz* to record the youngster. He did two albums for *Pacific,* two for *MGM,* one for *RCA Victor* and a pair for *MPS.*

Subsequently, Alexander has usually preferred the trio format, but has often teamed up with vibraphonist **Milt Jackson** for club and concert appearances. Among his favourite pianists are Nat Cole, Oscar Peterson, Art Tatum, Ahmad Jamal, Fats Waller, Eddie Heywood, Erroll Garner and Wynton Kelly. *Monty plays a happy brand of piano which reflects his sunny Caribbean background.* An eclectic musician, Alexander has borrowed wisely from other stylists and is perhaps closest in feeling to the late Wynton Kelly. He generates a satisfying swing, and his improvisations are engaging without being glib. He is technically gifted, conscious of the jazz piano tradition, and rhythmically very fresh in his approach.

Monty Alexander has penned some catchy original tunes including *This Dream Of Mine, Monticello* and *Zing!* which title sums up the inherent energy in a typical performance by the pianist. There is nothing weird or far out about Alexander's music. He is concerned with communicating with his audience, be it via a Chopin *Nocturne* or a piece from his homeland such as *Brown Skin Girl.* An Alexander trademark is an occasional dip into the body of the piano as he draws his fingers across the strings.

Recommended records:
Monty Alexander/Zing!
RCA Victor LSP-3930
Monty Alexander Trio/We've Only Just Begun
MPS BASF 25103
Monty Alexander/Here Comes The Sun
MPS MB 20913
Milt Jackson And The Monty Alexander Trio
Pablo 2310 804
Milt Jackson/That's The Way It Is
Impulse AS-9189
Monty Alexander/In Tokyo
Pablo 2310 836
The Monty Alexander 7/Jamento
Pablo 2310 826

Monty Alexander

Ray Brown

(RESOLD)
Mickey Roker

Ray Brown

Raymond Matthews (Ray) Brown. Bass/Cello/Composer/Author. Pittsburgh, Pennsylvania, October 13 1926.

A student of both piano and bass, Brown completed his high school education in 1944, and his first professional experience comprised eight-month spells with the bands of Jimmy Hinsley and Snookum Russell. He quit the Russell band in 1945 and went to New York with the intention of taking up an offer to go with the **Andy Kirk** Orchestra.

On his first night in New York, Ray and a cousin went down to 52nd Street and dropped into the Spotlite Club where Coleman Hawkins was playing. Hawk's pianist, Hank Jones, was an acquaintance, and as he and Brown chatted, trumpeter **Dizzy Gillespie** walked in. Jones introduced Brown to Dizzy who invited the bassist around to his house the following night for a rehearsal. That was how Ray became a member of Dizzy's quintet that included **Charlie Parker**, **Bud Powell** and **Max Roach**, whose percussion duties were later taken over by Stan Levey. Brown replaced the erratic Curley Russell in the group at the Three Deuces. A couple of weeks later **Milt Jackson** was added to the group. In December they left cold New York for a residency at Billy Berg's Club in Hollywood. Pianist **Al Haig** was called up to take over the keyboard role from the unstable Bud Powell. After the unhappy California episode, Brown continued to work with Gillespie in New York as a member of the sextet and then as a member of Dizzy's second big band. He was prominently featured on small group and large ensemble versions of *One Bass Hit* and the follow-up title *Two Bass Hit*.

Ray confesses that he was the 'least competent guy' in the sextet, but the others made something out of him. 'That's why I think that's a fantastic sextet; everybody in there turned out to be something else.'

Towards the end of 1947, Brown left the Gillespie orchestra. He had recently married singer **Ella Fitzgerald**, and took over the leadership of her accompanying trio; Dizzy's band was preparing for its first European tour so Roy resigned.

Before describing Brown's subsequent career, it is worth recalling that his original bass inspiration was Jimmy Blanton. 'I can remember clearly as a young boy,

standing outside a neighbourhood bar, listening to "Things Ain't What They Used To Be" and always waiting to the end to hear the last two bass notes. I was playing piano at the time, but I was continually fascinated by the bass,' says Brown. Blanton played the instrument like nobody had before. Oscar Pettiford (four years Brown's senior) was also inspired by Blanton's records with Ellington, and eventually played in the Duke's orchestra. Brown fulfilled a lifelong ambition when he was able to perform some of the original **Ellington**/Blanton duo pieces with the Duke for an album, recorded 18 months before the pianist's death. On this session (and many others) Ray Brown revealed himself as the true musical heir to Jimmy Blanton, the first authentic bassist with a thoroughly modern conception.

Ray toured widely with Ella Fitzgerald (the couple were divorced in 1952) and Jazz at the Philharmonic in the late 1940s and early 1950s. In 1951 he joined the **Oscar Peterson** Trio and remained a member of this highly successful unit for some 15 years. The Peterson trio, apart from its own recordings, backed all the top jazz soloists with JATP and Norman Granz' *Norgran/Verve* labels – from Charlie Parker, Stan Getz and Ben Webster to Coleman Hawkins, Lester Young and Gerry Mulligan, and not forgetting Ray's old friend Milt Jackson.

Since 1966 he has been based in Hollywood, recording prolifically for film, television and jazz assignments, still finding time for his sporting passion – golf. He and Milt Jackson co-led a quintet/sextet for annual engagements, and in the 1970s Brown was also a member of the LA Four (with Bud Shank, Laurindo Almeida and Shelly Manne). He also organized a number of West Coast concerts, and toured widely abroad, occasionally reuniting with former employers Gillespie and Peterson for concerts and/or records.

No amount of commercial work has blunted his keenness to play jazz. While he occasionally uses electric bass if required, Brown firmly believes in the traditional sound of wood and strings. 'Nowadays if you read a review of a performance or a recording and the bass player plays fast or high and plays some good solos he will get special merit, but if he just lays down some good time, with a good sound and good intonation, he may not even be mentioned.'

To Brown, tone, time and intonation are

the basics. He has more technical facility than many of the young bassists who flash their wares at every opportunity. English jazz writer Benny Green has described Brown as 'the most outstanding instrumentalist of his kind', and few would quarrel with that evaluation.

Of the records made under his own name, the first were among the finest, featuring as they did a contingent from the Gillespie band (including Dizzy himself) and friends Hank Jones and Milt Jackson. He made a series of albums for Verve between 1956 and '64, a collaboration with Milt Jackson coming off especially well. His best known composition is *Gravy Waltz,* with a vocal by Steve Allen. The piece was recorded by singer Bill Henderson, backed by the Peterson Trio, in 1963. A number of other vocalists also recorded this catchy tune. Among many gleaming solos that litter Brown's recording career, one of the best was on a 1948 side by Charlie Parker. Brown's classical opening to his statement on *The Bird* shows his taste in finding the perfect musical quotation for this heady context.

When you have been hailed as a master at the age of 20 (as Brown was) it is sometimes difficult to live up to such early recognition in later life. Brown has maintained his position as perennial poll-winner with dignity, maturity and musical authority. Alun Morgan wrote in *Jazz On Record* (1968): 'Ray Brown is certainly one of the finest bass players active in any musical field. Fortunately he may be heard on literally hundreds of records, and it is obvious that he is one of the most consistently good musicians jazz has ever known.'

Recommended records:
The Dizzy Gillespie Story
Savoy MG 12110
The Definitive Charlie Parker, Vol 1
Metro 2356 059
Sonny Rollins/Way Out West
Contemporary C 3530
Bill Henderson/With The Oscar Peterson Trio
MGM SE 4128
The Poll Winners
Contemporary C 3556
Duke Ellington/Duke's Big 4
Pablo 3210 703
Duke Ellington – Ray Brown/This One's For Blanton!
Pablo 2335 738

B.B. King. Sometimes you are so carried away by the music that something slips in that's outside your conscious control. This one I made so fast that I wish I should have had a stopwatch just to see how fast.

B.B.King

B.B. King

Riley B. (B.B.) King. Singer/Guitar/ Clarinet/Composer. Indianola, Mississippi, September 26 1925.

Came from a musical background: grandfather played bottleneck guitar, father Albert King and mother Nora Ella Pully were singers. Born on a plantation between Itta Bena and Indianola, one of five children. From the age of four he sang in local churches and was later in school spiritual quartet.

Quit school to work on plantation, though continued to sing in church choir. Taught himself guitar and formed the Elkhorn Singers to work in local churches (1940-'43). Some radio work in Mississippi just after World War II but moved to Memphis in 1946, busking in parks until able to obtain gigs in bars and clubs.

In late 1940s got a regular radio job as musician and disc jockey (billed as 'Riley King, The Blues Boy From Beale Street'). His famous initials actually stand for 'Blues Boy'.

In 1952 King was heard for the first time in Chicago and New York. King became internationally known during the late 1950s, touring the USA with considerable success. He was *the blues singer who influenced so many of the white rock and roll singers and groups,* receiving somewhat belated recognition in 1969 when he toured with the **Ike & Tina Turner/Rolling Stones** Show.

King's guitar work and singing are of equal interest and importance to the camps of rock and roll, blues and jazz. This enabled him to appear with universal acclaim at jazz and pop festivals and blues conventions.

Since the early 1970s he has toured internationally, taking Europe, Africa and Japan by storm and playing at several Newport Jazz Festivals.

King has written scores of original blues compositions to show his immense versatility with the twelve-bar form. A perennial winner of magazine polls in the USA and Europe, he was elected to the *Ebony* Blues Hall of Fame in 1974.

King is revered for both his vocals and guitarwork. As a guitarist he once cited his favourites and influences as Django Reinhardt and T.-Bone Walker. But other influences would include his cousin, blues singer Bukka White, Joe Turner, Jimmy Rushing, Al Hibbler, Blind Lemon Jefferson and Lonnie Johnson. In turn King inspired an army of singers and guitarists including Eric Clapton, Mike Bloomfield, Jimi Hendrix, Magic Sam and his namesake Albert King.

The late Ralph Gleason described B.B. as the best blues singer of his generation and the 'master of the blues guitar'. King has been seen in many television shows and a number of films. His publications include *BB King Songbook, Blues Guitar Method* and *The Personal Instructor.*

B.B. has proved to be the most popular and influential of the modern black blues artists and it is difficult to see what more he can achieve having reached the pinnacle within his field. Blues expert Paul Oliver has described King's electric guitar style as fluent but sometimes flashy, and noted that B.B.'s themes invariably centre around 'woman trouble'. Oliver, in his book *The Story Of The Blues* (1969), states: 'The very first notes of a performance bring screams of delight from his (King's) audiences and his sung phrases trigger off immediate responses from his ecstatic listeners.'

King has been heard only rarely in an instrumental jazz context. One such occasion was at a Newport In New York jam session at the Yankee Staium in 1972 when he joined jazzmen Joe Newman, Clark Terry, Illinois Jacquet, Zoot Sims and fellow guitarist **Kenny Burrell** for a memorable *Blue 'n' Boogie* and struck up an interesting and all-too-brief partnership with Burrell on *Please Send Me Someone To Love.*

B.B. King has made hundreds of singles and many LP albums. In this extensive output he maintains an enviable consistency.

Recommended records:
B.B. King/Blues In My Heart
Crown 5309
B.B. King/Blues Is King
HMV CLP 3608
Newport In New York '72,
Vols 5 & 6 Cobblestone CST 9027/CST 9028

Sonny Rollins

Theodore Walter Rollins. Tenor/Soprano Saxophones/Composer. New York City, September 7 1930.

Rollins showed little interest in music as a young boy. As a nine-year-old he started piano lessons, at the instigation of his mother, but he stopped going after a month or two. He attended PS 89, then went to Benjamin Franklin High School from where he graduated in 1947. Three years earlier he had taken up alto saxophone, encouraged by a cousin who played the instrument.

In his teens, Sonny was drawn to jazz, but he was more interested in art at that time. His preferred saxophonist was Coleman Hawkins, and Hawk became something of an obsession with the youngster. He would wait on the tenorman's doorstep, just to catch a glimpse of and have a fleeting word with Hawk. Rollins still treasures a photograph that Hawkins autographed to him in 1945.

After leaving school, Sonny joined the Musicians' Union and began taking casual engagements around New York. 'I wasn't certain about music, though,' Rollins recalled years later to Lester Koenig. 'My interest began to pick up at the time I made my first records in the latter part of 1948 with Babs Gonzales. After that I recorded with J.J. Johnson, Fats Navarro and **Bud Powell**. I also started writing. J.J. recorded my first tune, *Audubon.'* By now Rollins had effected the transition to tenor saxophone, and his early recordings show that he had fallen under the influence of Charlie Parker.

His tone and style on tenor show a distinct Bird flavour and suggest that Sonny listened long and hard to Parker's only solos on tenor, made at a Savoy session under **Miles Davis**' name. By a strange quirk of fate, on the only occasion Rollins recorded with Parker, they both played tenors and Miles Davis was leader! Sonny worked with drummer **Art Blakey** in 1949, and was heard with Tadd Dameron and Bud Powell in 1950 – the year he made his first visit to Chicago where he played with a brilliant local drummer, Ike Day. Rollins' playing in mid-century was rough and unfinished, but sufficiently impressive to immediately affect many young saxophonists. J.R. Monterose told me that after hearing Rollins for the first time he promptly went home and threw away all his Stan Getz records!

In 1951 Rollins was featured with Miles Davis and appeared on the trumpeter's first extended performances issued by *Prestige Records.* In 1951 Rollins also made the first dates under his own name and subsequently was heard with

B.B. King. He tries to get the audience going even more. A real professional. The jam session here not only has to do with the interplay between musicians themselves but with bringing the audience to new heights of ecstacy.

Sonny Rollins
Laren's Jazz festival

13-8-77

Thelonious Monk, Kenny Dorham and **Elmo Hope**. Then he returned to Chicago for an eighteen-month stay, doing a good deal of his playing at The Beehive club. Meanwhile he was studying all kinds of music, not only jazz. His Chicago 'exile' ended in November 1955 when **Max Roach** and **Clifford Brown** persuaded him to take over from Harold Land in their quintet. Land had tired of touring and wished to return to the West Coast. Eight months later the co-leader, Brown, was killed in a car accident, and Rollins was stunned by the loss of his front-line partner who was just 7^1/$_2$ weeks Sonny's junior. Rollins stuck with Roach until May 1957 when he left to lead his own groups and resume his musical studies.

Rollins, along with John Coltrane, was one of the most copied saxophonists of the 1950s, and in 1957 he made a number of albums on which he was accompanied by only bass and drums, enjoying the freedom that the absence of a pianist allowed him. Nicknamed Newk, because of his resemblance to Don Newcomb, Rollins a large but gentle man, was hailed by the critics for his magnificent 1956 LP *Saxophone Colossus* which fully defined for the first time his mastery of the tenor and introduced three of his compositions, *St Thomas* (now a jazz standard), *Strode Rode* and *Blue Seven*.

Rollins had a hard, sometimes harsh, tone and there was a sardonic ring to some of his work. He would distort melodies and insert hilarious quotations from other songs into his solos. The faster the tempo, the better Rollins liked it. On such albums as *Newk's Time, Way Out West, Tenor Madness* and *A Night At The Village Vanguard*, Rollins sent his stock soaring. But he was criticized for what some listeners heard as off-hand honking on a mis-matched session with the Modern Jazz Quartet in 1958. Others heard those sides as Sonny's caustic musical comment on the MJQ.

Rollins' capacity to surprise took a new twist in 1959. At a stage when his jazz star was riding high, he withdrew from public performance and became something of a recluse. He actually wanted a breathing space to re-evaluate music and his place in it. During this period the Rollins Legend flourished. As Sonny immersed himself in the beliefs of Rosicrucianism, he practiced his playing in the seclusion of the pedestrian walk of the Williamsburg Bridge, above New York's East River.

Sonny's dramatic return to activity in late 1961 was marked by the release of a new album, fittingly titled *The Bridge,* and a new quartet including guitarist **Jim Hall**. There was greater discipline, tenderness and authority in Rollins' work; some of the rough edges had disappeared. Rollins explained that his work-outs on the bridge were not weird or mystic. He merely sought privacy and had no wish to disturb others by his solo improvisations.

With a lucrative *RCA Victor* contract, Rollins embarked on a series of stimulating recording sessions with the likes of Ornette Coleman's sidemen **Don Cherry** and **Billy Higgins**, his idol Coleman Hawkins and Herbie Hancock. He inspected, and largely rejected, the innovations of the avant garde, following his own personal path.

He resumed touring and ventured overseas to Japan (1963), Germany, France, England (1965).

At that time Sonny had his head shaved, and he was to appear with a curious Mohican hair style. His new recording affiliation was with the *Impulse* label for which he made three LPs including the music he composed for the soundtrack of the 1966 British film *Alfie*. There was another six-year recording hiatus and from 1968-'71 he again retreated out of the public eye. He privately visited Japan and India, studied yoga, zen and the theories of Ghita, re-emerging once again in 1971, refreshed and renewed by years of reflection.

Possibly due to the upheavals in jazz during those years, Sonny's new return failed to make such an impact, although his *Milestone* album, *The Cutting Edge,* gained the Grand Prix du Disque in France. Rollins had taken up soprano saxophone and experimented with the varitone, along with electronic accompaniment. His playing, always variable, verged on the vapid at times. His 1972 *Next Album* hinted at what was to follow, with piano and bass electrified and a conga drummer cluttering up the rhythm department. His solos tended to be self-indulgent and lacked the ferocity of the *Saxophone Colossus* period or the clarity of *The Bridge* phase of 11 years earlier.

Rollins has subsequently surrounded himself with competent but unremarkable players. A case could be argued for Rollins and some of his other contemporaries — Jackie McLean, Walter Bishop, Miles Davis even — regrouping

and reassessing their former values. Sonny has been a consistent member of the international jazz festival circuit for more than a decade.

There will surely be more exciting jazz from him in the future than we have been offered of late. Sonny has won many jazz polls, and was elected to the *down beat* hall of fame in 1973.

Recommended records:
Sonny Rollins, Vol 1/Vintage Sessions
Prestige 24096
Sonny Rollins/Saxophone Colossus
Prestige PRST 7326
Sonny Rollins/Worktime
Prestige PRST 7246
Sonny Rollins/Three Giants!
Prestige PRST 7291
Sonny Rollins, Vol 2
Blue Note BLP 1558
Sonny Rollins/A Night At The Village Vanguard
Blue Note BLP 1581
Sonny Rollins/More From The Vanguard
Blue Note BN-LA 475-H2
Sonny Rollins/Brass & Trio
Verve V/V6-8430
Sonny Rollins/Way Out West
Contemporary C 3530
Sonny Rollins/Newk's Time
Blue Note BLP 4001
Sonny Rollins/Tenor Madness
Prestige PRST 7657
Sonny Rollins/The Bridge
RCA Victor LSP-2527
Sonny Rollins/What's New?
RCA Victor LSP-2572
Sonny Rollins/The Alternative Rollins
French RCS PL 43268
Sonny Rollins/Sonny Meets Hawk
RCA Victor LSP-2712
Sonny Rollins/The Standard Sonny Rollins
RCA Victor LSP-3355
Sonny Rollins On Impulse!
Impulse AS-91
Sonny Rollins/East Broadway Run Down
Impulse AS 9121

123

Sonny Rollins. One of the first drawings I made of a jazz musician. I was still so ignorant in the field that I forgot to ask for his signature.

The jazz life

Down and out

When the French pianist/bandleader Henri Renaud travelled to New York in the winter of 1953/54 to record some of his favourite American contemporaries, he was bemused by what he found. His idol Duke Jordan, the pianist in Charlie Parker's best quintet, was ekeing out a living by giving piano lessons to a few students. He had no regular employment and had never made a recording session under his own name. Later on, Jordan virtually vanished from jazz for 11 years and took a job as a cab driver to make ends meet. Renaud also learned that the distinguished trombonist J.J. Johnson had lately been working in a factory, and other major bop figures were clerks in post offices or labourers on building sites. George Wallington, a rising piano talent, would soon turn his back on jazz altogether to enter the family's air-conditioning business. Guitarist Tal Farlow, when jazz gigs failed to materialize, fell back on his skills as a signwriter. In some cases musicians deliberately turned away from jazz, no longer willing or able to cope with the seamy, seedy side of the business. Others were harried and hassled by narcotics investigators or prohibited from working by the New York licensing authorities' refusal to grant them a cabaret card.

Nightlife

The environment in which they have to work and the pressures they are under are key factors contributing to the poor health and early demise of jazz players down the years. To survive to three score and ten demands an iron constitution and a will of steel in jazz. People possessing exceptional creative talent are not necessarily well-balanced, 'normal' individuals, and proclivities towards wildness and irresponsibility are bound to be expanded by the abnormal life pattern of jazz.
Just consider the routine. They sleep when most people are at work. They must hit the stand and face an audience at 9 or 10 pm. The customers expect to be thrilled and excited from note one, but the players are starting 'cold' and may feel nervous or depressed. Given just that circumstance, is it surprising that a musician will take stimulants so that he feels good and is not intimi-

dated? It is not easy to simply switch on deep emotions and expose them to strangers, but that is the stock-in-trade of the jazz improvisor.
His fears and insecurities make him easy prey for the evil, unscrupulous elements that flutter around night people like moths drawn to bright light. Ruthless club owners, rip-off managers, agents and bookers, calculating record producers, drug pushers and a nasty array of fawning hangers-on as well as the loud degenerates who know nothing and care little about what they are there to hear are some of the characters jazzmen must deal with on a daily basis.

Records and recording

The organized crime syndicates of America took a grip on entertainment outlets during Prohibition, and that hold has never been released. The tentacles spread throughout the industry. They are the bookers, managers, sheet music owners, record companies, club proprietors. It may be to their advantage to have artists hooked on drugs because that makes dependence and manipulation much easier. It is no secret that in the 1940s, when the use of narcotics in jazz was so widespread, musicians were given an 'advance' in the shape of a bag of heroin. Royalties and copyrights failed to benefit the musicians; dues simply weren't paid and tunes were registered in the names of people who had never written a note in their lives. A few months after the session, the company would contact the musician and point out that he owed them money because sales had never reached the break-even point. The firm would suggest he must therefore do more recordings to pay them back. More drugs would be offered as an inducement, and so the crazy cycle continued with musicians getting ever deeper into debt as their drug dependency increased. Of course this did not apply to all recording concerns. There were straight, honest men who always gave the artists a fair shake, and probably erred on the generous side to their own financial detriment. Streetwise musicians, who had experienced deception and exploitation in their business dealings, could hardly be blamed for fighting back and doing their share of conning when the opportunity arose. But when they found

Sippie Wallace. She was born in 1900.
Probably one of the oldest living blues singers.
She came dressed in a 1900 outfit too. A grand
old lady.

125

agents or record company executives they could trust, lasting working relationships were formed. It cannot have been easy for the late Lester Koenig, of Contemporary Records, to stay patient with strung-out addicts like Hampton Hawes and Art Pepper, but such was his faith in their creativity that he stood by them over very many years, and it is due to Koenig's persistence that their recorded legacies are so impressive.

The hazards for the independent record producer in setting up a session need to be appreciated. He has booked a studio, engineer, the supporting musicians, someone to take photographs, a writer to pen the liner notes, an artist to design the jacket. But then his star fails to arrive. He is faced with the decision of trying to salvage a date from the lesser names present, or writing off the whole enterprise and losing several thousand dollars. In that situation – and it has happened to men I know – he can be forgiven for feeling bitter or thinking about retirement! But these dedicated 'midwives' to jazz generally don't give up; they love the music and the musicians (despite their frailties) too much. And the real enthusiasts are equally forgiving. If their trumpet king fails to show up at a club, they realize there has to be a reason. So they will catch him next time, and if it's a good night feel rewarded twofold.

Jazz artists who have been put upon, duped and robbed are naturally guarded, suspicious and occasionally hostile to strangers offering them the earth. Too many broken promises and let-downs have taught them to count no chickens. But they are philosophical about disappointments. There is no future in storing up resentment about the past. Any pent-up angers can be released, in the proper context, within music. Bassist Charles Mingus certainly had his stock of grudges against what he considered society had done to him, but those feelings of rage and frustration were put to good use in composition and performance. Mingus kept despair at bay by his creative instinct, which was not confined to music but also embraced poetry and autobiographical writing, even painting in his last years.

On the road

While many nightclubs deserve the description 'upholstered sewers' with their poky dressing-rooms and grim back-stage facilities, some jazz rooms do offer modern, acceptable conditions. Ronnie Scott's Club in London is a model in this respect, and this may help to explain why musicians are always glad to return there. Overall, though, jazz instrumentalists have to endure working accommodation that would not be tolerated by performers in other branches of entertainment. One can imagine the response of pampered sportsmen to the drab and downright dirty cubbyholes where music-makers are supposed to relax between sets. To blot out this inescapable squalor a bottle of booze may be a vital part of the travelling musician's baggage.

The touring aspect with a succession of mind-numbing journeys from town to town, city to city, is another wearysome aspect of the musician's lot. To survive he must perforce leave his home and family. As a single, there is the anxiety of meshing with a rhythm section he may never have met before in a strange club in a place he has not visited for years. As part of a group or large orchestra at least some company is afforded, yet it might not be welcome at all times. In a group of people who are strongly individualistic, clashes of temperament are unavoidable, loyalty and brotherhood notwithstanding.

A place to settle

The bystander sees no more than the tip of the iceberg – a gathering of fashionably dressed fellows playing three or four sets during an evening. It doesn't seem like hard work. This picture ignores all the heartburn and hammering of rehearsal, the boredom of a long, hot uncomfortable journey by car, bus, train or plane, the arrival in yet another faceless hotel room. Time for some snatched winks of sleep, then it's back to the grind. On some of the snakes and ladders-like European tours, taking in 23 or more cities with a minimal number of rest days, it is understandable when a musician wakes up and wonders where he is and what the hell he is doing, following a crazy, frenetic map that allows him scant time to examine the country in which he finds himself. And after such intensive activity for a limited period, he is liable to return home without prospect of work for weeks at a stretch. He yearns to find a long-running residency, such as saxophonists Dexter Gordon and Johnny Griffin enjoyed at the Montmartre Jazzhus in Copenhagen during the 1960s. A place where he can settle and concentrate without worrying if his saxophone has been transferred to the wrong aircraft and is sitting in an airport luggage department 500 miles away.

Travelling is a way of life to a leader like Lionel Hampton who, in his mid-70s, covers almost as many miles as notes he plays. Hampton got used to the continuous movement on road and rail as a member of the Benny Goodman Orchestra. On leaving Goodman, Hamp formed his own orchestra in November 1940 and has been on the move ever since. His only break from regular playing was for a couple of months in the autumn of

Chet Baker

1955 when he was laid up, recovering from injuries suffered in a band bus accident. Duke Ellington and Count Basie showed similar stamina in their prolific criss-crossing of international geographical routes.

The Hampton bus crash raises another spectre that haunts musicians – the risk of death or severe injury on the road. Car accidents have killed a long list of musicians – Clifford Brown, Richie Powell, Bob Gordon, Doug Watkins, Dave Lambert, Bessie Smith, Stan Hasselgard were some – and maimed many more. Jazzmen are aware of the dangers and conscious that the chances of being involved in a serious crash are increased in proportion to the amount you drive. And driving in the early hours, after work and alcohol, reduces the odds.

The crime element

The criminal elements that feed off musicians – and in rock and roll they are as active as in jazz – might appear less obvious in Europe than in the USA, but they exist. Thieves and exploiters are not confined to New York, Chicago or Los Angeles. Dizzy Gillespie, bringing a band to Europe for the first time in 1948, was bilked by a crooked promotor. Additional engagements had to be sought to pay for the band's return tickets.

The late Julian 'Cannonball' Adderley, with great courage and candour, told in a magazine article how he had been enslaved by a Mafia-owned record company which at one time cornered a virtual monopoly of jukeboxes in the mid-West. Establishments that failed to play this concern's records were visited by thugs and the juke-boxes smashed up. Coercion ensured that exploitation could continue unchecked.

The small print in contracts effectively bound artists hand and foot to the company, and the screw was tightened if a whiff of success was scented. The system of 'owning' artists had already been tried and tested through the Hollywood contract system. A wise head like Sonny Stitt avoided contracts like the plague. He was content to remain a free agent, recording when and for whom he wanted. Experienced, organized and intelligent men of the calibre of Dizzy Gillespie, Oscar Peterson and Miles Davis know all about the crooks that infest the music business. They will deal only with straight operators whose words and handshakes are worth more than a pile of contracts.

One of the harmless and actually quite useful pursuits of jazz buffs is the compilation of discographies – detailed, and wherever possible, complete lists of an artist's work including band personnels, locations, dates, matrix numbers and titles recorded. I was compiling one such listing of a particular musician who, for a while, had been contracted to a company of dubious reputation. When I visited their New York office in the summer of 1963 and innocently asked if I could make photocopies of session sheets to fill out some important gaps and clear up arguments about line-ups, the receptionist promptly called out an 'executive'. A short, squat, cigar smoking individual appeared and started to grill me. Who was I representing? For what purpose did I want the information? Who the hell did I think I was? And so on. The information was confidential, and it was none of my business who had played on those records. And after that, I was brusquely told to leave. No reputable firm, understanding the obsessions of jazz collectors and realizing the importance of discography, especially when reissues are being compiled, would act in this manner. There was obviously something to hide, and that's why the executive behaved in this aggressive way. Incidentally, the facts I was seeking remain a mystery 20 years later.

Discrimination

Although top musicians prefer playing at concerts and festivals rather than in clubs, some of the best jazz continues to emerge from the intimate surroundings of a relatively small room where the band and audience are close. Trumpeter Miles Davis thinks nightclubs stink, as club owner Max Gordon recounts in his autobiographical *Live At The Village Vanguard*. Davis can make more from one college date than a club could afford to pay him in a week. 'I can't stand the whole fuckin' scene,' said Davis referring to the club environment. 'The cats comin' around, the bullshit, the intermissions. I hate intermissions. On a college concert I do two short sets and I'm through. I don't have to hang around, listen to a lot of bullshit.' Not many of Davis' contemporaries are in a position to be so selective, and some actively dislike the polite atmosphere of a concert in a huge hall.

Festivals are fun, and ever since the first Newport Jazz Festival in 1954 the idea of listening to 'jazz on a summer's day' outdoors has been appealing. The well-planned festival is a great coming-together of musicians from diverse styles. Hearing them play together, possibly for the only time, is intriguing. But certain festivals have grown too large, and when so much talent is presented, and concerts clash, the enthusiast is left frustrated. But if there is 'something for everyone', why complain? It is surely better to be spoiled for choice, rather than have a narrow and perhaps unsatisfying selection.

Albert Collins and A.C. Reed at the North Sea Jazz Festival.

Albert Collins & A.C Reed 17-7-'82

Discrimination against the blacks is not a phenomenon peculiar to the USA, where the Afro-American has lived under the cloud of rank prejudice and overt disadvantage for centuries. In its most savage form prejudice meant slavery, but abolition of that barbaric concept failed to give the Negro equality under the Law or in Society. Integration has been a long, slow fight that continues to this day. Anyone under the delusion that no sections of the white population believe in their innate superiority need look no further than that insidious, profane body, the Ku Klux Klan, whose very existence points to the fragility of so-called civilization.

The black jazz musician has not escaped the insults, the bullying, the physical attacks, the put-downs, the inferior housing, the unemployment and the whole 'back-of-the-bus' treatment that blacks in America have struggled against. But the musician, being more of an individualist, has almost instinctively rebelled against these illogical injustices. Duke Ellington did it by his sheer dignity and sophistication. By his wit, charm and intellect he could put any 'cracker' in his place. Dizzy Gillespie's humour, wisdom and truth have also silenced many a boozed white rowdy. The jazz environment was a dangerous one when Dizzy was coming up, and he and many contemporaries were forced to carry a pistol or a knife for self-protection. When co-leading with Oscar Pettiford a group at the Onyx Club on 52nd Street in 1944, three white sailors shouted an insult and bassist Pettiford waded into one of them. In short order, the two musicians were surrounded by a hostile group of seamen. Dizzy drew his carpet knife to hold them off while Oscar made good his escape. On another occasion, a white patron pulled a knife on Dizzy in a club, and Charlie Parker intervened. The hazards for Dizzy and his contemporaries are no less real today. There is always one nut who wants to prove his 'superiority'.

When the Ellington orchestra played white high society spots like the Cotton Club in Harlem, the black performers were not permitted to mingle with the white audience. The musicians were expected to be up on the stage or in a back room – another version of the master/servant idea with the stage the equivalent of the plantation hut or the domestic basement. But ten years later, a rising generation of black players were not about to accept this back-door nonsense. Drummer Art Blakey has recounted in Robert Reisner's *Bird: The Legend of Charlie Parker* a graphic incident at a St Louis club after he joined the Billy Eckstine Orchestra. The owner instructed the musicians not to fraternize with the customers. Despite the inhibiting presence of gangsters with guns on their hips, the bandsmen ignored the dic-

tate of the owner of the well named Plantation Club. And when Charlie Parker started smashing glasses, pointing out they were 'contaminated' because fellow musicians had drunk from them, the band's engagement came to a swift end! But it needed that sort of fierce reaction – and great courage – to break down the stupid and archaic barriers.

Cracks in the colour line

For years there were separate 'Locals' – one for whites, the other for blacks – of the American Federation of Musicians. Union segregation! So of course there was little official contact. To his lasting credit, Benny Goodman hired Lionel Hampton and Teddy Wilson in his hugely popular Swing orchestra of the late 1930s. He later employed the black guitarist Charlie Christian. Artie Shaw hired the magnificent black jazz singer Billie Holiday for a spell and ran headlong into prejudice from bookers. Shaw also had trumpeter Roy Eldridge who was featured with Gene Krupa's Band from 1941-'43. It was these three – Goodman, Shaw and Krupa – who helped to crack the colour line in big bands.

The small bebop combos of the 1940s were integrated almost from the start, since the Dizzy Gillespie/Oscar Pettiford quintet of 1944 had a white pianist in George Wallington. When Dizzy took a sextet to California the following year it was a mixed band. As Dizzy tells it in his autobiography, *Dizzy:* 'People noticed I had two white guys in the group – Al Haig, piano, and Stan Levey on drums. I guess because it seemed strange during the time of segregation. Almost everyone disregarded the fact that both cats were excellent musicians and devotees of the modern style. I didn't hire them because of their colour but because they could play our music.' Haig had turned down an opportunity to tour the Southern States with Gillespie's big band in a package show called Hep Stations '45 because he anticipated the venom that could have been released by his appearances with a black band in that part of the country; Dizzy and the rest of his men would have been given a hard time. A few years later when the white trumpeter Red Rodney was working for Charlie Parker on a Southern tour, they found a novel way of circumventing the colour problem (see Red Rodney's biographical entry). But, for the most part, a white musician working for a black leader was more than redneck club owners and police could swallow. A mixed band could expect persistent harassment and worse if they ventured into cracker country. The Syndicate stranglehold, coupled with a brutal law enforcement 'service', made a city such as Miami a place

130

J.B. Hutto. It was during a blues festival. He sat in the dressing-room for a long time like a pink statue looking like he'd been stuffed and mounted. That's also part of the jazz life: waiting for your turn to go on. It was probably his last gig. He died not too long afterwards.

J.B. Hutto
12.12.'82
Paradiso

for the black jazz player to avoid. When the jivey white humourist and pianist Harry, 'the Hipster', Gibson tried to run a club and present black groups in Florida, he was rapidly under threat from mobsters with rival establishments and the police who stepped up demanding protection money. 'Man, you couldn't tell the difference between the cops and the gangsters down there,' Gibson told me. He was forced to close down and quit.

How the whities stole it

A more subtle form of prejudice was evident in California during the 1950s when 'West Coast Jazz', synonymous with white musicians, enjoyed considerable popularity and commercial success. Superb black players – Teddy Edwards, Dexter Gordon, Wardell Gray and Sonny Criss among them – could find no way into this jazz boom. All the gigs were going to Art Pepper, Bob Cooper, Jack Montrose, Bud Shank and other white players. The 'cool' West Coast sounds were portrayed as the white players' great contribution, but the real architect of the cool, Miles Davis, was 3,000 miles away in New York. It was perfectly understandable that a fine saxophonist of Sonny Criss' calibre felt bitter at seeing men of inferior talent rack up piles of recording dates and plum engagements. And the rage musicians felt when their original ideas were blatantly stolen and reaped a big dollar harvest for the pirates! Thus Charlie Parker's riff blues, *Now's The Time,* turned up with a few altered notes as *The Hucklebuck,* a huge hit record for another artist. A Bud Powell composition of the late 1950s emerged with slight amendments as a chart-topper for a British entertainer a couple of years later. The melody – quite obviously Powell's – was credited to a pop songwriter. Such outrageous practices continue to occur, but without a specialist lawyer and the time and energy to fight musical plagiarism cases through the tortuous litigation process, the wronged composer has no chance of receiving his due.

Copyright

Jazz composers have been ripped off in other ways – by established stars agreeing to record their tunes only if they receive a 50 per cent piece of the action; the hard-up writer has little option but to accept this type of 'take-it-or-leave-it' offer, especially when a cash inducement is dangled before him. He can only hope that his name will get on the record label and sheet music and make him a 'commodity' so that he can drive a harder bargain next time.

Not before time, matters have improved in the matter of copyrighting of music and performances. Many jazz musicians have their own publishing companies, but of necessity they need to employ trustworthy business managers to keep a watchful eye on their affairs in the areas of royalty payments and copyright dues.

Dizzy Gillespie *(Dee Gee),* Charles Mingus *(Debut),* Lionel Hampton *(Hamp-Tone)* were three of the pioneers who tried to establish their own recording companies. But the touring jazzman invariably finds it next to impossible to keep track of ancillary enterprises when he is away travelling for much of the year. Hampton was fortunate in having a shrewd business partner in his late wife Gladys, but the musician-owned labels usually end up being bought out by one of the major companies. The biggest headache has always been distribution; if you haven't got the store outlets there is no future. The shoelace operation is doomed to failure. The jazz mystic Sun Ra has had his own recording company, *Saturn,* for years, but eventually he leased a number of the masters to a larger, established company. Listeners were clamouring for the *Saturn* LPs, but couldn't buy them anywhere except through a mail order address. It was a passport to obscurity and Sun Ra realized it. A co-operative musicians' record venture was the *Strata-East* label, but the initial enthusiastic glow of the venture soon wore off, and the familiar complaint of people not being paid started to be heard.

Pianist Kenny Drew and saxophonist Sahib Shihab launched their own *Matrix* label, and without overstretching themselves, seem to be making a modest success of the enterprise. Leasing masters to overseas firms is a vital aspect of this Denmark-based company. Drew and Shihab are taking care of business with the label plus their own publishing outlet *Shirew.* Perhaps they won't make a fortune but they will present music they believe in, affording the artist an uncompromising platform.

There's no business...

Jazz listeners and critics (who are almost all part-time and generally write about the music because they love it) are hard taskmasters. Not in judging a performance but in readily condemning a player who is patently seeking commercial success. What they fail to comprehend is that musicians also need financial security, and perforce must compete within a vast entertainment field. To gain economic stability they may need to make concessions.

Louis Armstrong and Fats Waller were two of the early

Lonnie Johnson
WALKING BLUSE
I WOLK UP THIS MORNING
FILLING A ROUND FOR MY
SHOES. WELL YOU NO
ABODE I GOT THESE
WOLKING BLUSE.

Lonnie
to THE
.T.

Lonny Pittiford American Folk Blues Festival Paradiso   18 in '83 Paradiso.

jazzmen who discovered that their talent for comedy gave them an appeal far beyond the narrow confines of the jazz world. Nat 'King' Cole, a superb jazz pianist and acknowledged influence on many piano players during the 1940s, found that his light, husky voice could earn him a fortune, so he became a vocalist who also played occasional piano. Frenchman Sacha Distel, a nimble jazz guitarist, made it as a romantic crooner in the early 1960s and he remains popular with the middle-aged audience. More recently, Donald Byrd, Freddie Hubbard, Herbie Hancock and Stanley Turrentine have earned large sums by working in fashionable styles — jazz rock, crossover, jazz funk — and who can blame them? Many years ago Donald Byrd, referring to Louis Armstrong, said when he reached old age he did not want to be toting a trumpet around. As a young man, Byrd was constantly criticisized because of his presence on so many records. As if he could be castigated for trying to pay his way! Byrd's early work was sometimes frail, but because he was almost omni-present on the album scene people stopped listening and failed to hear the remarkable artistic progress made by the trum-

peter. Some of his finest work, especially on the *Blue Note* label, was passed over. It wasn't too long after this that Byrd 'went commercial' only to incur more critical wrath. But then at least Donald could laugh all the way to the bank. The latest phenomenon to spring from a hard core jazz background is the excellent George Benson, a scintillating guitarist who, like Cole and Distel, had a most pleasing singing voice. Benson has made a fortune, but he's still a 'jazzer' at heart and in a documentary film about Tal Farlow it was refreshing to hear George paying tribute to the older man (and a white man at that). Benson commented that no guitarist would think of trying to 'cut' Tal Farlow because of his astounding technique. Cynics might say that Benson can afford to be generous with his praise; equally a man in his position need not pay tribute to anybody. He is a star. Jazz musicians who opt for more lucrative employment will always be put down, and risk the hostility and jealousy of the other 'bloods'. It's one price for fame. Professionals like Oscar Peterson and Dizzy Gillespie, whose names are known internationally, have unashamedly made records of a popular nature, but they put jazz first. When Peterson was already a star 30 years ago, he would always plug fellow pianist Hampton Hawes, who worked the same jazz rooms, to audiences. Hawes, strung out on dope and wrestling with the resultant problems, never forgot Peterson's support and many kindnesses. Dizzy, too, has offered a helping hand to many less fortunate musicians. They are all part of the same brotherhood. That sense of fellowship and fraternity overrides and compensates in great part for the negative aspects of the jazz life which have been discussed in this chapter.

Wit

Allied to the bonds of friendship is the real sense of comedy and the ridiculous shared by musicians. They tend to stand slightly apart and see the wry, ironic side of life. They love the practical joke, told deadpan, and putting people on. Before a young player is fully accepted into a band he must show he can take a jibe in the right spirit. The 'bop joke' illustrated the kind of straight-faced humour that is so much a part of jazz. It was usually a long, convoluted story with a surprising twist in the tail. There is one about an audition for trumpeters in a famous band. There are at least 20 top men lining up to grab this envied first trumpet chair, and as they are strutting their stuff in walks an unknown cat in a raggedy suit with a trumpet wrapped in newspaper. Of course he's the last to step forward for audition. The punch-line of the bop joke is that the unknown sounded terrible! Another gag from this genre recounts the disaster that befell a band working on a liner which hits an iceberg. The band keeps playing in true Titanic tradition as the ship slowly sinks. They are the last to go down, and just before they go under the saxophonist removes the instrument from his mouth and addresses his colleagues thus: 'Where is James C. Petrillo when you need him!' This was a reference to the one-time president of the American Federation of Musicians whose contribution to improving the jazz artist's lot was a large zero.

The language

In jazz, musicians have always used their own special coded language to exclude the squares, punks and straights. A whole vocabulary, much of which has passed into general usage, was invented. Like the music itself these words are constantly changing. When they pass into mainstream speech, you can be sure they are no longer in usage in jazz circles. Lester Young was supposedly a master of hip talk which was a down-beat,

cryptic form of communication in which a single word by a subtle use of intonation could assume an entirely different meaning. Young was way ahead of inflation — he used to call a dollar a cent! A droll, laid-back man who called everyone 'Lady' or 'Baby', Lester was the first jazz hipster, relaxed, inscrutable, three steps ahead of the game. Superficially nothing bothered him; he epitomized the cool cat, and his detached manner served as a model for the young players of the 1940s whom he referred to as 'the kiddies'. But this uncaring demeanour masked a deeply troubled and unhappy man who was peremptorily written off by the jazz establishment after he quit the Count Basie Orchestra. Nonetheless, the presence of the President, as he was dubbed after emerging the victor from a Kansas City jam session in which even Coleman Hawkins had to bow to his artistry, is still felt in the fabric of the music and its offbeat humour.

Dizzy Gillespie is an adroit deployer of shafts of wit. His off-the-cuff remarks can have an audience laughing at prejudice, because he is able to show up racialists for the absurd idiots that they are. Possibly this approach is more effective than righteous tub-thumping.

The name of the game

With a suitcase and tuxedo in one hand and an instrument bag in the other, the musician travelling as a 'single' cuts a lonely figure. In a foreign town, far from home, grappling with an unfamiliar tongue, he instinctively heads for the nearest bar in search of casual companionship and to keep from brooding on the demanding, draining and daring profession he has chosen. He is a prism reflecting a very particular musical spectrum; the way he refracts those 'colours' has to be entirely personal. The life scars him, but he must stay loose, keep open his powers of transforming vibrations heard, seen and felt. He will still climb on a podium somewhere that night and bare part of his soul before strangers. If it goes well, he will feel good, but tomorrow could be even better. If it's bad — with a thrown-together and falling-part rhythm section — tomorrow will loom as another ordeal. He will take the money and run.

He may have felt obliged to play what he thought the audience wanted to hear, and that assails his conscience. Like the famous trumpeter who got trapped in a commercial groove and was serving up his usual programme of hits on which the tread was wearing decidedly thin. A lone voice in the packed theatre shouted out: 'Why don't you play some jazz?' After a moment's pause for thought, the leader enquired: 'Is that what you all want to hear?' Cries of 'Yes, yeh!' Said the trumpeter: 'That's what we'll do then. We're sick of playin' this shit!' And it was undiluted jazz for the rest of the evening. Jazz players — though they don't show it and might be the last to admit it — seek a response, attentive listeners and a little respect. Polite applause is not enough. When trumpeter Jon Eardley worked a well-known jazz room — the sort of place where non-listeners go to be seen — an especially noisy group of diners talked at the top of their voices throughout a set. As the music ceased, they cheered and clapped with gusto. Eardley gave them a fixed smile and this backhanded compliment: 'Thank you, ladies and gentlemen, for being a really *attentive* audience!' The cutting implication of his comment was lost on that moronic contingent, refugees from a conference, out on a spree.

The insults, the slights, the rank discomforts, the touring grind are unpalatable parts of the jazz life. But as saxophonist and club owner Ronnie Scott says in his autobiography, *Some Of My Best Friends Are The Blues*: 'I think you have to have some kind of a sense of humour to be a jazz musician, otherwise you'd go potty sitting in band coaches and trains for hours on end.'

Unfortunately the life is such that it can (and has) wrecked men's minds and bodies. In a perfect world the creative, improvising musician would be able to play just what he wanted, when he wanted. There would be no economic worries. The pleasure he gives is immeasurable, but he is mostly under-rewarded in coin. Arts subsidies and bursaries are inadequate in size and quantity. Meanwhile, out there, the musician's struggle goes on. There is nothing romantic about survival, and that's the name of the game.

Joe Bowie

*Joe Bowie. Trombone/Composer/
Vocalist. St Louis, Missouri, 1953.*

Worked with several jazz ensembles in
his hometown, and moved east after
touring the club circuit with bluesman
Albert King and Little Milton. It was as a
live backing band, for New York funk
band, James Chance and The
Contortions, that Defunkt (Bowie's group)
was originally formed in the summer of
1979. Through his acquaintanceship with
James Chance, Bowie was asked to
assemble a brass section to accompany
The Contortions. He went one better,
forming a complete band which very
quickly began to eclipse its mentor in

terms of popularity. As its title suggests,
Defunkt aims at the funky, commercial
end of the market, but the music, loud and
electronic, does not entirely by-pass jazz.
Bowie's trombone playing reflects an
interest in the avant garde; there is
nothing smooth about his work. Several
years before the noisy emergence of
Defunkt, Joe Bowie made a duo album in
Toronto, Canada, with saxophonist **Oliver
Lake**. On that 1976 session, critic Barry
McRae found: 'The trombonist's playing
permanently captures the feeling of the
blues, with its inherent mixture of sorrow
and anger.'
People who admired Bowie's
experimental music were doubtless
disconcerted at his sudden reappearance
in a jazz/funk bag and the trombonist's

search for chart acceptance: 'They'll have
no choice but to accept me, 'cause I'm
not gonna go away.' Defunkt had a
large-selling single in the shape of *The
Razor's Edge,* but it is difficult to square
Bowie's former style with what he now
plays. The band records in New York and
London, and frequently makes forays to
Europe to appear at both jazz and funk
venues.

Recommended records:
Joseph Bowie-Oliver Lake/In Concert
Sackville 2010
Defunkt
Hannibal Records HNBL 1301
Defunkt/Thermo Nuclear Sweat
Hannibal Records HNBL 1311

*Wynton Marsalis. His signature too speaks of
erudition. A perfect piece of calligraphy that
adds dimension to the drawing.*

Wynton Marsalis

Wynton Marsalis. Trumpet/Flugel-Horn/ Composer. New Orleans, Louisiana, October 18 1961.

Son of Ellis Marsalis, pianist, composer and jazz educator. Given his first trumpet at the age of six by Al Hirt, but did not take up the instrument seriously until he was 12. After a year's practice and study developed into a highly promising soloist. Astounded everyone by playing the Haydn Trumpet Concerto with the New Orleans Philharmonic at 14, and two years later performed the Brandenberg Concerto No. 2 in F Major with the same orchestra. Thorough education in classical music.

Joined **Art Blakey**'s Jazz Messengers and was rapidly recognized as a superb jazz trumpeter in the tradition of Clifford Brown and Miles Davis. Made many albums and tours with Blakey, and signed a recording contract under his own name for *CBS Records.* Played with the Herbie Hancock Quartet and VSOP II, a re-creation of the Miles Davis group of the mid-1960s. Has recorded classical and jazz albums for *CBS* and won praise from critics of both idioms. Feels that working with Blakey was important to his jazz development, as has been experience with Herbie Hancock, Ron Carter and **Tony Williams**. Favourite trumpeters include Clifford Brown, Louis Armstrong,

Don Cherry, Miles Davis, Freddie Hubbard, Woody Shaw and Fats Navarro.

Recommended records:
Art Blakey & The Jazz Messengers/Live At Bubba's
Who's Who In Jazz WWLP-21019
Art Blakey In Sweden
Amigo AMLP 839
Herbie Hancock Quartet
CBS 22219
Wynton Marsalis/Think Of One
CBS 25354
Wynton Marsalis
CBS 85404
Fathers And Sons
CBS 85786

North Sea
10.7.83

Be beautiful within
Bobby McFerrin

Tony Williams

Anthony Williams. Drums/Composer. Chicago, Illinois, December 12 1945.

Studied music from age 10 in Boston. His drum tutor was Alan Dawson, the highly advanced and technically brilliant percussionist. Saxophonist Sam Rivers also counselled him on matters musical, and the pair participated in a series of experimental concerts with the Boston Improvisational Ensemble. Rivers has recalled that he first met the drummer when Williams, then only 13, sat in with Sam's band on a gig in Cambridge, Mass., around 1959: 'Even at thirteen Tony knew where he was all the time.' Another saxophonist, Jackie McLean, was responsible for persuading Tony to move to New York in December 1962. Williams jobbed with McLean and was heard by trumpeter **Miles Davis** who immediately hired him for a new quintet he was forming. Thus the famous rhythm section of Herbie Hancock (piano), Ron Carter (bass) and Williams (drums) was born. Williams soon made his recording début with trumpeter Kenny Dorham, and he was to serve as the percussionist with the Davis group from 1963-'69, appearing on all Miles' records during that period and touring the USA, Europe and Japan with the unit.

Listeners were amazed by the originality of the 17-year-old when he burst upon the jazz scene. Influenced by Elvin Jones, Roy Haynes, Billy Higgins, Philly Joe Jones and of course Alan Dawson, Williams *brought a new looseness and freedom to jazz drumming* which fitted the changes taking place in the music at that time. While his playing was ideal for established mainstream soloists of the day, such as Dorham and Donald Byrd, it served admirably to propel the avant garde excursions of Grachan Moncur, Sam Rivers and Jackie McLean. Williams made the first album under his own name for *Blue Note,* the label which launched so many jazz careers. The record, called *Life Time,* was widely acclaimed. Tony won the *down beat* critics' poll New Star award on drums in 1964. Williams left the Davis group to form his own band, Lifetime, featuring **John McLaughlin** (guitar) and Larry Young (organ/synthesizer/keyboards). The unit featured an eclectic mix of chord-based and free jazz and rock; it

139

Bobby McFerrin. His voice calls to mind an instrument which he pantomimes at the same time as he is doing here with the bass. A phenomenal vocalist!

was a very loud group. Ted Dunbar subsequently replaced McLaughlin, and another line-up featured the leader's father, Tillman Williams, on tenor sax. Lifetime was re-formed in 1975 with Allan Holdsworth (guitar) and Alan Pasqua (keyboards).

Many critics felt that Williams' own playing deteriorated after he left Miles Davis. They missed the marvellous perception of time and subtle shading which were the hallmarks of his best work. The rock rhythms offered virtually no challenge to a percussionist of Tony's powers. There were approving noises from the writers' lobby when Williams threw in his lot with VSOP (the Miles Davis group of the sixties but with Freddie Hubbard in place of Miles) in the mid-1970s.

Williams renewed his long-standing associations with Herbie Hancock and Ron Carter in the 1980s with VSOP II which has the extra dimensions provided by the talented **Marsalis** brothers. Sam Rivers, who has keenly followed Williams' development, once offered this appraisal of his protégé: 'As he's matured, what most impresses me about Tony is the emotional content of his playing. No matter how technically fascinating he becomes, you're always aware of his sensitivity and of the emotional power behind all that technique.'

Bassist Butch Warren once described *Williams as: 'The best young drummer in years. New York needed a new drummer,* because most of the guys seemed to be falling into the same groove. This guy, however, is fresh and he's so together. He's strong melodically as well as rhythmically, and he has a fine sense of dynamics. He never overpowers you. His playing is just plain beautiful.'

Williams reached a plateau of perfection in the Davis years with the Herbie Hancock album *Maiden Voyage* containing some of the most influential and beautiful drumming of the 1960s. What followed was not always palatable. Dave Gelly took him to task in a *Jazz Journal International* record review (December 1978): 'As for what's happened to A. Williams since, it doesn't bear thinking about. That superhuman grip on time, that uncanny sense of percussive density just collapsed under the weight of powerhouse rock. An immense talent snuffed out in its prime.' But all was forgiven, as Gelly was the first to acknowledge, when he reviewed VSOP II in 1983. Williams seems to have put aside the rock years for more demanding

endeavours. That is sweet music to the ears of connoisseurs of jazz drumming, because Tony Williams at his best is a prince among percussionists.

Recommended records:
Kenny Dorham/Una Mas
Blue Note BST 84127
Herbie Hancock/Empyrean Isles
Blue Note BST 84175
Tony Williams/Life Time
Blue Note BST 84180
Sam Rivers/Fuchsia Swing Song
Blue Note BST 84184
Herbie Hancock/Maiden Voyage
Blue Note BST 84195
Miles Davis/Miles In Berlin
CBS S 62 976
Miles Davis/Miles In Tokyo
CBS Sony SONX 60064-R
Miles Davis/E.S.P.
Columbia CL 2350
Miles Davis/Miles Smiles
Columbia CL 2601
Herbie Hancock Quartet
Columbia C2 38275

Ray Charles

Ray Charles Robinson. Singer/Piano/ Organ/Alto Saxophone/Composer. Albany, Georgia, September 23 1930.

Went blind at age six. Enrolled in State School for the Blind in St Augustine, Florida. Learned braille and took up piano. Early influences were Baptist Church music and the blues he heard played around Greensville. Listened to Art Tatum and was impressed by the boogie-woogie pianists Pete Johnson, Meade Lux Lewis and Albert Ammons. Liked the country blues of Tampa Red, Blind Boy Phillips and Washboard Sam. An early model was Nat 'King' Cole. As an 11- and 12-year-old Charles could play and sing much of the Cole repertoire. Also delved into composition and arrangement. Began jobbing in Florida at 15 and two years later formed a trio in the Nat Cole style that appeared on TV in Seattle. Made first records in 1948. Worked with rhythm and blues group of Lowell Fulson in California for 18 months. Recorded with **Jack McVea**, Marshall Royal and Maurice Simon. Developed own emotional style of singing, reflecting his blues roots. Signed for *Atlantic Records* in 1952. First hit (before he joined *Atlantic*) was *Baby,*

Let Me Hold Your Hand. At that time he was still using piano/guitar/bass instrumentation and singing in the Nat Cole/Charles Brown vein. Worked as a single for a couple of years.

Played New York and then moved to New Orleans for a spell, then resumed touring. Formed own band in 1954 with **David 'Fathead' Newman** (saxophone), Joe Bridgewater and Clanky White (trumpets), Jimmy Bell (bass) and Bill Peeples (drums). Ray Charles' remarkable and rapid rise to fame happened suddenly in the mid-1950s when he hit on the idea of adapting spirituals he had sung in his childhood to a rhythm and blues setting. He mixed in a blend of blues and popular tunes, and injected a strong jazz feeling into his performances. *I Got A Woman* was one of his recast spirituals, with lyrics by trumpeter Renolds Richard, and it proved to be a smash hit for Charles in 1955.

Charles reckoned his band worked around 315 days a year, and that meant long months on the road.

Their first LP, issued in 1957, contained instrumentals in jazz, pop and gospel styles. By this time Ray had developed as an arranger, and he had a keen ear for new instrumental talent. The gutsy saxophonists from the Charles stable included **Hank Crawford**, Don Wilkerson and Fathead Newman. But the ensemble's main selling-point was the distinctive vocal style of the leader. He really knew how to 'sell' a song, but he was at his most potent when delivering blues and spirituals in his own arrangements. His piano style, while acknowledging Nat Cole and Hank Jones, also mirrored his intense feeling for gospel music.

In 1959 Charles made his first recording with strings, along with his début at Carnegie Hall on the same bill as Billie Holiday. At the end of that year Ray signed for *ABC-Paramount,* for whom he cut one of his biggest records, *Georgia On My Mind.* This transformed him into a hot commercial property, and there were more successes to follow – *Ruby, Hit The Road Jack, I Can't Stop Loving You, Born To Love, Busted, Crying Time, What I Say, Take These Chains From My Heart, That Lucky Old Sun.*

Charles displeased some jazz critics with his switch to a more popular style, but he was now an international figure and toured France, Belgium, Sweden, Germany and Switzerland in mid-1962 – the first of

Ray Charles. I had to draw him by pen light. We were, so to speak, two blind men held together by a piece of black chalk.

Ray Charles
'op de fast'

Nol Sea 9-7-8?

Jon Faddis
8-7-8s
North Sea

many such excursions to the Continent. Charles had been addicted to narcotics since the age of 16, but after a much-publicized 'bust' in Boston, Ray decided to kick the habit, and he was able to finally renounce heroin. He formed a new big band and re-formed the Raelets. Ray Charles resumed his position in the upper echelons of the music/ entertainment scene in the late 1960s and has been there ever since. He appeared as an actor in *Ballad In Blue* and recorded the sound-track themes for two other impressive pictures, *The Cincinnati Kid* and *In The Heat Of The Night*.

Charles has always enjoyed collaborating with jazzmen, and the two albums he taped with vibraphonist **Milt Jackson** are excellent, enabling us to hear Ray expounding on the alto saxophone. On this horn he was influenced by Buster Smith, the Texan who is said to have inspired Charlie Parker. In the 1970s, by which time Ray Charles had become a very rich man with his own private aircraft and a large holding in the *Tangerine* record company, he could afford to dabble with his love for jazz. The large orchestra he formed in that decade was a superbly well-drilled and musical aggregation, featuring **Blue Mitchell** and other fine soloists. The two albums (listed below) they recorded for *Tangerine* show where Ray's heart really lies.

Not surprisingly, Charles, who had judiciously borrowed from black sacred and secular music, rock and roll, country and western, jazz and any other style that took his fancy, also inspected the possibilities of jazz/rock, though found little to interest him there. Charles had been amalgamating various forms to suit his own ends for years. That was why he confused and bemused the purists. They could not understand why such a powerful blues singer would want to toss off a light-weight pop song – and enjoy it! His stance is that he's open to all good music if it fits the parameter of his personal taste and style.

'Sure I'm a real singer. But I know goddam well that I can interpret anything – country, blues, jazz – except opera. And I'm not so sure I couldn't do that if I set my mind to it,' he stated in his autobiography.

His unusually varied discography, covering three and half decades of record studio appointments, supports his contention. Apart from widening his musical horizons, Charles also extended

his stage technique and built up a complete show around himself, the band and the glamorous Raelets.

Joe Williams, an outstanding big band singer of jazz, blues and popular material, once said of Ray Charles: 'The president of the Soul Society... brother Ray Charles. As far as I'm concerned, he is by far the greatest exponent of blues and feeling and what we call soul. If he's feeling good, he really makes you feel better than anyone else, and if he's feeling bad, he can make you cry. His musical taste for the thing he does is impeccable.'

To fully understand the complexities of Ray Charles, the man, readers are referred to his excellent autobiography (written with David Ritz), *Brother Ray: Ray Charles' Own Story* (London, 1979).

Recommended records:
The Ray Charles Story
Atlantic 2-900
The Great Hits Of Ray Charles On 8-Track Stereo
Atlantic SD 7101
Ray Charles-Milt Jackson/Soul Brothers
Atlantic 1279
Ray Charles-Milt Jackson/Soul Meeting
Atlantic SD 1543
Ray Charles/Genius + Soul = Jazz
Impulse A-2
Ray Charles Presents David Newman/Fathead
Atlantic 1304
Ray Charles And Betty Carter
ABC-Paramount 385
Ray Charles/My Kind Of Jazz
Tangerine TRCS 1512
Ray Charles/Jazz Number II
Tangerine TRCS 1516
Ray Charles/My Kind Of Jazz, Part 3
Crossover CR9007
Ray Charles/True To Life
Atlantic SD 19142

Jon Faddis

Jon Faddis. Trumpet/Flugel-Horn/Piccolo Trumpet/Piano. Oakland, California, July 24 1953.

Family is musical. One sister is a singer, the other a pianist. Started on trumpet, taking private lessons. Also played in grammar school, but only began getting interested in the instrument at age 11 or

12. As a 15-year-old studied with Bill Catalano who made Faddis aware of the playing and writing of Dizzy Gillespie. Further studies with Carmine Caruso. Was at the Manhattan School of Music 1972-'73 studying with Mel Broiles, outstanding first trumpeter in symphony orchestras and a colleague of Charlie Parker's in the 1940s. Completed studies – piano, harmony, theory – with jazz pianist Sanford Gold in 1975.

Worked in rhythm and blues groups around Oakland in mid-1960s. Bill Catalano arranged for him to sit in with rehearsal bands led by Rudy Salvini, Cus Cousineau and Don Piestrup in San Francisco. Upon graduating from high school in 1971, Faddis joined **Lionel Hampton** for a six-month hitch. Recruited to the trumpet section of the **Thad Jones-Mel Lewis** Band in February 1972 and stayed for 3½ years, making a tour of USSR with the orchestra. Worked with **Gil Evans** in 1972, and also played with **Charles Mingus**, touring Europe with him in the summer of 1973.

Teamed up with fellow trumpeter Chuck Mangione for a series of concerts from 1972. Appeared with his idol **Dizzy Gillespie**, who regards Faddis as a protégé, at the Vanguard and Half Note clubs in 1974. Achieved an ambition by recording with Gillespie at the 1977 Montreux Festival.

Faddis soon gained recognition for his exciting, all-action playing, superb command of the trumpet and great musicality. Made a remarkable duo album with pianist **Oscar Peterson** as part of a prestigious *Pablo* series. Also made his début as a recording leader for the *Pablo* label. Co-led an interesting session with saxophonist Billy Harper on the *Trio* label. And demonstrated his versatility as a soloist with pianist Randy Weston's orchestra.

Faddis impressed many listeners in the 1970s by his virtuosity and obvious respect for the jazz trumpet tradition. Leonard Feather and Ira Gitler in *The Encyclopedia Of Jazz In The Seventies* (Horizon Press, New York, 1976) summed him up thus: 'Gillespie's musical son', Faddis, with his great range and fire, is one of the most promising of the young crop of musicians to come to light in the '70s. As he moved towards a more personal expression his potential seemed vast.' The 1974 Peterson-Faddis collaboration convinced British critic Alun Morgan of the trumpeter's worth.

143

Reviewing the *Pablo* album he wrote: '...Faddis is one of those remarkable soloists who come along about once in every two decades. He seems to have sprung, fully-formed and mature, from the womb with enough technique for an entire trumpet section and the taste and ideas to match.' Morgan was surprised to hear Faddis using freak tonal effects beloved by Cootie Williams and Rex Stewart, and observed that on a performance of *Things Ain't What They Used To Be,* Jon punched out D flat 42 times to make up a complete chorus of this B flat blues, 'and they are all clean and high too!'
Ruminating about Faddis' leadership debut, *Youngblood,* Alun Morgan had further pertinent points to make in *Jazz Journal* (August 1976): 'Away from the obvious influences Faddis is refreshingly impressive with *a broad tone in the lower register, an almost casual approach to accuracy on the high notes and a frighteningly competent way of ripping out strings of semi-quavers at fast tempo.* He has joined the small coterie of young trumpeters who seemed destined for greatness from the very outset.'
Jon Faddis continues to make occasional concert appearances with his mentor Dizzy Gillespie in the 1980s. Rarely has a great musician had such a persuasive and compelling disciple!

Recommended records:
Oscar Peterson & Jon Faddis
Pablo Super 2310 743
Jon Faddis/Youngblood
Pablo Super 2310 765
Thad Jones-Mel Lewis Orchestra/Suite For Pops
A & M Horizon SP-701
Dizzy Gillespie Jam/Montreux '77
Pablo 2308 211
Charles Mingus And Friends
Columbia KG31614
Charles Mingus At Carnegie Hall
Atlantic SD 1667
Randy Weston/Tanjah
Polydor PD 5055

Illinois Jacquet

Battiste Illinois Jacquet. Tenor/Alto Saxophones/Bassoon/Singer/Composer. Broussard, Louisiana, Oktober 31 1922.

Birthplace is near New Orleans. Jacquet was only six months old when the family moved to Houston, Texas, and that's why Illinois is identified with the 'Texas School' of tenor players. His father was a bassist and his brother Russell, five years his senior, played trumpet. Started on soprano and alto sax (which he occasionally used professionally) before switching to tenor. Learned his craft during late 1930s in bands of Lionel Proctor, Bob Cooper and Milton Larkins. Moved to West Coast with Floyd Ray Orchestra, and then joined **Lionel Hampton** band. Jacquet was a star before the age of 20 due to his powerful solo on Hampton's *Decca* version of *Flying Home.* Jacquet continued in big band work as a featured soloist, first with **Cab Calloway** (1943-'44) and **Count Basie** (1945-'46). His solos of importance with Basie included *Mutton Leg, The King* and *High Tide.*
Jacquet subsequently led his own groups, toured with Jazz At The Philharmonic, occasionally enlarged his small group to big band size, and also worked as a single. Although he grew to maturity in the Bebop Era, Jacquet's chief influences were the swing tenormen Chu Berry and Herschel Evans. Lester Young and Coleman Hawkins only marginally touched him.
Illinois was identified as a big-toned tenor who could turn on an audience with wild honking and screaming solos, and it was this ability that Norman Granz wanted from him for JATP in which he often blew tenor battles with **Flip Phillips**. This was his commercial side. At root, Illinois is a fine jazz improvisor capable of majestic solos at medium and fast tempo, and a fine, controlled approach to ballads.
His early bands employed such splendid musicians as trumpeters Fats Navarro and **Miles Davis**, saxophonists John Brown and Leo Parker, trombonists J.J. Johnson and Henry Coker and drummers **Denzil Best** and Shadow Wilson. Brother **Russell Jacquet** was in the 1940s band, and other regular associates down the years were baritone saxophonist Cecil Payne, bassist Al Lucas and pianist Sir Charles Thompson. A poll organised amongst musicians named Illinois as the 'greatest' on tenor sax which helps to explain why he is known as 'The King' in saxophone circles.
Jacquet's feel definitely stems from the Swing Era. *He has always possessed an unusually rich tone with a nice vibrato and when he swings he attacks.* Dexter Gordon, and through him Sonny Rollins and John Coltrane, learned a good deal from Illinois (Dexter and Jacquet were section mates in that Hampton outfit more than 40 years ago). Jacquet, who appeared in the classic *Jammin' The Blues* movie (1944), showed his tremendous capabilities *after* JATP ran out of steam through a series of impressive albums for *Cadet, Prestige, Epic, Black Lion* and *Sonet.*
In 1959 he acquired a bassoon and studied with Manuel Zegler of the New York Philharmonic. By 1965 he was using it on gigs, and he has featured the instrument on several recordings to telling effect. But it is as a tenor player that Jacquet really ranks high.
Critic Bob Porter once wrote: 'As far as influence goes one might say that Jacquet is the great unnamed influence. Is there really a tenorman anywhere, on an R&B gig, who doesn't in the course of an evening play something that Illinois did first?' Illinois has also penned many original compositions. Here is a selection: *Bottoms Up, Port Of Rico, You Left Me All Alone, Sassy, Jivin' With Jack The Bellboy, Goofin' Off, It's Wild, Jumpin' At Apollo, Merle's Mood, King Jacquet, Jet Propulsion, Embryo, Riffin' At 24th Street, Symphony In Sid, B-Yat, Hot Rod, Adam's Alley, Ydeen-O, Black Foot, Big Music, Teddy Bear.* Illinois Jacquet is, thankfully, a King, who shows no sign of abdicating!

Recommended records:
Illinois Jacquet/Flying Home
Polydor 46862
Illinois Jacquet/1947-1950
RCA 430.705
Illinois Jacquet/Desert Winds
Argo LP 735
Illinois Jacquet/The Soul Explosion
Prestige PRST 7629
Illinois Jacquet/The Blues; That's Me!
Prestige PRST 7731
Illinois Jacquet/Bottoms Up
Prestige PRST 7575
Illinois Jacquet/The King!
Prestige PRST 7597
Illinois Jacquet/Genius At Work
Black Lion 30118
Howard McGhee/Illinois Jacquet/Here Comes Freddy
Sonet SNTF 714

Illinois Jacquet. He noticed me drawing him during a gig at the Nick Vollebreght's Jazzcafé When he finished his solo the grabbed the drawing off my board and enthusiastically showed it to the audience and I got a round of applause

Jean Baptiste
Illinois Jacquet
you are the greatist I.J.

28 oct 82

Arthur Blythe 80

Arthur Blythe. He was so big that every instrument had to look small in his hands. Calm power is what his playing and this drawing emanates.

Congratulations
and best always

[signature]

6 Aug 86
de Meeuwart

[signature]

Gerry Mulligan

Gerald Joseph Gerry Mulligan. Baritone & Alto Saxophone/Clarinet/Piano/ Composer/Arranger. New York City, New York, April 6 1927.

Brought up in Philadelphia where, as a teenager, he wrote and arranged music for a radio band led by Johnny Warrington. Moved to New York City to play baritone sax and arrange with the **Gene Krupa** Orchestra. Krupa recorded the Mulligan composition. in the bop style, *Disc Jockey Jump.*

A tireless performer at jam sessions, Mulligan scuffled for several years before becoming an important member of the **Miles Davis** 'Birth of the Cool' band which played a two week-engagement at the Royal Roost in 1948 and subsequently made three sessions for *Capitol* in 1949 and 1950. 'I was lucky to be in the right place at the right time to be part of Miles' band. I'd been on the road a couple of years with various bands by that time, but with Gil Evans' encouragement I decided to stay in New York,' Mulligan recalled to Simon Korteweg more than 20 years later. Evans' apartment behind a Chinese laundry became a gathering place for the avant garde of the day. Mulligan played baritone sax on all three *Capitol* dates, and contributed *Jeru, Venus De Milo* and *Rocker* to the band's book; he also arranged *Darn That Dream,* a vocal for Kenny Hagood.

The Davis experience had a profound influence on Gerry's career and, like Miles, saxophonist Lee Konitz and pianist John Lewis, he would spread the 'cool' gospel — or at least his personal distillation of it — in the ensuing years. Mulligan loved the dense, cloudy sound achieved by the Davis instrumentation. His own 1953 nine-piece ensemble was an extension of the *Capitol* band. As Mulligan explained: 'The tentet is essentially my original quartet with **Chet Baker** combined with the ensemble instrumentation of the Miles Davis Nonet.'

The quartet had been formed in the summer of 1952 when Gerry moved to California and teamed up with trumpeter Chet Baker. Interestingly the first track they made together had Jimmy Rowles on piano, but the group leaped to fame as the first modern combo *without* a pianist. The unit lasted a couple of years but registered several hits including *Bernie's Tune, My Funny Valentine* and *Walkin'*

Shoes. These tracks ensured rapid national and international fame for both Mulligan and Baker. Gerry formed the tentet as a rehearsal band which would serve as an outlet for his writing talent. Baker was subsequently replaced (after leaving to form his own quartet) by valve-trombonist **Bob Brookmeyer** and then another trumpeter, **Jon Eardley**, came in. Eventually both Brookmeyer and Eardley plus tenor saxophonist **Zoot Sims** were members of a Mulligan Sextet which still had no official pianist, although the leader himself would often provide chordal accompaniment for the other horns.

Mulligan visited Europe in 1954, '56 and '57. The late 1950s found him recording with a wide variety of soloists such as Thelonious Monk (an uneasy alliance, this), Paul Desmond, Ben Webster and Johnny Hodges. He formed a new band, with Art Farmer on trumpet, which appeared in the film *I Want To Live,* and Mulligan was a guest soloist with the Duke Ellington Orchestra at the 1958 Newport Jazz Festival.

Another significant milestone for Gerry was the formation in 1960 of his Concert Jazz Band, a fourteen-piece orchestra which amplified the work of the tentet and recast some of the arrangements Gerry had recorded 10 years previously for *Prestige.*

In 1968 Mulligan embarked on a series of tours with pianist **Dave Brubeck**, following another spell at the helm of a small group. Gerry formed another large ensemble, called The Age of Steam, in 1972. Reunited with Chet Baker for concerts and recordings in 1974. In the mid-1970s Gerry played in France and Italy and was present on Quincy Jones' soundtrack for the picture *Hot Rock.*

Slim, bony-faced and recently sporting a ragged beard, Mulligan is an acknowledged master of the baritone saxophone, but in his own sphere one feels that he obtains the greater satisfaction from composing for and directing hand-picked bands to perform his ever challenging scores. Indeed Mulligan's instrumental virtuosity has tended to obscure his considerable ability as a writer. While he may dally with small groups, every few years Gerry is driven to work on a larger canvas and produce new music of his own.

Michael James, in a penetrating study of Mulligan's recorded work in *Ten Modern Jazzmen* (1960), assessed Gerry's

contribution thus: 'Engaged in a continual struggle to externalize as fully as possible the contradictions of the human predicament, he (Mulligan) has willingly used every means at his disposal to translate to terms at once personal and valid for us all that ultimate sense of release which is the vision of every creative artist. So entire a resolve speaks most eloquently for the generousness of his design.'

Mulligan's work on baritone shows a keen awareness of earlier jazz styles, and a number of observers have drawn attention to his genuine feeling for New Orleans jazz. *But good as his soloing has been on occasion, it is in the realms of composition that Mulligan has offered his most mature and substantial contributions.* His superior ability as an orchestrator was evident in the songs he arranged for the 1947 Claude Thornhill Orchestra — *Poor Little Rich Girl, Sometimes I'm Happy, Poor Butterfly* etc.

As a composer his more memorable efforts, in addition to the items for Miles Davis, have included *Westwood Walk, A Ballad, Flash, Simbah, Ontet* (adapted from George Wallington's *Godchild*), *Decidedly, Funhouse, Roundhouse, Kaper, Mullenium, Id's Side, Four And One Moore, Crazy Day, Turnstile, Sextet* and *Revelation.* More recent works are: *An Unfinished Woman, Grand Tour, By Your Grace, It's Sandy At The Beach, Song For Strayhorn* and *Country Beaver.* Mulligan has retained a singularly independent stance in the matters of jazz playing and writing. His bluff baritone is in complete contrast to his carefully crafted charts — two sides of an invaluable jazz coin.

Recommended records:
Gerry Mulligan/Historically Speaking
Prestige PR7251
Miles Davis/Birth Of The Cool
Capitol 5C05280798
Gerry Mulligan Tentette
Capitol 5C05280801
The Gerry Mulligan Song Book
World Pacific ST1237
Gerry Mulligan Quartet
World Pacific 1207
Mulligan Meets Monk
Riverside RLP 12-247
Gerry Mulligan Sextet
EmArcy MG 36101
The Concert Jazz Band
Verve MGVS 68388

Sun Ra

Le Sony'r Ra/Sonny Blondt/Herman Blount/Sun Ra. Piano/Organ/Clavioline/Percussion/Electric Keyboards/Synthesizer/Rocksichord/Sun Harp/Composer/Arranger. Birmingham, Alabama, May ? 1915.

Mystic, self-styled prophet, keeps much of his past shrouded in mystery. Admits to being born under Zodiac sign of Gemini. Claims: 'I studied music under the guidance of Nature's God, and this study is yet in being.' Privately tutored while at college by Mrs Lula Randolph, of Washington, DC. Started in music at high school and credits John T. Whatley as a help. Played piano in **Fletcher Henderson**'s band at the Club de Lisa, Chicago, 1946-'47.

Gathered kindred spirits around him in Chicago and many of these fine players, such as saxophonists Pat Patrick, **John Gilmore**, trumpeters Dave Young, Art Hoyle, bassist Vic Sproles, were charter members of their leader's so-called Sun Arkestra. Sun Ra founded his own record company, *Saturn,* as an outlet for his work, but a couple of early albums were issued by the Chicago-based *Delmark* concern.

Wrote music for documentary movie, *The Cry Of Jazz,* and in the 1960s moved to New York. Made a rare appearance as a sideman on vibraharpist Walt Dickerson's quartet LP, *A Patch Of Blue.* Became associated with the avant garde group, the Jazz Composers' Guild, but his music was much closer to the jazz tradition than most of the free players within the guild. Ra's piano playing reflects a penchant for Thelonious Monk while his early writing showed him to be a devotee of Tadd Dameron's composing and arranging style. The nature of his Arkestra evolved and expanded and what started in 1956 as a tentette with typical Dameron instrumentation grew into a sixteen-piece band including a half dozen percussionists. The nature of the performances changed too into 'jazz theatre' with a troupe of dancers, singers, an occasional fire-eater and spectacular use of colourful costumes and lighting effects. The Arkestra became a show, an experience, a carnival but with the music still the focal point.

Ra, who pioneered the use of electronic instruments in the 1950s, was severely criticized for these theatrical trappings by jazz purists, but more broad-minded audiences loved every moment of the entertainment which has also encompassed the use of film within the performance. The leader himself continues to sport exotic, outlandish garb, but it is hard to comprehend why any of this visual stuff should be seen as detracting from his music. Some of the criticism of the Arkestra has been as ephemeral as the musicians' unusual apparel!

Sun Ra is undoubtedly a cult figure, and his influence beyond his own circle of players appears to be small, but he has created a body of imposing and impressive music, incorporating the use of many offbeat musical effects. He is treated reverentially by his 'court', and within the confines of the Arkestra company there can be no doubting who the priest figure is. In some of his statements ('I paint pictures of infinity with my music'... 'Inter-galactic music concerns the people of the galaxies'... 'It is really outside the realms of the future on the turning points of the impossible'... 'Music has wings. It moves upon the wings of intuition and thought'... 'The sound of it rushes like a wild thing and takes its place as the core of even the minutest part of being') Sun Ra recalls another eccentric free spirit, Moondog (Louis Hardin). Jazz has — and should have — room for such characters, for they enrich the music.

His numerous compositions include *Future, New Horizons, Sung Song, Brainville, Planet Earth, Saturn, Rocket Number Nine, Astro Black, The Cosmo-Fire, The Stargazers, Outer Spaceways Inc, Friendly Galaxy* and *Nebulae.* In his role as a jazz 'Extra Terrestrial', it is not surprising that not everyone treats him kindly or takes him seriously; but the man's music does warrant close study and to dismiss it is to lose an absorbing perspective on jazz writing and improvisation. It is the opinion of this writer that the first two albums listed below comprise the best examples of Sun Ra's *jazz* activity.

Recommended records:
Sun Ra/Sun Song
Delmark DL-411
Sun Ra/Sound Of Joy
Delmark DL-411
Sun Ra
Impulse A 59255
Sun Ra Arkestra
Polydor 2460106
Sun Ra
Blue Thumb BTS 41

Sun Ra. I sat very close to him as he sat on stage tucked away among palm trees behind the piano, looking a little awkwardly clad in that quasi spacesuit-outfit. But this medicine man sure is some eminent pianist!

'There are about a thousand ways to play a single note.'

'Get into the note. That's the reason I could read the first time I saw music. I had given myself over to the music.'

'The moment is the thing. Everything changes according to where the sun is, the stars are, the moon, how many people are in the room — there's a delicate tension that exists when you play an instrument.'

'My music is not about understanding; it's about feelings.' (Sun Ra)

Jimmy Raney. The expression of someone who drinks in his own music. He plays very internally.

Jimmy Raney

James Elbert (Jimmy) Raney. Guitar/Composer/Singer. Louisville, Kentucky, August 20 1927.

Son of a well-known journalist, Raney studied with A.J. Giancolla and Hayden Causey. It was Causey who recommended Raney to replace him in the band of **Jerry Wald** in New York City during 1944. Pianist in this band was the slightly older **Al Haig** who took Raney under his wing. It was the start of a collaboration between Raney and Haig that lasted intermittently until the pianist's death in 1982.

Raney's chief early influence was Charlie Christian (1919-'42), although he also admired Django Reinhardt and, later, Tal Farlow.

After a couple of months with Wald, Raney moved to Chicago where he worked with Max Miller and **Lou Levy**, and met **Lee Konitz**. Jimmy returned to New York to join the **Woody Herman** Orchestra and toured with the band from January to September, 1948.

Unfortunately there was a recording ban in that year, but this did not prevent Raney playing on many undercover disc sessions for independent labels with Al Haig, **Wardell Gray**, singer Harry Belafonte, Allen Eager and Ray Abrams. He was heard with clarinettists **Buddy DeFranco** and **Artie Shaw** in the late 1940s, and spent a couple of months with vibraharpist Terry Gibbs before joining the **Stan Getz** Quintet in 1951. This group is still reckoned by many to be the finest Getz has ever led, containing as it did Haig and Raney and the super rhythm team of Teddy Kotick (bass) and Tiny Kahn (drums).

Jimmy's next assignment was a year with **Red Norvo**'s combo, including a European tour which afforded him the opportunity to record under his own name in Paris. For a number of years Raney was with the Jimmy Lyon Trio, resident at the Blue Angel Club in New York. He was also heard with Teddy Charles and valve-trombonist Bob Brookmeyer.

After playing in Broadway shows such as the *Thurber Carnival,* Jimmy was reunited with Stan Getz 1962-'63, and did studio work with occasional jazz LPs. He returned to his hometown in the late 1960s to teach and work outside music, with just the occasional jazz job. Made a number of trips to New York in the 1970s and during one visit recorded again with his longtime friend Al Haig in November 1974. They did another album the following year, and gradually Jimmy eased back into the jazz scene, touring Europe several times, going to Japan as a member of the *Xanadu* All Stars, and recording for *Xanadu* and *SteepleChase*. Became a special favourite of audiences in The Netherlands where his friend Gerry Teekens arranged several visits and supervised Raney recording dates for the *Criss Cross* Jazz label. On a number of LPs Raney has been joined by his talented guitarist son Doug who is much influenced musically by his father.

Raney's sound has been described as pure, soft and slightly dulled, and cloudy and soft-edged. He uses amplification sparingly to achieve his particular sound. *His approach is gentle, melodic, lightly swinging. His lines are long, often complex and always compelling.* Raney took over where Christian left off and became *the* guitar influence. Among those who acknowledged Jimmy's example were Grant Green, Jim Hall, Attila Zoller, Pat Martino, Wes Montgomery, René Thomas and Jimmy Gourley.

A diffident man, Raney is an earnest student of the sciences and his grasp of complex theories would surprise many people.

He is a gifted composer, and tunes credited to him include *Signal, Motion, We'll Be Together, The Flag Is Up, Lee, Five, Minor, Samba Teekens* and *Jim's Tune.*

His most ambitious recorded work is *Suite For Guitar Quintet* which was taped in 1957 but not released until 1972. More recent pieces from the Raney pen include *Chewish Chive And English Brick, Jonathan's Waltz* and *Momentum.* But perhaps his best known chart is *Parker '51* which the Getz group recorded in that year.

Raney's mature style has often been likened to the guitar equivalent of Lee Konitz' saxophone conception, and the two musicians do have a similar approach to pure improvising. If anything, Jimmy's work has improved with age, and today his music has reached a level very close to perfection. Fortunately, the one person unlikely to accept that statement is Raney

himself who can be counted on to strive for higher quality. That is the nature of this influential pacesetter of the guitar.

Recommended records:
Jimmy Raney/Featuring Bob Brookmeyer
Japanese ABC
SR(M) 3033
Jimmy Raney/Strings & Swings
Muse 5004
Al Haig-Jimmy Raney/Special Brew
Spotlite LP8
Al Haig-Jimmy Raney/Strings Attached
Choice CRS 1010
Jimmy Raney/The Influence
Xanadu 116
Jimmy Raney/Live In Tokyo
Xanadu 132
Jimmy Raney/Solo
Xanadu 140
Jimmy Raney & Doug Raney/Stolen Moments
SteepleChase SCS 1118
Jimmy Raney/Raney '81
Criss Cross Jazz 1001

Al di Meola

Al di Meola. Guitar/Mando-Cello/Drums/ Miscellaneous Percussion/Vocal/ Composer/Arranger/Leader. New Jersey, July 22 1954.

Started off playing drums and discovered he was a 'natural' percussionist. Switched to guitar but had to work hard at this instrument. He believes his drumming experience influenced him to use more rhythms than most other guitarists. Early guitar training was with jazz musician Robert Aslanian who emphasized reading, picking technique, and technical proficiency rather than riffing. Di Meola learned to play rock and roll as well as jazz and pop, and listened to Larry Coryell, Doc Watson, Kenny Burrell and George Benson.

In 1971, he enrolled at the Berklee School of Music in Boston, majoring in instrumental performance. Was soon playing with the Barry Miles Quartet which was recorded by a friend, Mike Buyukas, on a date in New Jersey. Pianist **Chick Corea**, at that time the mainspring of a group called Return To Forever, heard the tape and was impressed by the guitarist. Di Meola re-enrolled at Berklee to study

arranging until a few months later, in 1973, he was invited by Corea to attend a rehearsal of the group in New York. 'At the time Chick was my favourite musician and Return To Forever was my favourite group,' Al later recalled. After a weekend rehearsing, Al made his debut with RTF in a Carnegie Hall concert the following night. He was 19 and received a standing ovation to launch his musical career in the major league.

In the next two years Di Meola, Corea, **Stanley Clarke** and **Lenny White** comprised one of the most interesting units attempting to fuse jazz and rock. They toured consistently and recorded three successful albums, two of which featured Di Meola compositions. When Corea broke up the group in 1976, Di Meola was already working on his first solo LP, *Land Of The Midnight Sun.* It was followed by the albums *Elegant Gypsy* and *Casino,* both of which were consecutively named 'best album of the year' by *Guitar Player* magazine. Those three records racked up sales in excess of 1.3 million copies around the world. There was a gap of a couple of years before Di Meola came out with a new double album, *Splendido Hotel,* featuring his first guitar concerto, *Isfahan,* his debut as a vocalist, and an intriguing collaboration with a popular guitarist of the 1940s and 1950s, **Les Paul.** As an exclusive contract artist to *CBS,* Al was assured of good promotion and lucrative treatment from the company. He was a star by his mid-1920s.

Di Meola has firmly resisted being pigeonholed, and his music encapsulates jazz, rock, Latin and classical styles. His technique incorporates alternate up-down flat picking rhythms, the use of four fingers on his left hand for chording, and muting with his right hand palm, fingertip and fingernail. In 1980, Di Meola stated: 'My technique has gotten better. I hear it more advanced. The speed is better, the accuracy. The phrasing is a bit more advanced than it was a few years ago. I pick every note. When I play anything that's fast, it's all picked.' As German jazz critic Joachim. E. Berendt wrote in his *Jazz: A Photo History* (New York, 1979; Frankfurt, 1978): 'Di Meola plays with the power and volume of contemporary jazz-rock, but he tempers this style and transforms it into *tone poems rich in emotion and sound.'*

Among Al's influences, apart from those already cited, are such diverse musicians

as John Coltrane, Larry Coryell, Ralph Towner, Julian Bream and Igor Stravinsky. An imposing and free-ranging list. On records, at least, Di Meola aportions set spaces for improvisation. 'I don't like a solo to go on for too long. A solo should be worked out in the sense that it must hold one's attention. It can get boring if it goes on too long, no matter who it is. A solo has to be a gem, not just a good solo,' he says. This is an interesting departure from the attitudes of the 'free' players of the 1960s who would solo for 20 or 30 minutes in an exploratory way, but invariably their inspiration would dry up. Rock musicians are probably more attuned to the importance of relative brevity than their jazz contemporaries, many of whom have interpreted the long playing record/tape as a medium for playing long. The 78 rpm record imposed a self-discipline that has escaped an entire generation.

Di Meola is untypical of *his* generation in his catholicity of taste and awareness of so many different phases of music. He is equally at home on electric or acoustic guitar, but leans more toward the former. 'The composition is the thing,' he declares. 'And the melody is what's going to hold people's attention. That's what I'm after. I've established a following and now I want to reach more people.' How he achieves this goal will continue to provide stimulating listening in this decade and, hopefully, for many years after that.

Di Meola has already displayed his versatility by duetting with figures as disparate as the Spanish flamenco guitarist Paco de Lucia, and the legendary pop stylist Les Paul, lured out of retirement to combine with Al on a version of *Spanish Eyes*. Di Meola is 'commercial' yet an explorer. He has a growing audience and has won admirers in the jazz and rock camps. The sky would seem to be the limit for a young man who is seasoned in his craft but continues to learn and expand his knowledge and experience.

Recommended records:

Al Di Meola/Land Of The Midnight Sun
CBS 32027 Columbia PC 34074
Al Di Meola/Elegant Gypsy
CBS 81845 Columbia PC 34461
Al Di Meola/Casino
CBS 32071 Columbia PC 35211
Al Di Meola/Splendido Hotel
CBS 88468 Columbia C2X36270

Al Di Meola/Tour de Force (Live)
CBS 25121 Columbia FC 38373
Al Di Meola/Friday Night In San Francisco
CBS 84962 Columbia FC 37152
Al Di Meola/Electric Rendezvous
CBS 85437 Columbia FC 31654
Return To Forever/Romantic Warrior
CBS 81221 Columbia PC 34076

David Murray

David Murray. Tenor/Alto/Soprano Saxophones/Flute/Bass Clarinet/Composer/Leader. Berkeley, California, February 19 1955.

A musical and religious background. His father played guitar in church while his mother was known throughout the USA as a pianist in the Sanctified Church. Both parents were important influences on him musically. Raised in the San Francisco Bay area, David played in the Missionary Church of God and Christ. He remains a spiritual person who believes in a Greater Force and a life hereafter.

At the age of 12 he got interested in rhythm and blues and led groups playing in this vein as a teenager. In this period he met trumpeter/composer Bobby Bradford and Black Arthur through a friendship with drummer and writer Stanley Crouch. During college vacations, Murray had his own group with trumpeter **Butch Morris**. Murray's musical horizons were expanded by two years of piano lessons with Margaret Kohn at Pomona College where he studied music.

At the age of 20, and firmly into jazz, David moved to New York in 1975. Made an immediate impact on the New York scene, leading his own groups at Sunrise Studio, Studio We, Studio Rivbea and Yale University. His confidence was apparent in the solo recitals he gave. Murray was a welcome guest with the groups of pianist **Cecil Taylor**, trumpeter Don Cherry and saxophonist **Anthony Braxton** – all 'senior' members of the avant garde from the 1960s. He also worked with drummer **Sunny Murray** (no relation), but was soon heading his own groups on a regular basis.

Murray, who was born just over three weeks before the death of Charlie Parker, cites 'Bird' as an influence, along with Sonny Rollins, Archie Shepp, Albert Ayler, John Coltrane, Duke Ellington, Ben Webster, Coleman Hawkins, Bobby Bradford, Black Arthur and Stanley Crouch. Also admires the late Paul Gonsalves, and has worked on unusual saxophone techniques opened up by Albert Ayler. Rather like Chico Freeman among his contemporaries, *Murray is unusual in that he has great awareness and knowledge of jazz instrumental history.*

A longtime advocate of Murray's playing has been the British critic Barry McRae who has referred to the 'integrity of Murray's musical conception, and the coherence of its realization'. According to McRae: 'It is true that Murray's music repeatedly proclaims its disaffection with traditional procedures, yet lyricism still remains at its heart.'

Murray has made several successful tours of Europe, recording in England and Switzerland where he was celebrated for his solo concerts. In the 1980s he has been heard with his old friend Butch Morris and other talented young players like pianist Anthony Davis and trombonist **George Lewis**. Though primarily acknowledged for his tenor saxophoning, Murray has not been found wanting on alto and soprano, flute and bass clarinet. Reviewing a mid-1970s solo recital by Murray for *Coda* magazine (April 1976), Roger Riggins enthused: 'Murray was able to widen the parameters of the music: pitch, intensity, duration and timbre were exploited to provide the listener with a variety of moods and tone colours, and his method never lacked assuredness.' And further: 'Murray's solo work can hardly be compared with anyone else's, although if pressed for directives, Hawkins or Rollins come to mind. Murray's overall advantage on the saxophone has to do with his range and his exquisitely beautiful tonal sense in the upper register of his horn. He achieves these breathtaking sinus (pure) tones on the top of his horn with such ease, assurance and depth of feeling that one is simply left sentimentally restored while listening.'

Murray played the leading role in a play by Stanley Crouch entitled *Saxophone Man*, and has been featured in a number of TV programmes in both Europe and the USA. He already has a substantial list of compositions to his credit including: *Shout Song, Roscoe, Flowers For Albert, Sweet Lovely, BC, Rag Tag, Both Feet On The Ground, Miss Sweet, Suite For Yellowman Warrior, Low Class*

155

Al di Meola. The contemporary scene: a stage full of cables, strings, cords and PA systems.

To Pete —
Excellent images!
Keep up the good work
Please
David Murray
'86

Conspiracy, Dewey Circle, Ballad For A Decomposed Beauty, Welcome To The Set, S.B. And C Follies.

Murray does not restrict himself to his own material; he can sometimes be heard playing the works of Thelonious Monk and even classic popular songs. Still only in his twenties, David Murray continues to develop and is now an accepted stylist within his chosen area of music – 'free jazz'. His purpose is not to have audiences whistling his melodies as they leave the concert hall but to make them feel alive and stimulated. To this end he seems to be winning. Murray, wrote Barry McRae (*Jazz Journal International*, May 1980), 'thinks in strong superstructures while setting out to embellish them with rhetorical niceties'.

Recommended records:
David Murray/Ming
Black Saint BSR 0045
David Murray/Solo Live, Vols 1 & 2

Cecma 1001/1002
David Murray/3D Family 1978
Hat Hut Records U/V
David Murray/Live At The Lower Manhattan Ocean Club, Vols 1 & 2
India Navigation IN 1032/1044
David Murray/Sweet Lovely
Black Saint BSR 0039
David Murray/Low Class Conspiracy
Adelphi Jazz AD 5002
David Murray/Flowers For Albert
India Navigation IN 1026

Ronald Shannon Jackson

Ronald Shannon Jackson. Drums. Fort Worth, Texas, January 12 1940.

At the age of five he started to study piano, but became more interested in the drums. In 1958 he was one of the Lincoln University school band in Jefferson City,

Missouri – along with **Julius Hemphill**, Lester Bowie, **Oliver Nelson** and Bill Davis. First work as professional with James Clay and the Red Tops. In New York he met Albert Ayler. Made his first recording with Charles Tyler in 1966. Played with **Charles Mingus**, McCoy Tyner, Kenny Dorham, Joe Henderson, amongst others.

Ronald Shannon Jackson on his own group, The Decoding Society: 'The Decoding Society is an awareness body formed to decipher, organize and present humanitarian messages of the Arts.'

Recommended records:
Ronald Shannon Jackson/Barbecue Dog
Antilles AN 1015
Ronald Shannon Jackson/Eye On You
Abouttin AT 1003
Ronald Shannon Jackson/Mandance
Antilles AN 1008

157

Dave Murray. He was one of the first persons to write his appreciation on the drawing. Signature and comment not only add to the authenticity of the drawing but often improve its composition.

Hey Piet
You capture Rhythm
You capture life M.M.R.C.
capture Marks Shannon 6/10/83

Ronald Shannon Jackson

Jazz talk

Alligator: (1930s) term used by black jazzmen, particularly in New Orleans, referring to white jazz musicians, jive people or jitterbugs.

Armstrong: a very high note or a series of them, especially on a trumpet.

Back-door man: a married woman's lover who is, incidentally, a legendary figure in blues numbers.

To have a Ball: to enjoy yourself.

Belly fiddle: guitar.

Blow (one's) ass off: to play music superlatively.

Blow the gig: to fail to appear for a one-night musical engagement.

Blowing session: (1950s) a jazz session where improvisation is the orientation.

Bread: money.

Burn (someone for bread): borrow money.

Businessman's bounce: term of derision; music played by society bands.

Canary: female jazz vocalist, especially one who sings with a band.

Carve: (1920s-'40s) to outplay another musician in a musical competition.

Clam: a misplayed note.

Clambake: a jam session (not in the groove).

Clinker: (since the 1930s) in jazz, an error in playing; at one time also referred to the leg chain that bound one convict to another in a chain gang.

Clound Nine: complete contentment.

Cook: (1930s and after) in jazz, to play with great inspiration; to be in the spirit of a situation.

Cooking with gas: doing something well.

Crumbcrusher: a baby.

Crumbs: a small sum of money.

Crumbsnatcher: a baby.

Cut it: a successful recording.

Day gig: any non-jazz job.

Did: job (mostly a one-night stand).

Dog tune: song of questionable musical quality.

Dots: sheet music.

Down with one's ax: get around on one's horn.

Fats: jazzman.

Faust: an ugly girl.

Feed: (1940s) in jazz, chords backing a soloist.

Feel a draft: to feel hostility directed against oneself.

Fingers: a jazz pianist.

Fish horn: a saxophone.

Flag waver: a familiar tune.

Fluff: to play a wrong note.

Freak lip: a brass man who can play three octaves for three hours at least.

Freeby: something for nothing.

Frisking the whiskers: (1940s) the 'warm up' playing musicians do before swinging into a full jam session.

Funk: (1950s) the 'soul' quality in black music, the melancholy mood of the blues.

Fuzz: the police.

Gas: anything enjoyable, satisfying.

Gas pipe: (1940s) a trombone.

Geets: dollars.

Gig: originally a jazzman's job; later it came to mean any kind of job.

Gray boy: white man.

Grease your chops: eat.

Historical eyes: outdated, passé.

To stay Inside: to play within the established chord structure of a tune.

Jam session: (1930'-40s) an occasion where jazz musicians get together to play strictly for their own pleasure.

Kick (it) around: to improvise music freely and relaxedly.

A Lame: a square.

Left people: fingers of a pianist's left hand.

Left town: died.

Licking the chops: (1940s) the tuning up musicians do before a jam session.

Licks: (1920s-'40s) very jazzy musical notes.

Licorice stick: (1930s-'40s) a clarinet.

Lipton's: fake or poor marihuana.

Lit (it) up: to bring an instrument into tune.

Living room gig: in jazz, a TV appearance.

Long green: over $ 1,000.

Long underwear: musicians who can play only 'as written'.

Mellow like a cello: beautiful.

Mickey Mouse band: band that sounds as if it is playing background music for an animated cartoon.

A Monster: an inordinate player.

Mugging heavy (or light, lightly): (1930s-'40s) in jazz, the term refers to the beat, its quality.

Mulligrubs: the blues.

A Needle dancer: a heroin addict.

On the Nod: sleeping; usually in a standing or sitting position.

Other man: the liquor dealer.

Pork chop (music): slow, earthy blues music.

Pots (are) on: (1950s) in jazz, means the music is very beautiful.

Rain on (one): complain, bother someone.

Rusty dusty: the buttocks.

Scare: to play music with originality and skill.

Short: automobile.

Short line: not enough money.

Skin: handshake.

Skypiece: hat.

Smoke them out: (1950s) to be really fantastic, especially in making good music.

Make Snakes: play very fast.

Talk: (1920s-'40s) when a jazzman is really communicating through his music people often cry out; 'Talk to me!' Or they might say: 'He's saying something!'

Tear (it) up: (1920s-'40s) in jazz, to give a great performance.

Threads: clothes.

Woodshed: (1930s) in jazz, when a musician practises his instrument in privacy.

(Source: Clarence Major: Black Slang.)

159

Ronald Shannon Jackson: 'Hey Piet, you capture rhythm, you capture life.'
'Thanks, Shannon.'

Tito Puente

Ernest Puente Junior. Drums/Vibraphone/Timbales/Piano/Alto Saxophone/Leader. New York City, April 20 1925.

Son of immigrant couple from Puerto Rico. Studied composition and arranging with Richard Benda. Worked with Noro Morales and Pupi Campo, one of the pioneers of fusing jazz with Latin American rhythms. From 1945-'49 Puente was employed by these and many other big time bandleaders in the Latin field. A multi-talented musician, he was particularly admired for his vibraphone and timbales playing, but also gained respect with his chunky piano underlays for sections and soloists, and his well structured arrangements which showed more than a tinge of jazz influence. Formed his own band in 1949 and has been an important leader in his chosen style for more than 3^1/$_2$ decades. Puente's outfit in the 1950s played unadulterated mambo, with little evidence of the Cuban feel which permeated so many Latin groups of that period. Tito was billed as 'The Mambo Kid' and enjoyed a huge following among the Puerto Rican community when it packed the Palladium on Broadway, New York. Apart from piano and bass, the band was composed entirely of trumpets and drums, an aggregation known as a 'conjunto', or jam band.

The late Marshall Stearns, who was quite an expert on Latin music, reckoned that Puente had one of the finest bands working in the mambo style. They would serve up piping hot cha cha chas and brassy mambos which were meat and drink to the exciting dancers who displayed their intricate steps on the floors of New York's ghetto ballrooms. The Palladium was actually down-town, only a few doors from Birdland, headquarters of bebop. There was a good deal of cross-fertilization of ideas between the boppers and Latin rhythmic 'juggernauts' at this venue.

Puente would alternate with other successful leaders of the genre, Machito and Tito Rodriguez, at the Palladium venue. And all three men appeared as leaders at Birdland. Puente would usually have a jazz soloist or two in the ranks to add pep to his performances. As his band grew in versatility, its popularity increased with fans of both Latin-American and jazz music. Puente revealed his fascination with jazz when he recorded an album for *RCA Victor* entitled *Puente Goes Jazz*. Critic John S. Wilson wrote of this LP: 'There are several surprisingly good big band performances here – direct, forceful, often genuinely hot – when the band digs into uptempo material using its Latin rhythms simply as accents to what are predominantly jazz pieces.'

In 1958 Puente, a staunch admirer of the large jazz orchestras of Woody Herman, Stan Kenton and Count Basie, teamed up with Herman for a successful South American tour and an album, *Herman's Heat And Puente's Beat* which again illustrated that, in the right hands, Latin Jazz had considerable possibilities. Tito, who has employed such jazz soloists as trumpeter Bernie Glow and saxophonist **Dave Schildkraut**, once recorded a tribute to jazz drummer Tiny Kahn called *Tiny – Not Ghengis*. He has never been short of work, but with the boom in 'salsa' (Puerto Rican music spiced with jazz) in the 1970s, Puente was once again to the fore, converting rhythms old and new to his own ends. After Machito's successes in Europe, it was obvious that Tito had to be brought over. He was, and proved to be equally popular with festival audiences on the Continent.

Whether directing his ensemble through one of his own arrangements, stepping out front to take a hot timbales solo or conjuring up a moody atmosphere on the vibes, Tito Puente is a musician to be respected. He regards Dizzy Gillespie as the master of Afro-Cuban music and jazz. But when it comes to the mambo Tito is no longer 'The Kid' – today he is definitely 'The Mambo Maestro' and surely 'The Sage of Salsa' too.

Recommended records:
Puente Goes Jazz
Victor LPM 1312
Woody Herman-Tito Puente/Herman's Heat And Puente's Beat
Everest 5010
Tito Puente/Puente In Love
Tico LP 1058

Percey Heath

Percy Heath. Bass/Viola da Gamba. Wilmington, Delaware, April 30 1923.

Eldest of three musical brothers, he was brought up in Philadelphia. Played violin in school orchestra. Army in 1943 and then 2^1/$_2$ years as fighter pilot in US Air Force. After World War II attended Granoff School of Music in Philadelphia and studied bass. First job with Hollis Hoppers, and then became the house bassist at Philadelphia's Down Beat Club. Joined trumpeter **Howard McGhee**'s sextet late in 1947, and the following spring went with the band to the Paris Jazz Festival.

Heath soon established himself in the forefront of the second wave of bebop bassists inspired by Oscar Pettiford, Ray Brown and Jimmy Blanton. He worked with Fats Navarro, **Miles Davis**, J.J. Johnson and others before joining **Dizzy Gillespie**'s sextet in June 1950 and stayed with the trumpeter for two years. In 1951 the Modern Jazz Quartet was in embryo, recording under **Milt Jackson**'s name for *Savoy*. Ray Brown was on the first session, but Heath got the job for the next two dates. The group officially became the MJQ at the end of 1952 with pianist **John Lewis** taking over as musical director. It proved to be a most durable group lasting for more than 21 years – an incredible span for a jazz combo.

Heath was the bassist for the duration. Within this intimate chamber jazz context, Percy formed a telepathic understanding with leader Lewis, vibraharpist Milt Jackson and drummer **Connie Kay**. *Heath's resiliant bass lines, his flexibility and sense of shading* were constant co-ordinating factors in the unit's balance and success. His flawless technique, *rock steady beat and mellow tone* were much admired by fellow bassists. Jazz with the MJQ called for Percy to develop a sound arco facility, too.

When the quartet disbanded in July 1974, Heath freelanced, working with his saxophonist brother Jimmy and singer **Sarah Vaughan**. For a time the three Heath brothers – drummer Albert 'Tootie' is the youngest – had their own band with pianist Stanley Cowell in the 1970s. The brothers had recorded together on a number of occasions in the early 1960s. Percy also did engagements with his longstanding collaborator Milt Jackson.

A tall, lean man of sober mien and easy movement, Heath has devoted more than 3^1/$_2$ decades to the bass, straying only very occasionally into the compositional field. His expertise has been used on recordings by Charlie Parker, Dizzy Gillespie, Thelonious Monk, Clifford

160

Tito Puente. Those quotation marks around Jr are pretty. He sure ain't as young as he used to be!

To. Pite-
Wishing the greatest
of Artistic achievements —
Your boy
Tito Puente "Jr"

29 mai '82

Percy Heath
11 juli
'81

Brown, Sonny Rollins, Ornette Coleman, Miles Davis, J.J. Johnson and many others. So his credentials are impeccable. When the MJQ were persuaded to reform for a Japanese tour, Percy was back in his old spot in 1982. The group simply took up where they had left off in '74 and after a hugely successful New York club engagement in the spring of 1983 they were soon making the European rounds again. Reviewing the MJQ for the London *Observer* (May 1, 1983), Dave Gelly wrote: 'It wasn't until hearing Percy Heath with the MJQ that I fully realized what has happened to the double bass in recent years. Players nowadays invariably use a built-in pickup that feeds directly into an amplifier. Heath doesn't; he simply has a microphone placed near the bridge. The result is wonderful — a real bass sound, quiet but perfectly defined, the noise that jazz bassists always used to make, and preferable to the ugly whine we get these days.' Since Heath is something of a purist and fussy about tone, his shunning of spurious over-amplification is right in character.

Recommended records:
Milton Jackson/The First Q
Savoy SJL 1106
Modern Jazz Quartet/First Recordings!
Prestige PRST 7749
The Complete Milt Jackson
Prestige PRST 7655
Jimmy Heath/The Quota
Riverside RLP 9372
Jimmy Heath/Triple Threat
Riverside RLP 9400
Dizzy Gillespie/Modern Jazz Sextet
Japanese Verve MV 1124

Machito

Frank Grillo Machito. Vocal/Maracas/ Leader. Tampa, Florida, February 16 1912. Died on a tournee in London, April 16 1984.

Machito was brought up in Cuba where he was known as a singer and rhythm player, rather than a leader. Worked with all the top Cuban bands of the 1930s. From 1929 onwards made frequent trips to USA, making the move permanent in 1937. Spent much time at Harlem's Savoy Ballroom listening to the bands of Duke Ellington, Count Basie, Benny Carter, Fletcher Henderson and Chick Webb.

Sometimes the drummer Webb would allow Machito to sit in and spice up the rhythm. Meanwhile Machito was employed by such leaders as Xavier Cugat and Noro Morales as singer and sideman.
Organized his own band late 1939/early 1940 with the idea of fusing Latin music and American jazz. Trumpeter Mario Bauza, a friend of Dizzy Gillespie's, helped to set up the new ensemble, and was lead trumpeter and featured soloist. The style that was to emerge in the mid-1940s as Afro-Cuban was still a few years in the future, as Machito and his sixteen-piece band earned a respectable living from playing Latin music for dancing.
Gillespie and **Charlie Parker** were fascinated by the irresistible rhythms of the Cuban drummers and frequently sat in with Machito's band.
In 1948 the *Roost* label released a performance by Machito featuring bop trumpeter Howard McGhee and tenorman **Brew Moore**. It became a cult hit in jazz circles. McGhee and Moore were both featured with Machito in an engagement at the Royal Roost, and that recording of *Cubop City* sold a lot of copies. During the successful Royal Roost gig, **Milt Jackson** (vibraharp) was also an occasional guest with the band.
In 1949 Machito recorded for Norman Granz' *Clef/Norgran* label with Charlie Parker and Flip Phillips as principal soloists.
When I caught up with an edition of the Machito Orchestra in 1963, two members of the saxophone section were Danny Turner (alto and flute) and Cecil Payne, baritone bulwark of the 1940s Dizzy Gillespie Band. Payne toured Latin America with Machito too. Also in the band were **Chino Pozo** (conga) and Paul Serrano (trumpet.
During the 1950s Machito made many records, many for dancing but a few with high jazz content spotlighting jazz players like **Cannonball Adderley**, Herbie Mann, Eddie Bert, Curtis Fuller, Doc Cheatham and Joe Newman.
A short, garrulous and gregarious man with an accent thick enough to cut with a bread knife, *Machito's bands were the musical equivalent of heavy, steam-driven locomotives; once they started moving they were relentless and unstoppable.*
Afro-Cuban music is concerned primarily with rhythm. The various band sections pile up layers of sound, producing an

hypnotic effect. The trumpets play with a wide vibrato and the piano adds a florid flourish in solo passages. The rhythms are complex, but cushion the jazz soloist. Stan Kenton was heavily influenced by Machito, so much so that when he recorded *The Peanut Vendor*, a brassy arrangement with a Cuban beat, he insisted that Machito and Jose Manguel, another fine percussionist, should play on the date.
The Machito-Mario Bauza partnership flourished for 35 years. Bauza quit the band at the end of 1975 because of a disagreement. He had switched from trumpet to alto saxophone in 1958. Despite their differences Machito admired him as a 'great musician' and recognized his part in effecting the Afro-Cuban/Jazz coalition.
In the late 1970s Machito's style of music, more conveniently re-named as salsa, enjoyed a resurgence. Machito resumed his recording association with Norman Granz and toured Europe to considerable critical acclaim.
Machito was a key figure in the evolution of an interesting musical diversion — Afro-Cubop. The coming together of those contrasting yet complimentary modes of expression was explosive when they collided, merged and coalesced. Across the years, the reverberations are still felt and sound remarkably potent. Machito, master of the mambo and regius of the rumba, regarded the union of two different musical approaches with a twinkle of affection. After all, he brought them together and watched, with satisfaction, as Gillespie, Stan Kenton and others absorbed the Cuban rhythmic factor into their styles.

Recommended records:
Charlie Parker/Verve Years, Vols 1 & 2
Verve 2-2501/2-2512
Machito-Chico O'Farrill-Dizzy Gillespie/Afro-Cuban Jazz
Verve 2-2522
Machito/Latin Soul Plus Jazz
Tico CLP 1314
Machito-Herbie Mann/Afro-Jazziac
British Vamp SRCP 3002
Stan Kenton
Creative World ST 1047
Dizzy Gillespie-Machito/Afro-Cuban Jazz Moods
Pablo 2310 771
Machito & His Salsa Band Live At North Sea '82
Timeless Records 168

163

Percy Heath. I can vaguely remember a concert the Modern Jazz Quartet gave in the Amsterdam's Concertgebouw, a long time ago. This time he was wearing a polo shirt but I still saw the same gentleman dressed in a tuxedo. He radiates a combination of a man of distinction and one of force.

Mucha
P to
to Tocca
Machito

Machito and his Salsa Big Band 29 mei 82

Stan Getz

Stanley (Stan) Getz. Tenor Saxophone. Philadelphia, Pennsylvania, February 2 1927.

First musical instrument he tried was bass, then switched to the unlikely bassoon. Attended the James Monroe High School in the Bronx, New York. Took up tenor sax and was playing wedding gigs around the Bronx at the age of 12, worked with Richard Himber at age 14. Quit school at 15 to join Dick 'Stinky Rogers' band, but the truant officers caught up with him and returned Getz to school.

At 16 he was working with legendary trombonist **Jack Teagarden** who took out guardianship papers on the saxophonist to keep the school authorities at bay. Stan played with Bob Chester and Dale Jones and spent a year (1944-'45) in the bubbling cauldron of the **Stan Kenton** Orchestra. Further practical experience gained with Jimmy Dorsey, Benny Goodman, Randy Brooks, Buddy Morrow and Herbie Fields.

The baby-faced tenor player moved to California in 1947, working with bassist Butch Stone and leading his own trio at the Hollywood Swing Club. In September of that year joined the newly-formed **Woody Herman** Herd, becoming a member of the famous 'Four Brothers' saxophone section with Zoot Sims, Serge Chaloff and Herbie Steward (subsequently replaced by Al Cohn). Getz' early records under his own name showed him to be under the spell of Dexter Gordon, but by the time he soloed on *Early Autumn* with the Herman band, he had a markedly personal style based upon the 'teachings' of Lester Young. That performance and others demonstrated Stan's penchant for cool ballads. His approach to jazz was and is essentially gentle and melodic, but he can swing with the best.

After leaving Herman, Getz led small groups – quartets or quintets – featuring pianists like **Al Haig**, Duke Jordan, Horace Silver and Johnny Williams, and guitarist **Jimmy Raney**.

Went on tour of Scandinavia in 1951 and recorded there with Swedish musicians. Getz' work was admired around the world by the 1950s but his personal life was a mess. Getz was one of many in his musical generation who fell victim to narcotics addiction. In 1954 desperation led him to try to rob a drugstore, using his hand to simulate a gun. He fled when his bluff was called. He was arrested and while awaiting trial attempted suicide in his cell. Stan at that time had a 70-dollar-a-day habit which he was fortunately able to break and straighten out. For once, the law showed clemency to a great musician.

After doing studio work in New York, he again ventured to Scandinavia in the autumn of 1955 but was taken seriously ill and could not work for six months. Resumed touring on returning to the US and appeared in the *Benny Goodman Story* movie (1956). Moved to Copenhagen in 1958 and stayed there for three years. Though by then possibly the most popular saxophonist of his generation (he consistently won magazine polls from 1953), Getz was still a tireless player at jam sessions, relishing the competitive push provided by men like **Sonny Stitt**.

In 1957-'58 Getz toured and recorded with Jazz At The Philharmonic ensembles. Pressed to name his favourite saxophonists, Getz came up with Lester Young, Herbie Steward, Zoot Sims, Al Cohn and Charlie Parker (Getz and Parker often shared the same rhythm section but sadly never recorded together).

Stan's style was in eclipse when he returned to the US at the start of 1961, for by that time the major new sax influences were the hard-edged tenors of John Coltrane and Sonny Rollins. However, Getz was on the brink of his biggest success. In 1962 he joined forces with guitarist **Charlie Byrd** to make, on the face of it, an unprepossessing album of Brazilian sambas penned by Antonio Carlos Jobim. Two of the tracks were *Desafinado* and *One Note Samba*. The album became one of the biggest sellers in jazz history, and those individual titles were hits in the singles market. So the Bossa Nova was launched as an international sound, with Getz' melodic bent perfectly suiting the simple, sweet melodies. The craze swept America, but to Stan it was a valid fusion between jazz and Brazilian music. He persisted with it, recording with **Joan Gilberto** (guitarist/composer), pianist Jobim and singer **Astrud Gilberto** whose fetching, unpretentious voice, accompanied by Stan's tenor, made the perfect combination. *The Girl From Ipanema* by Gilberto and Getz was a huge pop chart success in 1964.

Getz also made two important albums, arranged by Eddie Sauter, appeared in several films and received the ultimate accolade in establishment acceptance by recording with Arthur Fiedler and the Boston Pops Orchestra. As a jazz soloist he seemed to go from strength to strength, making a magnificent quartet album, *Sweet Rain,* with **Chick Corea** (piano), Ron Carter (bass) and Grady Tate (drums) in 1967, after leading another satisfying group including **Gary Burton** (vibes), Steve Swallow (bass) and Roy Haynes (drums) the previous year. Stan's playing was slightly revised from the mid-1960s onwards and his tone assumed a sharper edge. Somehow he has always managed to sound contemporary without being actually influenced by current trends in jazz. He refused to flirt with other instruments or experiment with electronics. His 45-year involvement with music has been dedicated to adding further majesty to his mastery of the tenor saxophone, and honing *a lyricism which, at its best, possesses a fineness and logic comparable with Jimmy Raney's cultured and carefully structured guitar conception.*

Recommended records:
Stan Getz/Opus De Bop
Savoy SJL 1105
Stan Getz/Prezervation
Prestige PRST 7516
Stan Getz/It Might As Well Be Spring
Vogue VJD 573
The Stan Getz Quintet At Storyville, Vols 1 & 2
Vogue LAE 12158/12199
Stan Getz-Chet Baker/Stan Meets Chet
Verve MGV 8263
Stan Getz/Focus
Verve MGV 8412
Stan Getz/Big Band Bossa Nova
Verve MGV 8494
Stan Getz/Live At Montmartre
SteepleChase SCS 1073/74

Chet Baker

Chesney H. (Chet) Baker. Trumpet/ Flugel-Horn/Singer. Yale, Oklahoma, December 23 1929.

After his family moved to California in 1940, Baker started his musical training at Glendale High School, playing trumpet in

166

Stan Getz and Chet Baker in the Singer Concertzaal at Laren. The same music as 25 years ago, only the heroes 25 years older.

Beautifully done —
Thanks
Chet Baker
—83—

the marching and dance bands. He spent four years in the Army, playing with the 298th Army Band in Berlin and Presidio Army Band in San Francisco. Also studied theory and harmony at El Camino College. Baker worked briefly with **Charlie Parker** when the saxophonist was on the West Coast in 1952, and that same year joined baritone saxophonist **Gerry Mulligan**. His fame spread overnight following the release of the pianoless quartet's first recordings.

Baker led his own groups or toured as a guest soloist from 1953, and for the past 30 years his musical career has been persistently interrupted by personal problems associated with drug addiction. His frequent brushes with the law in Europe and the USA have all been occasioned by narcotics offences, and he has seen the inside of too many jails. Baker's personal appearance is a mirror of the anguished experiences that have beset his life. *Baker at his best is a stylistic descendant of Bix Beiderbecke, although his tone and spare phrasing show more than a trace of admiration for Miles Davis.* He is a melodist; his improvisations are not mere mechanical exercises through a chord progression but new melodies in themselves.

His early compatriot Gerry Mulligan has said of him: 'Chet was one of the best intuitive musicians I've ever seen. We used to get some remarkable things going.' And pianist **Russ Freeman** thought that at his best Baker was as good as anyone including Charlie Parker and Dizzy Gillespie.

Baker sustained a serious setback in 1968 when he was viciously beaten up by thugs. He lost his teeth and did not play for two years. Of slight, frail physique, Baker has found it increasingly difficult to play for extended periods. What energy he can muster seems to be directed solely into music, but he is still capable of intensely beautiful playing, and while his is a sad, haunting trumpet or flugel-horn sound it is neither bitter nor self-pitying in its emotional content.

Recommended records:
Chet Baker In Paris (1955-1956)
Blue Star 80704/5
Chet Is Back!
French RCA PM 31256
The Touch Of Your Lips
SteepleChase SCS 1122
Rendez-Vous
Bingow Records BGW 04

No Problem
SteepleChase SCS 1131

Clarence 'Gatemouth' Brown

Clarence Brown.
Singer/Guitar/Harmonica/Violin/
Mandolin/Bass guitar/Drums.
Vinton (Calcasieu Parish), Louisiana,
April 18 1924.

He was named after his father, Clarence Brown, who was a local musician. His half-brother James 'Widemouth' Brown was also a singer and guitar player and his brother Bobby played drums. Three weeks after Clarence was born, the family moved to Orange, Texas, where he was raised. As a child he was already interested in music and it was his father who taught him to play guitar and violin. Through the thirties he joined William Benbow's Brown Skin Models as a drummer.

During the 1940s he worked with Hart Hughes' Orchestra (still as a drummer) and from 1947 on he recorded under his own name for Don Robey's *Peacock label* from Houston, Texas. *Peacock* owner Don Robey took a special interest in Gate as the two pioneered Robey's entry into the record business together. Gate was T-Bone Walker's main challenger as blues guitar king of The Southwest, when Gate wasn't going into one of his many trick-bags. Guitarist/singer Lonnie Brooks summed it up for authors Robert Neff and Anthony Connors in their book *Blues: 'That Gate can do more with a guitar than a monkey with a peanut.'*

During the mid-50s Gatemouth made some extensive tours with singer **Big Mama Thornton**. During the '60s there was a lull in his career, but the '70s appeared to be the decade of Gate's revival. In '71 he did a European tour, recording an album for the French *Black & Blue* label, being followed by several albums in The States that featured him with blues and jazz musicians as well as some country and bluegrass heroes. Gatemouth toured Europe (even Russia!), Japan, Africa and The United States extensively and signing a record contract with *Rounder* records in 1981 resulted in the Grammy award winning album 'Allright Again', which has been followed by the release of a second *Rounder* album 'One more Mile' as well as the re-release of his

old *Peacock* recordings. 'The Sheriff' (as many people call him, due to his preference for Sheriff outfits) continues to be one of the most influential blues artists.

Recommended records:
The Original Peacock Recordings
Rounder 2039
Allright Again
Rounder 2028
Live In Concert/Int. Jazzfestival Bern
Schweizerischer Bankverein LP P19831

Johnny Coles

John (Johnny) Coles. Trumpet. Trenton, New Jersey, July 3 1926.

Largely a self-taught musician, Coles began playing at the age of 13. Emerged from the ranks of rhythm and blues bands led by the likes of **Eddie Vinson** and **Bull Moose Jackson**. Had his own band briefly but was then featured with **Tadd Dameron**, **James Moody** and **Gil Evans** orchestras. Also played with **Charlie Mingus** on several important recordings. Though his tone is small and far removed from brassy brashness, Coles is a most gifted player with an ear for the unusual melodic turn of phrase. He has often figured prominently on recordings by **Gil Evans** who made him featured soloist on one session. Affectionately known as 'Little Johnny C' (his height is only five feet four inches), Coles has made surprisingly few LPs under his own leadership. Yet **Duke Ellington**, with whom Coles worked for several years, had a high regard for him.

The late Duke Pearson, another pianist with great respect for Coles, once wrote: 'Johnny Coles is a warm individual with a personal approach to each note or phrase he plays. A painter of very beautiful patterns.' Coles has shown his perception on such diverse material as the 1927 Bix Beiderbecke composition *Davenport Blues*, John Lewis' *Django* and Randy Weston's perky *Hi-Fly*.

Recommended records:
Johnny Coles/Little Johnny C
Blue Note BST 84144
Gil Evans/Out Of The Cool
Impulse A-40
The Individualism Of Gill Evans
Verve V-8555

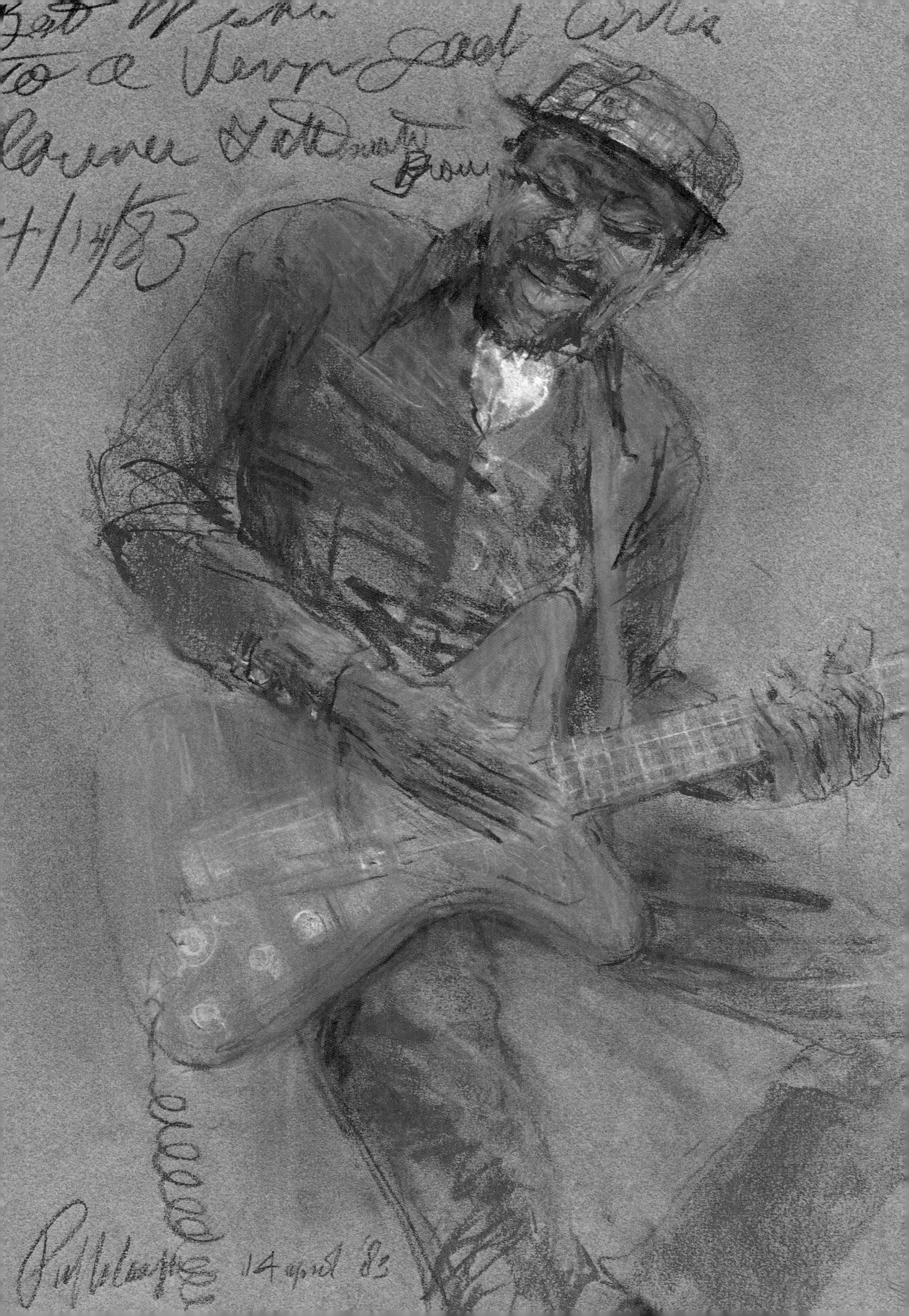
4/14/83
14 april '83

IT'S A GREAT
PICTURE!
Johnny Carbo

21 nov '82

The jazz line

A wordless melody

A hand, a hand with a pencil. Motionless, it hangs over the white paper. Then suddenly something appears: a couple of lines, a sentence, a few notes. And the outsider asks himself how they got there, where they came from.

Artists are not in the habit of being able or wanting to answer this. The one says it comes from the inside. It comes as a gift, says the other, as if someone were living inside him who guides his hand. Yet another claims it is a matter of an unconscious process, faster than those of conscious thought.

Even in this era of advanced brain research, the workings of the creative process still remain a mystery. Computers still cut a pretty poor figure when it comes to writing poetry or playing chess. But sometimes someone comes along who seems to lift the veil enough to afford us a glimpse.

Nadjezjda Mandelstam, widow of the famous Russian poet Osip Mandelstam, noted in her *Memoires* the following observation of the poet Anna Achmatova: 'At first a constant kind of wordless melody sounds in your ears, initially totally devoid of form, but becoming increasingly precise.' (...) 'At a certain moment words presented themselves through the melody and then the lips began moving. There is probably a similarity between the way composers and poets work and that the performance of words is the critical instant which distinguishes these two forms of creativity from one another.'

Anyone engaged in a creative endeavour should recognize the moment before the hand proceeds, the words arrange themselves, the notes fall into place: it has got something to do with a trance, the sensation of a sensibility quicker than the intellect.

The language of the body

Maybe something exists outside language, drawing, composing or improvising which forms the source from which all these activities issue. Maybe it is better not to use the term 'source' but to speak of a 'field', an electrically charged field of criss-crossing brain impulses. Let's call it the 'Language of the body'. Art would then be the translation of this body language, the echo of a primeval language of which the grammar is known but not known, since we ourselves are the grammar.

Over the years a lot of Western forms of artistic expression have become removed from this language of the body. Art became predominantly a matter of reflection, a stylizing of emotions, not the direct expression of them. However there are a couple of artistic means of expression suitable for presenting that language of the body with a minimum of distortion. Within this framework I am referring to the arts of drawing and improvisational music (or as it is more widely known: jazz). Jazz is practically the only form of Western music which has not lost contact with the language of the body. Presumably because of its non-Western origin. Its basis lies in African culture which views the body itself as an instrument capable of directly expressing itself through dance, song and rhythm.

This close connection to the physical is also what gave jazz a bad name in a puritanical American society while at the same time explaining its rising popularity in a time in our culture when the body has again come to demand its rights.

Expression

The musical practice of jazz distinguishes itself radically from that of composed music. The jazz musician lays complete emphasis on expression, the classical musician on mastery of the instrument. The former speaks entirely on his own behalf, the latter is a mediator between the composer's score and the audience. The jazz buff has the feeling of almost personally knowing his favourite players while the appreciation of a classical composer takes place on a much more abstract level. That's why the jazz world is so full of anecdotes, photographs and other documents which all emphasize the personal and unique character of its makers. In a way this book is one more proof of this. But there is more to it than that and that is because what we have here is a unique combination of two art forms Piet Klaasse's drawings seem to bring together.

Johny Coles. When I showed him his picture I expected him to be shocked, but he thought it 'great'.

A high state of alertness

In response to my question as to just what improvisation was, a jazz musician once answered: 'It's the knowledge in your hands.' What he meant was that he could play 'without using his brains'. The choice of what to play was not determined by the intellect but through intuition, fed by years of study and knowledge of one's musical material, for in jazz too the old axiom holds true: without limits there is no freedom.

Generally speaking, when drawing you normally have the freedom to take as much time as you need to complete the sketch of your subject. If you choose jazz and jazz musicians as your subject you enter the realm of the immediate, the now (which is why jazz is also sometimes called 'instant composing'). You then must be able, just like the musician, to call upon the knowledge in your hands to enable you to give immediate form to what you see. 'It is,' says Piet Klaasse, 'a combination of drawing along to the beat with a completely open mind as well as being in an acute state of alertness. But of course everything goes wrong if your paws just haven't got it in them. You've got to have already drawn the formula of a hand so often because you don't get the chance to conjure it from reality with such a moving hand. It's got to be totally prepared.'

On many drawings you can see how the nature of the music not only determined the drawing technique but the choice of materials as well. The choice fell to the 6B graphite pencil to depict Art Blakey's drumming-power. 'You can only beat hard like that with such a very thick pencil. And you have to decide with which kind of paper he'll bounce off best and then I bounce along with him.'

Just as with a jazz musician decisions are made on the spot. That does not mean that all the drawings are purely registrations of the moment in the sense of a snap-shot. Klaasse sometimes worked at home on them when he did not have the opportunity to finish them off on the spot. He always tried to finish off a drawing as quickly as possible after a concert when the memory of the music was still fresh in his mind.

800 drawings in three years

In the meantime Piet Klaasse has become a well-known figure at the Dutch jazz venues and festivals. He considers himself lucky to be living in a country that is as relatively jazz loving as the Netherlands and which has afforded him the opportunity to make more than 800 drawings of roughly 350 different jazz musicians.

Despite that favourable jazz situation in the Netherlands it remains an astoundingly large production from that artist who is not exactly a spring chicken anymore. The circumstances under which he must work are often far from ideal. Bad lighting, packed audiences, overzealous ushers who try to remove him from the premises, but Klaasse no longer allows himself to be intimidated. By now he knows his way around Dutch jazz land.

It is a fascinating sight to see Piet Klaasse at work. The man with the friendly eyes enters the concert area largely filled with young people who ask themselves what an 'old goat' like him is doing there. Under his arm a plywood drawing board on which his choice of drawing paper is held by two elastic bands. He keeps his pencils, chalk and pastels in the compartments of a black plastic fishing tackle box. Piet nestles himself close to the stage, lets the music penetrate him and then embarks on the lightning fast journey which is made even more difficult because there is not one musician in the world who stays put playing in the same position for more than a minute.

'I try to carry on working on those parts of the body that *do* stay put in the same position. Sometimes I make a second drawing after the first one. But there's something more. The composition of the head is determined in such a way (I could even model it in clay) that I can make it plastic even though I usually only view it from a single angle. That means that I can make a drawing as though I were looking based on another angle than the one I'm looking from. It is seeing supplemented with spatial knowledge, the compass of the head.'

The autograph as graphic

Most of the sketches include the autograph of the musician portrayed. Klaasse decided to include them not only to add to his sketches' authenticity but also as a means of observing the musician to check for any missing details in the quieter surroundings of the bar or dressing-room. Klaasse does not view the musician's autograph and/or other texts as an intrusion upon his work but rather as a complement in that many musicians react quite inventively to any 'spots' he may have missed. Occasionally the placement of the autograph actually forces him to reconsider the drawing which sometimes leads to an improvement.

Portraying jazz musicians in action has traditionally been the province of photographers who register each and every movement with their fast films. Their ubiquitous presence at jazz concerts is often a nuisance.

This is me

Buddy Guy North Sea 9-7'83

Klaasse has always tried to position himself as modestly as possible. That is why at first he drew in a smaller format than the present (50 cm x 32.5), but the larger format gave his hand that much more room to 'draw along with the music'.

Motional drawing

Piet Klaasse developed the skill of drawing moving things at an early age. As a schoolboy he performed as a quick sketch artist. In effect he had been drawing jazz musicians for a long time.

Just after World War II the first jazz musician he drew was Kid Dynamite, the American tenor sax player he saw perform in the Casablanca dance club on the Zeedijk in Amsterdam. Jazz music was a symbol of liberation from Nazi occupation, a period Piet Klaasse remembers less fondly.

As a teacher at an art academy just after the war he developed his own course in 'motional drawing'. The students were given assignments to make free sketches to the rhythm of jazz and other ethnic musics.

It was that freedom of drawing which brought Piet Klaasse back to the subject of jazz at the outset of the eighties. Meanwhile he had become a well-known artist and had created something of a furore as an illustrator

too. By nature an extremely critical yet modest man, he saw through his own limitations, which paradoxically enough had to do with his own virtuosity. He could actually draw too well.

'I'm still pregnant'

All the effort, the stumbling, the searching, making mistakes and then taking advantage of them, in a word: through jazz, *improvisation* crept into his drawings. As he himself put it, he has drawn himself 'over the threshold' with these jazz sketches. They share in one of the most attractive aspects of jazz: its lack of perfection, of completeness and the desire for change that is most indicative of the language of the body. Through that 'imperfectness' the listener, the spectator can enter into the music and the drawing.

That is what Miles Davis meant when he commented to a reporter: 'Tell them, I'm still pregnant.'

Eric Dolphy once said, during a radio recording in Holland on June 2 1964, shortly before his death: 'After the music is over, it's all gone in the air. You can never capture it again.'

An essential characteristic of jazz is its transcience. Fortunately, there are people like Piet Klaasse who try to do something about this.

174

Ansley Jackson. I remember the loud music
made me completely go soft. I made this
sketch almost 'automatically' on glossy
machine coated paper. The material in no way
slows down your hand. And so that's how a
lightning fast drawing technique is born.

Mojo Buford

George 'Mojo' Buford. Harmonica/Singer.
Hernando, Mississippi,
November 10 1929.

He started singing gospel and playing
harmonica in churches. No wonder,
because his father was a harmonica player
and his grandfather was a preacher. After
spending his youth in Mississippi he
moved to Memphis, Tennessee, to work
mostly outside music. From 1953 on his
residence was Chicago. During the period
1953-'55 he led his own band and he
called himself Muddy Waters Jr.
One year later the 'real' Muddy Waters
(McKinley Morganfield) asked him to play
in his band, which resulted in a long
off-and-on partnership with the father of
the Chicago Blues.

During the '60s and the '70s Buford made
several recordings under his own name
for a variety of, often local, labels and he
performed continuously in clubs in and
around Chicago as well as in Minneapolis
where he lived and worked for a while.
During his career he joined and rejoined
the **Muddy Waters** Blues Band during
the periods 1956-'60, in the sixties when
George Smith wasn't able to make it with
Muddy, in the early '70s and, finally, in the
summer of 1980, after Muddy had fired
his band, to form a new line-up. Buford
played with the Muddy Waters Band on
several Coast-to-Coast tours in The
States and he also visited Europe several
times with Waters to play a.o. at The North
Sea Jazz Festival at The Hague/Holland a
couple of times. He continued his job as
Muddy's harp player until the latter died
on April 30, 1983.

In the meantime Buford saw the release
of an album he recorded in '79, shortly
before he joined Muddy's band. Originally
the album was released by the local *Mr
Blues* label but the, more common,
Rooster label from Chicago re-released it.
Dick Shurman's liner notes give some
insight into Buford's qualities: *Mojo blows
strong, amplified harp, and his chromatic
work is full and effective. He's at his best
as an ensemble player. His voice,
surprisingly deep and powerful for a
person of his stature, and harp volume
come from the method he and James
Cotton use of drawing air from the belly.*

Recommended record:
Chicago Blue Summit
Rooster R 7603

ojo Buford. He's wearing a kind of sash. It
ned out to be a storage space for scores of
ferent harmonicas. A kind of musical
munition belt.

Bernard Upsen

Chris White

Leroy Vinnegar

Major Holley

In contrast to the concert grand piano which remains an immovable piece of furniture with a little man in front of it, the bass is an instrument of literally human size, shape and proportions.

17-3

Fela Kuti, four times. 'The' popstar from Nigeria
on tour with a large group including his 27
wives. They play with a mixture of traditional
African percussion instruments, electronic and
Western acoustic ones like the sax.

After the first tentative lines to determine the composition and posture comes the concentrated groping for the unique characteristics of the head. Then it comes fast and furious. Lines and stripes, scratches and dots rhythmically set down to the music's swinging beat. On some drawings the head and body are drawn more than once side by side, all seen from different angles. This is not done out of a need to create some semblance of modern art but was suggested by the great mobility of the models themselves.

In the course of a couple of years I switched from a paper format of 25 x 32.5 cm to the rather large one of 37.5 x 55 cm. A larger sheet of paper does not automatically mean more work. You can draw lines with more speed on a larger sheet of paper. So the drawings can often look more lively than the ones done on smaller sheets which force you to use more controlled lines. Just like the musicians you have got to warm up and by the end of the gig, in the throes of a chaos of sound and the conquest of the audience, I strike and scratch along to the swinging beat with my thick 6B graphite pencil.

The past two years I've begun using more and more coloured paper. Sometimes chosen because of the general impression the artist makes, sometimes because of something as trivial as the colour of a shirt or the dominant stage lighting. Or even more primitive: at my first blues concert I'd brought along several different shades of blue paper! By first selecting the darker and lighter shades, in a short time you get a surprising spatial effect. Allow me the illusion of thinking that the colour to some extent brings a person's character a little closer. Anyhow, paper is part of the picture.

181

Junior Wells. The moment I'd started drawing
that harmonica of his, he'd started singing
again. So I just let it go back and forth in the
drawing.

Blind Herman Foster

182

Blind Herman Foster

Steve Swallow
Carla Bley Band

Blind Herman Foster. Lou Donaldson's
accompanist for years. Here, after two earlier,
rather detailed drawings at the end of the
concert, two encores on his waterfall of notes.

4 - april '83

Katie's Worried Blues (spoken)
(traditional/lyrics by Katie Webster)

You know, I'm just tide,
T-I-D-E, tied,
that's not the way you really
spell it but...
that's the way I feel
I want you to know, I'm tired
of these men telling me the same old
thing, everyday.
Everytime they look in my face, they're
telling me something about:

'Woman your show is fine' and then
they're telling me: 'And you're pretty
too'...
I don't need them to tell this, I already
know this. Just as cute as I wanne be...
And he's always telling me... Well let me
tell you about this... Every Friday night he
comes home and he tells me, he's been
out there, drinking beer with the fellows,
but it's a funny thing that it must be some
funny kind of fellows, 'cause he always
comes home with a kind of lipstick on his
face of a kind I don't use... yeah...

And they have a perfume of a kind...
See I use my own brand and this stuff
they use doesn't smell like it... I know it's
not mine...
So I'm getting tired of this man telling me
this every Friday night and coming home
with this big silly grin on his face...

(starts singing the original blues classic
'Worried Blues':)
'Oh Lordy Lord, it hurts me so bad, but
someday baby,
Ain't gonna worry my life anymore...'

Katie Webster

Kathryn Jewel Thorne. Piano/Singer.
Houston, Texas, September 1 1939.

Her father Zyrus Thorne was a ragtime piano player from Chicago, who became a preacher in the late '50's. Her mother also played piano, so it's no wonder that Katie started singing in churches at an early age. She heard a Fats Domino song on the radio and tried to figure out on her parent's piano what Fats was playing, thus discovering her abilities to play piano. At the age of 15 she married one Earl

Webster. Their marriage ended in divorce after 7 years, but Katie still uses her first husband's family name. Later she married James Lewis, somebody outside the music business. In the late fifties Katie recorded as session pianist for labels from Lake Charles, Louisiana, and Crowley, Louisiana.
During the sixties she recorded under her own name for various labels from Crowley, Louisiana, owned by Jay Miller. She also recorded for Eddie Shuler's *Goldband* label from Lake Charles. Also during the sixties she sang for more than three years in **Otis Redding**'s band,

until Otis' untimely death in December '67. In '82 she made her first European tour and right now she has five albums out (three on European labels), is very successful during her at least annual club tours through Europe and is famous for her many '*Talking Blues*-songs'.

Recommended records:
Whooee Sweet Daddy
Flyright 530
Live + Well
Ornament 7.123

Irvin Stokes with the band of Illinois Jacket in
Nick Vollebrecht's Jazzcafé, Laren.

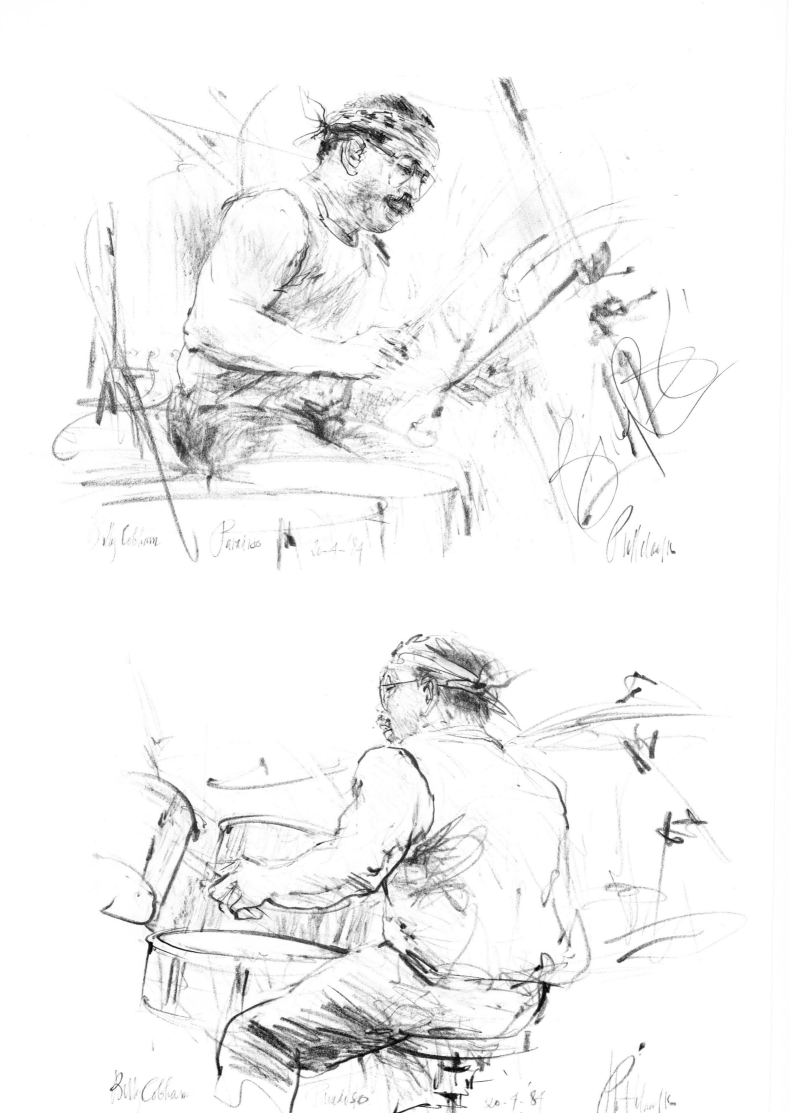

Billy Cobham   Paradiso   20-1-'87

Billy Cobham   Paradiso   20-1-'87

A new blues generation

The past two decades a great number of
blues musicians died, e.g. the fathers of
the Chicago Blues – Big Bill Broonzy,
Tampa Red, Little Walter, Howlin' Wolf,
Sonny Boy Williamson and Muddy
Waters. And it was expected that with
them the blues were dying out, but this
proved to be wrong.
In towns like Chicago, St Louis, Memphis
and San Francisco blues fans can still
enjoy 'live' blues at several spots, seven
nights a week. After their successful tours
to Europe and Japan, musicians like
Buddy Guy, Albert Collins, Junior Wells,
Katie Webster, Pee Wee Crayton and
Luther Allison returned 'home' to play
regularly at local clubs again.
An even more interesting fact is that

a whole new generation of blues
musicians – most of them in their
mid-twenties – is presenting itself. They
learned about the blues from their
predecessors or just picked things up at
'the club around the corner', adding their
own rhythm and words, reflecting the
world in the 1980s, to it.
One of them is **Valerie Wellington**, who
studied classical music but is now a
well-known blues vocalist. Her repertoire
comprises her own songs as well as the
older classics, including some of Bessie
Smith's and Ma Rainey's songs. Another
female vocalist who's on her way up is
Angela Brown, also from Chicago. A
third is harmonica player **Billy Branch**,
carrying on the important role the mouth-
harp played in the history of the blues. Yet
the son of harmonica player Carey Bell,

Lurrie Bell, seems to be the most promising young guitar player in the blues field,
playing a style that shows influences of
giants like B.B. King and Buddy Guy, but
also those Lurrie picked up from the late
blues/rock guitarist Jimmy Hendrix.

Recommended records:
**Valerie Wellington/Million Dollar
Secret**
Rooster R 2619
**Angela Brown a.o./Live At The Piano
Man**
Red Beans 003
**Lurrie Bell, Billy Branch a.o./Living
Chicago Blues Vol 3**
Alligator 7703
Billy Branch a.o./Sons Of Blues
Red Beans RB 004

187

*Billy Cobham. You can see he is a thrilling
mixture of immense force and great
tenderness. Stuck between back wall and
drums, I was especially confronted with the
immense – electronically amplified – force.*

Love =Blues=
Luther J. Allison

19-3-83

Luther Allison

Luther Allison. Guitar/Harmonica/Singer.
Mayflower (Faulkner Co), Arkansas,
August 17 1939.

Although Luther Allison was, like so many blues musicians, born in The South, being one of twelve children, it is Chicago's West Side that should be considered the birthground of his music. After moving to Chicago in the late '40s, Luther attended Farragut High School, where he learned to play guitar. During the mid-50s he played with the band of his brother Ollie Lee Allison (outside Luther the only member of the family who went into music). During the '50s and the '60s Luther developed his own style in guitar playing, under the influence of such West Side giants as Magic Sam, Freddie King and Otis Rush, whose guitar licks he mixed up with the work of a.o. B.B. King. His first step to a wider acclaim was made in 1966 when Luther recorded some songs for an anthology on the Chicago label *Delmark*. These recordings were followed by an album under his own name for the same label in 1969. Several Coast to Coast tours in The States were followed in 1976 and 1977 by two European tours. *It was during those two tours that he established himself as one of the strongest performers active in the field of blues today.* With his falsetto voice and his screaming guitar breaks as well as his occasional work on the harmonica he is able to sell out the biggest concert halls all over Europe and in The States. But outside Luther's vocal and instrumental virtuosity, it is his showmanship that makes his performances so incredibly dynamic.

After his first Delmark recordings, Luther entered the recording studios around the world several times to tape more albums for such labels as *Tamla Motown, Black & Blue, Album* and *Rumble Records*.
His albums usually reflect the repertory he features during his live performances in the sense that he mixes up some classic blues songs with a few new songs, written and composed by himself.

Among those fruits that dropped from his own pen, the slow blues called *Luther's Blues*, which he recorded in 1974, is without any doubt one of the highlights in his career.

Nowadays Luther Allison is an almost annual guest on Europe's most popular blues and jazz festivals, while he also plays on the most famous festivals and in the most populair blues clubs in The United States. And Allison still leaves every concert stage with sweat all over his body. Luther, explaining the reason for this: *'I am fightin' for world-wide recognition.'*

Recommended records:
Luther's Blues
Motown 523030
Gonna Be A Live One In Here Tonight!
Rumble RR 1001

Archie Shepp and Lester Bowie at the BIM-huis, Amsterdam.

189

Miles Davis 28 april '82

List of portrayed artists

135 George Adams	8 Von Freeman	156 David Murray
10, 116 Monty Alexander	167 Stan Getz	85 Sal Nistico
188 Luther Allison	6, 62, 65 Dizzy Gillespie	59 Always Big Voice Odom
127, 167 Chet Baker	29 Benny Goodman	102, 104 Oscar Peterson
192 Count Basie	87 Dexter Gordon	100 Horace Parlan
14 Art Blakey	23, 96 Johnny Griffin	133 Lonnie Pitchford
31, 32 Sugar Blue	173 Buddy Guy	81 Gerald Price
30 Hamiet Bluiett	94 Lionel Hampton	161 Tito Puente
146 Arthur Blythe	43 Herbie Hancock	150, 151 Sun Ra
136 Joe Bowie	10 Jeff Hamilton	152 Jimmy Raney
13, 189 Lester Bowie	162 Percey Heath	129 A.C. Reed
51 Jimmy Brewer	105 Billy Higgins	41 Max Roach
13 Ari Brown	177 Silas Hogan	117 Mickey Roker
169 Clarence Gatemouth Brown	178 Major Holey	122 Sonny Rollins
117 Ray Brown	52, 174 John Lee Hooker	24, 189 Archie Shepp
108 Dave Brubeck	22 Freddie Hubbard	59 Magic Slim
176 Mojo Buford	131 J.B. Hutto	56 Memphis Slim
36 Ron Carter	175 Ansley Jackson	44 Smokey Smothers
141 Ray Charles	38 Milt Jackson	183 Irvin Stokes
10 John Clayton	158, 159 Ronald Shannon Jackson	183 Steve Swallow
67, 96 Arnett Cobb	145 Illinois Jacquet	60 Queen Sylvia
186 Billy Cobham	35 Hank Jones	85 Buddy Tate
170 Johnny Coles	113 Philly Joe Jones	21 Koko Taylor
72, 85 Ornette Coleman	92 Duke Jordan	11 Charles Tolliver
129 Albert Collins	119, 120 B.B. King	98 James Blood Ulmer
9, 58 Johnny Copeland	26 Jimmy Knepper	178 Bernard Upsen
47 Pee Wee Crayton	111 Lee Konitz	78 Sarah Vaughan
165 Cecila Cruz	181 Fela Kuti	178 Leroy Vinnegar
85 Lou Donaldson	55 Lovie Lee	82 Eddy Cleanhead Vinson
49 Willie Dixon	101 Kirk Lightsey	124 Sippy Wallace
99 Grand Mixer D.St.	107 Abbey Lincoln	184 Katie Webster
16, 18, 190 Miles Davis	96 Eddie Lockjaw Davis	187 Valerie Wellington
22 Eddie Lockjaw Davis	164 Machito	180 Junior Wells
142 Jon Faddis	137 Wynton Marsalis	189 Frank Wess
70 Tommy Flanagan	75 Warne Marsh	178 Chris White
138 Bobby McFerrin	154 Al di Meola	139 Tony Williams
182 Blind Herman Foster	8 James Moody	90 Jimmy Witherspoon
33 Chico Freeman	147, 148 Gerry Mulligan	

191

'Most guys want to know about... well, they say
I'm rude, and that I turn my back on the
audience, and that I don't like white people.
And that I don't like the audience. But the thing
is, I never think about an audience. I just think
about the band.' (Miles Davis)

Colophon

Text: Mark Gardner
Editing and the article The jazz line: J. Bernlef

Typography: Casper Klaasse/Piet Klaasse

Lithography: Scanner Centre s.n.c., Pordenone (Italy)
Type setting: Graphique '84, Amsterdam
Printing: Smeets, Weert
Binding: Van Rijmenam, The Hague

The author wishes to thank the following persons, institutions and clubs for their generous help: Nick Vollebregts Jazz café, Muziek Centrum Vredenburg, de Meervaart, BIM-huis, Paradiso, Tros-sesjun, Scott Rollins, Rien Wisse, Wim van Eyle, Jazz Inn, Paul Acket and Wim van Woerkens/North Sea Jazz Festival.

In Memoriam   Count Basie 12.7.'81 North Sea

While care has been taken over the accuracy of album numbers for records recommended in this book, their availability cannot be guaranteed. Records are constantly being deleted, and just as frequently repackaged and reissued with new numbers. However, a welcome trend in the 1980s is the replica reissue. Thus in America, Europe and Japan, it is now possible to purchase Blue Note, Prestige and Riverside LPs, originally issued 20 or more years ago, in the same jacket design with identical album title and even the earlier number. Where the number has altered, the record keeps its title which makes tracing the disc relatively simple. We must thank the Japanese for this logical and convenient development. It is unfortunate that some of the multi-nationals, like Columbia/CBS, which give the same album a multiplicity of numbers across the world, are unable to rationalize and introduce a universal catalogue system. — M.G.

First published in Holland in 1984
by Moussault/Unieboek b.v., Weesp

First published in the United Kingdom in 1985
by David & Charles (Publishers) Ltd.

© Illustrations Piet Klaasse 1984
Moussault/Unieboek b.v., Weesp (Holland)

BRITISH LIBRARY CATALOGUING IN PUBLICATION DATA
Klaasse, Piet

Jam session: portraits of jazz and blues
musicians drawn on the scene.
1. Jazz music
I. Title   II. Gardner, Mark   II. Bernlef, J.
785.42   ML3506

ISBN 0-7153-8710-3